BEARER OF THE LIGHT

Vassula:
Mediatrix of Divided Christians

by
Michael O'Carroll, C.S.Sp.

Published and Distributed by:-

J.M.J. Publications
P.O. Box 385
Belfast BT9 6RQ
Northern Ireland
Fax: (0232) 381596

His Holiness Pope Paul VI has confirmed on
October 14, 1966, the decree of the Sacred
Congregation for the propagation of the Faith,
under number 58/16 (A.A.S.), permitting the
publication of writings about supernatural
apparitions, even if they do not have a "nihil
obstat" from ecclesiastical authorities.

1994   1st Printing (Canada) - 10,000

See back for the addresses of distributors

Պատրիարքարան Հայոց

ARMENIAN PATRIARCHATE

№

Թու ական
Date

Ms Vassula Ryden

Dear Ms Ryden,

It is an occasion of great pleasure and personal satisfaction for us to recognize in you a new catalyst of spiritual rejuvenation who can talk to our present generation in a most persuasive language, through the books you are publishing.

Your inspired mission of bringing the message of Christ to others is a source of profound joy to the Church. And your indefatigable zeal of drawing strength from and seeking regeneration and reinforcement in your Greek roots, should set an enviable example of dedicated fidelity, to our tortured youth.

In our days, at at time when crass materialism has taken such a deep root in the hearts of men, it is refreshing to know that all is not lost, that there still are among us people like yourself who are in communion with the Creator, and able to transmit to us the benefit of your inspiration.

We take pride in encouraging your ecumenical mission and pray for your success.

We look forward to reading your next book.

Meanwhile, we send you our blessings from the Holy City of God. and ask the Lord to keep you and guard you.

Archbishop David Sahagian

Archbishop David Sahagian
Chancellor & Grand Sacristan

ՓՈՍՏԱՐԿՂ 14235 ՀԵՌԱՁԱՅՆ 894866 ԵՐՈՒՍԱՂԷՄ ԻՍՐԱՅԵԼ
P.O.BOX 14235 PHONE: 894866 JERUSALEM ISRAEL

Dedication

To the Alliance of the
Two Hearts of Jesus and
Mary

FOREWORD

The writings of Vassula Rydén are now very widely distributed, in twenty-two languages. This remarkable demand dates from five years ago. Father O'Carroll, in a first book, analysed the thought content of the writings, making it clear that after her conversion from religious indifference over thirty years, she had no theological instruction whatever. Her mind was a complete blank on such things. But what she has written has profoundly impressed theologians of repute in different countries. It has also led to very many conversions.

In the present book Fr O'Carroll deals with Vassula's life before her conversion, expounds the immense importance of the Orthodox Church to which she belongs, with which the Catholic Church led by the Pope is seeking total mutual understanding and union; he illustrates the impact of her message on her worldwide Catholic constituency and he deals with the extraordinary phenomena which have been witnessed in her presence. He has words of advice to her critics and records some curious lapses from fairplay in journalism.

19 March 1994, Feast of St Joseph

TABLE OF CONTENTS

1

PREHISTORY OF A CONVERSION

God has often chosen to convert the world through converts. It may have been conversion from another religion to the Christian faith, as happened to St Paul; or from a life of indifference, even of sin, such as we can study in St Augustine. He has given us his personal narrative and reflection, a classic of its kind; we may well judge that he exaggerates in recounting his waywardness. Reflect how much was gained for the Church by Paul and Augustine in the years after their conversion and ever since.

In the history of all converts it is challenging to discern in the years preceding the capital event, signs of divine interest and care. This may have been protection in moments of danger; it may have been a way of life providentially controlled which would be a preparation for tasks ahead; it may have been exercise in skills which could be turned to a higher end in a new phase of life opened by the call of God and the response for which He was waiting.

We are dealing with two mysteries, the natural mystery of the human person, and the supernatural mystery of the Holy Spirit acting in a human soul. We have then to tread carefully. Let us do so in attempting to put together the varied items of Vassula's life before her conversion, which may prove enlightening.

Her family had a reminder of God's power in a secret healing tradition. This is a cure for hepatitis, held from generation to generation as a closely guarded secret. It has been proved efficacious to Vassula's certain knowledge. It may not always prompt an immediate religious response. But, as with others who have healing power that is naturally inexplicable, it fosters a sense of a reality not wholly bound by matter, though capable of affecting material things.

We come to Vassula's own life. To describe something that happened immediately after her birth she uses this enigmatic language: "I fasted on my first three days on earth for this mission." Let her explain: "I was born with my eyes well stuck together. It is very rare for a baby to be born with eyes stuck and even when they are, it is only for a few hours. Mine seemed to be stuck forever. The second day came and my eyes were still not opening. No one had seen the colour of them, or knew if I had any at all. My mother started to get worried and begged a Greek saint by the name of Paraskevi (which name incidentally means 'Friday') who is our saint for the eyes, to show her that I had eyes. She made a vow to this saint that if I had eyes, she would give me her name."

Within the family there was a difference of opinion about the name the child would have. Her grandmother who was to be her godmother had exercised a godmother's right to choose the name; she chose Vassiliki, her own mother's name, which Vassula's mother thought old-fashioned. She had wanted the name Claudia, but was now bound by her vow to a saint. Her prayer was heard. After three days the baby's eyes opened. So she has both names, Vassiliki, now known as Vassula and Paraskevi.

Many years later, on 1 May, 1992, God the Father explained it all to Vassula:

Ah Vassula, though you were a dried up driftwood ready to be thrown on the fire to be burnt, I came hurrying to you to save you. In the valley of death I have found you, making Me plunge into mourning. My cry turned the heavens into a state of alarm; the very memory of that sight still deeply grieves Me, such was the distress I endured. I was patient with you for many years, I called you many times then, but you would not listen; but greatly loving I did not make an end of you, I have shown you instead My faithfulness in your wickedness. The pain and injuries you were giving My Son were devouring slowly My Mercy. So great was your guilt and so many your sins that I was ready to avenge My Son's wounds by striking you. Ah Vassula, your Mother of Perpetual Help cried at My feet, shedding tears of blood for you; yes your Holy Mother favoured you and comforted Me. My Heart was deeply moved and My anger was removed by her tears; the tempest that had risen in Me was silenced. I, Yahweh, your Eternal Father, loved you with an everlasting love, since that day I created you and held you in my hands. Ah...never shall I forget that day how small you were. I said: 'I will drive the invader away from many souls through this small and delicate girl.' You and I made a pact together, that you would work for peace proclaiming My love to resound to the ends of the earth, and that through your weakness, I would rally those who would be on the point of perishing. I would make you fearless to threats and of invaders, and through you I would pursue and track down the renegades; then in you I would bring your generation to reconcile and unite... Since I was to encroach on My enemy's plans already, I had to bring your soul to consent with Me and strengthen you from the beginning. I said: 'sanctify yourself already and fast from your birth, this is what I desire: I shall not give you light at your birth, for three days and three nights you will remain in the dark; this is how you will fast.'

Then the heavenly Father went on to show how He had worked in Vassula's heart to bring her to Him in such language as:

> With everlasting tenderness I have pressed you on My Heart, making you
> Mine again. I swore to change your rebellious and unruly heart into a resting
> place for Me... I then removed your veil to honour My name and declared
> openly to My celestial hall that I Myself will fight those who will fight and
> persecute you, for now, I, your Creator, will be your husband and your only
> refuge. I would be He who confides in you and you in Me. I would make
> My words a fire in your mouth to proclaim them to the ends of the earth -
> all that you have learned, you have learned from Me. I, Yahweh, your
> Eternal Father, have embellished you, delicate little girl; I stoop at the very
> moment, down to you to lift your soul close against My Heart.[1]

God is master of time and by His power weaves a pattern coherent and consistent
across the years. This He showed to Vassula in His explanation of the apparent
tragedy of her very first days. He did so too in incidents which have been mentioned
in the first book I wrote about her, the vision of Jesus calling her to Him and the
vision of her mystical espousal.

As a child she also was allowed to see the agent of darkness. "When I was around
six years old" she writes "while lying in my bed and still being wide awake, I clearly
saw with my physical eyes in the dark, Satan's hands. Just a pair of hands. They
were the hands of someone who would be very old and thin. They came right in
front of me and were formed in a manner as when someone is intending to strangle.
They were heading for my throat and simultaneously 'something' pulled my head
backward. When I pushed my head back again, the hands had vanished; but they
had left my soul frightened. Next day I complained to my mother and, seeing how
frightened I was, she tried to convince me that it was not Satan at all, but our dear
Mother's hands - she was coming to comfort me. But I knew how I felt and whose
hands they were. I never spoke about this event anymore to anyone."

But, early in 1986 when this revelation (that is her messages) were still very new and
"I was with my angel in the beginning of it, and also now and then with God, Satan
tried to discourage me from writing and tried all sorts of tricks to deceive me. One
trick he played was to appear in a dream to my younger son. My son, frightened by
what he had seen and heard, came the following morning to tell me of his nightmare.
He saw himself lying in bed and near his bed a very old man was sitting in a chair.
These were his words":

> There was an old man sitting in the chair near my bed, and he looked very
> like the seer of the Asterix (cartoon) books; he had a long white beard and

---

[1]Volume III, p.10f.

appeared very mean. He was staring at me and said to me: 'Tell your mother to stop writing. If she will not stop writing, I will come back to you at night and will come for your throat. I will do what I wanted to do to her when she was young, and pull your hair from behind.'

"After these words were spoken he woke up. I recognised Satan and I complained to God about it. I even asked God to stop Satan from coming to my children to disturb them, if I had to continue in this mission. God immediately promised me that nothing of the sort will be allowed any more."

What was the point of these brief intrusions of the evil one in the life of Vassula and her son? Possibly to make clear once and for all the reality of satanic forces. Many years after the event of her childhood Vassula was shown hell and the demon by Jesus. Satan spat on the ground and she heard him say, "Now look what's coming to see us: worms."

Another curious event from Vassula's childhood is of interest in the light of future events. When she was about nine years old a family holiday was planned to Cyprus. One day as the family were on a visit to aunts and uncles, the children were playing on the verandah of their home while the elders discussed Cyprus. Let Vassula herself take up the story: "The more they were talking of Cyprus, the more uncomfortable I was becoming, to the extent that I could not stand it any longer. I got up, left the other children and went to the grown-ups bawling. Frightened they asked what was the matter with me. I said to them 'if we go to Cyprus, I will never come back again.' They all looked at my mother, and my grandfather who knew well how she would react, said to them, 'that holiday in Cyprus will never take place.' The trip to Cyprus was cancelled." A few days later, writes Vassula, "I had the vision of Jesus calling me. I told my mother, and she took it as a good sign." They went to Lebanon, but because of what had happened the mother kept a vigilant eye on her child while they were there.

That God watched over Vassula in the years of her apparent abandonment of Him is well illustrated by an incident which occurred when she was living in Lesotho. I give the story in her own words:

I woke up in the middle of the night and could not go back to sleep. Every time I was about to go to sleep I was like shaken and kept awake. I tried to use psychology. I thought that maybe something had happened during that day that disturbed my soul subconsciously. So to resolve the problem I started to go back in time to find out what happened that day. I went through the day's events to find out that nothing really special had happened to disturb me. Suddenly I found myself falling asleep and it must have been at the threshold of awakening and sleep when I was given a vision.

I saw hands clearly in front of me. These hands, I knew immediately, belonged to a burglar. He was touching the mosquito net of a window very near the main entrance and was trying to break in. It was very clear. Suddenly I was completely awakened by all that I saw. Then I immediately heard inside me a distinct voice speak to me. The voice said 'Stay where you are; do not get up yet.' A few seconds went by, then again, 'Do not get up yet.' The amazing thing was that I obeyed this voice. It had never crossed my mind to doubt of its authenticity. The other amazing thing was that I never asked myself who was speaking to me and how come I was obeying, as though I was conditioned. The voice suddenly ordered me in a very firm and definitive way, 'Get up now and look for them.'

I got up and tiptoed first to the back of the house. I peered through the window without lighting anywhere, and I saw no one. Then I tiptoed to our bedroom again and pulled the curtain quietly away. There right in front of me, standing fifty centimetres away, was a man whose profile I saw. I understood that he was covering the corner of the house in case someone would come from behind; he could signal this to his accomplice who was at the main door in front of the house, and had, in fact, lifted the mosquito net of the window near the entrance so as to reach the lock of the door.

With a loud voice to scare the one in front of me I said, 'Per, there is someone here!' At the sound of my voice he almost jumped out of his skin, gave the alert to the other one and ran away. There were three of them. An hour later we heard screams from our neighbour's house. They had managed to break in, and menacing them with knives and rocks had burgled them.

Vassula judges this to be the first time that she heard God's voice clearly in a locution. As she adds, it was well before her conversion.

Another significant incident occurred when she was living in Mozambique. At the time her husband was involved in a project sponsored by the Swedish government. It was not looked on favourably by the rulers of the country, marxists of stalinist loyalty. Their hostility was to give Vassula a taste of totalitarian ruthlessness. One night when she was alone in her residence, while her husband, Per, was in Rome on official business she was awakened and saw a number of people at the front of the house. She took them for young people working with him in the project which he directed. On opening the door she was surprised to hear them ask for Per. They would not believe her answer that he was in Rome, not there. One of them put his foot in the door when, thinking them burglars, she tried to block their entry.

They came in and the leader produced an identifying card, "Secret Police." What relief! But only for a moment. They were seeking her husband, whom they took for a double-agent - the last thing in the world Per Rydén would be, as anyone who knows him as well as I do will affirm. They would intern him, as they had done with his colleagues.

Refusing to believe that he was absent, they searched the entire house, going even through private papers. They did, however, respect her wish not to enter the room where her little boy, Fabian, aged four, was sleeping - their weapons would have scared him. They did not think her plea a scheme to hide her husband. They left at four o'clock.

Vassula waited until eight o'clock and then telephoned to the Swedish ambassador. He could have refused to act as Per was not a diplomat, but he rose to the occasion and behaved splendidly. He instructed Vassula, who was under constant surveillance, to take a few things in her car as if she was going to the beach, but to come straight to the embassy. With her son in the car she did so. Then the brave and thoughtful ambassador drove her personally in his own car, which was protected diplomatically, over the frontier to Swaziland. There she waited until the situation bettered. The ambassador, meanwhile, was not idle. Thanks to his wise measures, her husband was not molested. Eventually he could come to bring her home.

How many of those who read Vassula's writings and think of a sheltered mystic's life, far from the horrors of political manoeuvres with a threat of violence, have had any such experience, know from first hand what life was like in volatile third world situations? This is an integral part of Vassula's background. How many have had to travel by car for eleven hours at a time over rough roads to assure the necessary provisions for their families?

The Sudan, where part of Vassula's African career was passed, is remembered by her for a different reason. There she once narrowly escaped surgical amputation of her leg. Her left leg was cut by a piece of broken coca-cola bottle. It seemed slight and she gave it little attention. But it worsened showing signs of infection, so she treated it herself with a disinfecting ointment. There was no improvement and she had to call in a doctor. Cleaning the wound and antibiotics made no change, so she was hospitalized for there was danger of gangrene and amputation. There the remedy was drastic. Without anaesthetic the wound was deeply scraped, and then filled with gauze. The patient felt excruciating pain, more than she had experienced in child-birth. Ordinary pain-killers had no effect, so she was given morphine - an overdose accidentally which nearly led to her death by suffocation. She was rescued from possible death.

There is a happier memory of the African years. In the year 1973 Vassula was living in Ethiopia. A competition was announced for a stamp to honour the Emperor, Haile Selassie. Vassula who was at the time an experienced portraitist, felt not the slightest inclination to compete. But friends kept urging her to do so. She finally decided to follow their advice. She hastily made portraits of the Emperor and went to government buildings to submit them. When she met the government Minister responsible, the Minister for Telecommunications, she expressed the view that it would be quite understandable if a foreigner was not chosen. She was given assurance that the best design submitted would get the award. She left his office with the idea that she would not hear from that quarter again.

A month after she had given in her drawing she had a dream, which in retrospect she took for a vision. She saw seven priests on a height, all wearing the black clothes of their calling. I let her continue the narrative:

> I saw them all in profile and the last one I recognized; he was the Minister of Telecommunications. He turned and looked at me, left the line of priests who were walking one after another, and came running towards me saying: 'You won the competition. But if you knew how much I had to fight for you to win.'

> Next day the phone rang and it was the Minister. His first words were, 'You won the competition. But if you knew how much I had to fight for you to win.' I asked why did he have so much trouble. He said that the jury did not agree with him, not because of the drawing as such, but because of a condition they had laid down: if the drawing missed anything, was not complete, they would put it aside at once. The handkerchief in the pocket of the suit was missing in my drawing. The handkerchief had the symbolic initials of the Emperor, H.I.M., which stood for His Imperial Majesty, and these were important. Still, the Minister said, my portrait was far better than the one which came second - the difference was like night and day. He could not let it go by, so he argued a lot on my behalf, telling them that no one of the jury could know the Emperor better than he did - since he often dined with him, and saw his face so often.

> With that I had to add the handkerchief to my drawing. I could not figure out the symbols, since they were white on white. Advised by the Minister to go to the Emperor's sister and ask for a handkerchief, I went to her palace. Her maids told me that she was sleeping, which I told the Minister. He told me that I could go to the Emperor's palace; the symbol was on the fence all round it.

She was momentarily disturbed by one of the palace guards, but was able to reassure him. So she completed her drawing.

Haile Selassie himself wished to meet the winning artist. When the meeting took place, he presented her with a gold medallion of his ancestor, Menelik II. Fifty million copies of the stamp were issued in eighteen different denominations. An expatriate in Ethiopia, Vassula carries off the top prize in an international competition!

In Bangladesh Vassula was to meet the turning-point in her life. Before the encounter with her angel, which initiated the change, she was industrious in different sectors. Her mornings were spent in painting, the early afternoon was given to tennis and the evening to modelling and social functions. Some of her social activities she had to continue for her husband's sake. When she began to receive messages from the powers above she changed her life style drastically, but not entirely. Thus she was invited to play a part in a television drama. She considered it but thought that it would impinge on her time with her angel. So, at the last moment, she asked to withdraw and promised to look for someone to take her place. Her first choice was rejected as she was French and could not plausibly play a role which featured an Irish person. Then Vassula persuaded her sister Helen to go forward. She did so reluctantly, but was enthusiastically accepted and played the role.

When Vassula began taking dictation she did not abandon the friends of her previous life, who would not be easily attuned to such experience. Some welcomed the messages which she read for them and were deeply marked thereby. They have remained in contact with her since then. Outstanding among them was a French lady, Beatrice Fleury, who was in Vassula's milieu. They parted when Vassula came with her husband, Per, to Switzerland where he was posted by his organisation. The fortunes of life brought Beatrice to Switzerland too. She was dissatisfied with her first position, then Vassula persuaded her to seek a post in the World Council of Churches in Geneva. To her astonishment there was a vacancy, which she was offered at once. She works with *Faith and Order*, one of the great components of the WCC. There she has been an auxiliary to Vassula in her mission to promote Christian Unity.

As an addendum to these notes on Vassula's pre-conversion years I mention something which will show that she was not anti-religious, certainly not anti-Christian in the behaviour pattern she followed. She chose to donate one quarter of the proceeds of her first big artistic exhibition to a charity run by Catholic nuns. She wished especially to help provide saris and lungis to those in need. She continued the practice after her conversion. The local press was enthusiastic about her artistic talent. I quote from the *Bangladesh Observer* of 5 May, 1986:

> Mrs Vassula Rydén artist who last February exhibited her collection of oils and charcoals has - as promised - set aside 25 per cent of her sale to donate to the poor, buying for them 70 saris and 40 lungis. Rev Fr Samar Louis Cruze, Sister Claudie and Francis from St Patrick's Church and Holy Convent in Mymensingh and Fr Karl Edelmann from Dhaka accompanied Vassula and helped her organise the distribution in Kalduar village which is 12 miles from the Netrokona district headquarters. The whole village people greeted them warmly with songs and dances with their leaders Sontush Rongdi as well as Running Catechists Nicholas Gabil and Norbert Azim. Vassula distributed the saris and lungis to poor

Muslims and Christians alike.

A member of the Greek Orthodox Church practising charity to Catholics and Muslims: a good note on which to conclude.[1]

---

[1]Many years later Vassula discovered, in a message from Jesus that her elder son, gravely ill, in danger of death, had been restored to health by a special intervention of Our Lady.

2

EXTRAORDINARY SIGNS

In the first book which I wrote on Vassula's personality and mission I thought it better to give attention rather to the content of her messages. I did provide some biographical detail. I omitted analysis of one series of communications which she received from the Lord on the chastisement or purification which may fall on a world resolute in its apostasy. I treat of this theme in the present book. I have also for reasons overwhelmingly cogent drawn attention to the Orthodox and the enormous importance of Vassula as a mediatress between her Church and Catholics.

Having taken advice I have also decided to deal with a feature of Vassula's life which I had thought strictly private, not of interest to any but those very close to her, those she would herself choose as confidants. I have in mind the extraordinary signs which accompany her mission. I now see and she agrees that these special graces or phenomena are signs of divine intervention. Signs are for those called on to make an act of faith. I therefore deal with them here, briefly for reasons of time and space.

The inspired handwriting is such a sign. This has been dealt with adequately; attempts to interpret it as a form of "automatic writing", with a hint of satanic influence, have been countered by the expert judgement of J. A. Muenier and authoritatively by the French exorcist, Fr Curty OFM, who, in the exercise of his ministry has been able to observe "automatic writing", directly satanic. There is no resemblance whatever between Vassula's inspired script and this aberration; her writing, under dictation from Jesus, he styles hieratic.

Another sign of God's presence and power about Vassula is in the miracles of healing. She does not claim a ministry of healing. There have, nonetheless, been remarkable instances of healing at her meetings or as a result of her prayer. We must be guarded in using the word miracle. We should perhaps recall the procedure long established in Lourdes. There, an alleged miracle is studied only if there is proper documentation of a scientific kind. The responsible agency, the Medical Bureau, requests as part of its investigation a second appearance before its personnel of the beneficiary of the healing one year after the first examination. Should its judgement be favourable the case is referred to the International Commission or Jury of Lourdes which sits in Paris. Here there are experts specially chosen. Should they endorse the verdict of the Medical Bureau, the Bishop of Lourdes is informed and he passes the file to the Bishop of the diocese from which the healed person came. He may or may not publish the finding. Following this rigorous procedure only fifty-two miracles were declared authentic in the first hundred years after the apparitions. Thousands had been reported. Those who were healed were happy, though for one reason or another they may not have been included in the total.

Over five hundred cases of healing have already been reported from Medjugorje. How many will pass a severe examination of the kind made at Lourdes? Does this affect the lives of those who are freed from disease? In this spirit I mention some known cases of healing associated with Vassula. When she first spoke in Dublin, a lady afflicted with cancer came to ask her prayer. At the next meeting in the city the sick person was present, and she informed us that she had been healed. There is a young boy in the United States, John Curt Dow, who was brought by his parents to Vassula. In desperation she turned to the Lord and simply, spontaneously, cried out, "Do something." The disease was juvenile arthritis. There was a complete cure, which I was able to check a year later.

On the occasion of Vassula's first visit to Ireland she went from Dublin to Athenry, where she spoke in the church. A lady came to speak to her who had had terminal cancer and was partially healed during a visit to Lourdes. After her meeting with Vassula, on the night of 13 March, 1991 she was completely cured. I have had confirmation of the fact from her personally and from Fr Michael O'Malley, who was at the time pastorally responsible in Athenry.

During Vassula's visit to Stockholm, of which I shall write later, there was a surprising instance of healing. A young woman interested in her message wished to attend the meeting organised in a church. I was present, and checked the facts later. The young woman's mother, who knew nothing about Vassula, had to accompany her daughter because she was gravely ill, and could not remain alone at home. What happened was related to us next day by the daughter. First, the woman puzzled at the appearance of a "woman preacher", was startled to see a change in the speaker's appearance; she saw the face of Christ. Then she had a strange sensation of water rushing through her body - her ailment had some effect of this kind. She knew that she was instantly healed.

For the next case of healing I give the narrative as I received it from relatives of the favoured one:

> Little Angelique, resident at Orange in the Vaucluse in France, aged two years, had an inoperable cancerous tumour - the tumour was between the liver and a kidney. She had regular chemotherapy sessions. This treatment caused a slight diminution in the tumour, without eliminating it. It was also impossible to increase the chemotherapy doses in one so young... Her grand-

aunt Mary living in Neuchatel, made many pilgrimages to seek the cure of the little girl. In one of these pilgrimages Mary met Mme Alice Rey of Lens, who informed her about Vassula Rydén. In that week Mary was invited by Alice Rey to assist at a prayer meeting with Vassula in Villeneuve on 18 November, 1993. Very fervently they prepared an intention of prayer for little Angelique, to be confided in Jesus through Vassula. At Villeneuve on the evening of 18 November they passed their intentions, in an envelope, to Vassula. During the prayer vigil Alice Rey, her daughter Carole and Mary prayed very fervently. After Mass, in the parochial hall, while Vassula was reading the messages of Jesus and His Mother Mary, Mary saw a white headband covering Vassula's forehead, as one saw religious formerly - but it was only her forehead, not her hair. On their return to Neuchatel, on Friday 19 November, Mary had a telephone message from her sister to tell her that little Angelique was healed. The little girl had entered the hospital on Monday to pass various checks, and had come home on Thursday afternoon. The doctors on examining her had found but a spot in place of the tumour. For them it was a miracle.

Since the event of 17 October, 1917 in Fatima Catholics know of the "miracle of the sun." At certain moments the sun appears to spin, to revolve with rays of light shooting from it. Many people have seen this phenomenon in Medjugorje. They are just as reliable witnesses as any critic who would mock them on *a priori* grounds - as are those who believe in the miracles of the Gospel faced with sceptics who dismiss miracles on *a priori* grounds.

Pope Pius XII saw the miracle of the sun over the Vatican gardens some days after he had proclaimed the dogma of the Assumption, 1 November, 1950. He was a Pope of Fatima: he had been ordained bishop in Rome on 13 May, 1917; he had consecrated the world to the Immaculate Heart of Mary, in 1942; repeated the consecration for Russia, in 1952, in his Encyclical, *Sacro Vergente Anno*, addressed to the Russian peoples. He allowed Cardinal Tedeschini to state publicly at Fatima his vision of the miracle of the sun.

The "miracle of the sun" has occurred three times over halls where Vassula spoke or was about to speak. In the large hall at Notre Dame University, South Bend, Indiana: as I was at the entrance to the hall some people who had come from Dayton, Ohio, to hear Vassula came to relate their experience. They had seen the "miracle of the sun." They saw it spinning, and they saw some kind of coloured band surrounding it. They were very impressed. I shall report the event in Puerto Rico later.

Jack Rice, of whom I shall speak in the course of the present work, related to me the experience of two people who had come to hear Vassula at the meeting which, ecumenically motivated as always, he had organised in the grounds of his own manor in Kent. They have since written their testimonies. They too saw the changing appearance of the sun as it shone over the large marquee which Jack had erected to hold Vassula's audience. They too saw the "miracle of the sun." One must treat their testimony with respect.

We come then to something very different. This is the changing appearance of Vassula herself as she speaks before an audience. What does happen? People looking at Vassula see that her face assumes a different appearance. They see a face which is like that of Jesus. It is a face bearded, resembling that well known from the enhanced image taken from the Shroud of Turin. Some of those who saw this change could not believe their eyes. One lady, very distinguished in her country, admitted that she rubbed her eyes a good deal to make sure that she was not "seeing things." She finally, as she admitted to me afterwards, believed that Jesus had put His face in that of Vassula. Others had no difficulty in so interpreting what they saw. There is a case of one person who saw the change take place as she watched a video camera recording a meeting addressed by Vassula.

The testimonies which have reached me come from many different countries: the Philippines, Switzerland, Italy, France, Ireland, Greece, Holland, England, Canada, Sweden, United States, Mexico, South Africa, Puerto Rico. In each case there was no knowledge of any similar experience elsewhere. (See Chapter 9, *Testimonies*)

What significance have these phenomena? Have similar phenomena been previously reported? In reply to the second question there is a well-known case of St Catherine of Siena. Her spiritual adviser, Blessed Raymond of Capua, once went to visit her when she was ill. He was startled to see the face of Christ on her bed of pain in place of that of the saint. There are, probably, similar instances reported from time to time in the lives of other saints. But there is none known to us where the phenomenon takes place so frequently and with people of such diverse background, ethnic, cultural, religious. Among the testimonies which I have received there are two from priests, and two from Orthodox Christians, one from an Anglican; all the others are from Catholics.

As to the significance we should first perhaps ponder the words of Jesus himself. His Immaculate Mother had told Vassula that though her sufferings would be great, she will be like a "mirror reflecting Jesus' image... Jesus will suffer - upon you will show His sufferings." Jesus Himself on 10 December, 1990 spoke in terms most intimate to Vassula. It was a day on which she would make an act of consecration to His Sacred Heart. Among other things He said these words:

> I shall efface your 'you' altogether, if you allow Me. From now on, after your consecration to My Sacred Heart, you will worship Me from the depths of your heart, and serve Me with a fire inside you, you will serve Me in fidelity and more fervently than ever before. Weak you are, but My strength

shall sustain you. I will not allow you to lose sight of Me nor will I allow your heart to flutter elsewhere, your heart will look for Me alone and desire Me alone without ceasing. I shall make you dislike all that is contrary to My holiness and to My will. I shall sift you through to make sure that not one rival remains within you. From today, the bonds I have enlaced you with shall be tightened even more now by Me, I shall make your soul thirst for Me and your heart sick for Me your God. I am only waiting now to consume your whole being with the flames of My Heart and My love. Whatever you do from now on will be done for My interests and My glory and nothing for you. You shall from now on, in other words, be the slave of My Love, the victim of My Heart and the benefit of My pleasures, the toy of My soul. **I shall make your traits resemble Mine, from the sorrows when you see the deafness of souls and the agony to see them fall**. My Vassula I shall give your soul its fill. No, I shall not spare you from My Cross, like the Father had not spared Me. How can I? My affection for you is immeasurable, besides everything comes out of My generosity and My infinite love.[1]

It is clear from this message of Jesus that the absolute priority for Him is interior identification with Him. It is a Vassula totally given to Him, the "slave" of His love whom He will use, even by showing His physical traits, to draw others to Him. On another occasion He spoke to her in a similar vein:

Offer Me sacrifices, be generous, have I not been generous with you? Give Me now, as I have given you; offer Me sacrifices to appease My justice; build what I have given you to construct. Oh Vassula! Offer Me everything to assuage My thirst! Put your faith in Me; give those who wait for My Word My hymn of love; give so that all the earth's inhabitants may hear My merciful cry. I cannot ignore My children's supplication.

Vassula replied in these words:

Lord, I beg you to guide my steps in the truth and in the light.

Jesus replied:

You will continue then to minister before Me and I shall open your mouth to fill it with My words to glorify Me and **through you I shall produce a visible image of Myself**. I will touch the hearts of My people and even people who never knew Me will be blessing Me. Despise yourself and I shall not reject you. I, Yahweh, will save you.

---

[1]Volume II, p.255.

Jesus returned to the subject on 30 August, 1993:

> My peace will remain upon you, My angel, and like the sun rising over the sea, My Holy Face will be revealed through you and on you while you are caring for My interests. I shall manifest Myself in this manner too so that the islands, the mountains and every plain may believe that you are sent by the Most High, and I AM is the author of *True Life in God*, and that by means of your nothingness My Holy Countenance shall be revealed. I will leave an everlasting memory to those to whom I have willingly revealed Myself. I shall show Myself to your society. I shall not conceal that I AM is the author of *True Life in God*.[1]

A predictable response to all that has been here recorded is that those henceforth attending meetings where Vassula speaks will be pre-conditioned and looking out for some similar experience. Their imagination will do the rest. Admittedly this is a possibility, but such a possibility is no reason for silence on the signs God works. There is a guarded approach to the subject of miracles, because, in the case of functional disorders, suggestion may be a factor. But miracles occur. And so do the miraculous changes in Vassula's appearance.

---

[1] Communication of Vassula.

3

THE PASSION

Some time after her conversion Vassula began to experience the Passion of the Saviour. It would happen generally on Friday. It was witnessed several times by Fr James Fannan. I was a witness of the event twice at least, in Switzerland and in Pittsburg. It lasted for less than an hour, with Vassula lying on the ground quite obviously seized by a force that kept her body in cruciform position, totally rapt in attention to a reality beyond her immediate environment. She occasionally writhed as if in very great pain; the features of her countenance were gathered in a death-like stare. At times she would seem by her searching gaze to seek someone. She would lift her right hand as if to trace a blessing.

This experience had not taken place for eighteen months and it would appear to have ceased as a part of Vassula's mystical way of life. What happened in Omaha on 12 June, 1993 showed how uncertain are human judgements in this world of divine benefaction. I shall relate things as I saw them and then reproduce the testimonies of the other witnesses.

With Vassula and Fr Ljudevic Rupcic, OFM I was an invited guest speaker at conferences in Canada and at a Marian-Eucharistic conference in Omaha, Nebraska, which began on June 11, 1993. Vassula, Fr Rupcic and I were to speak on the afternoon of the following day. As we were free in the morning we decided to hold a meeting of those interested in the distribution of the English editions of *True Life in God*, and of the book I had written on her, *Vassula of the Sacred Heart's Passion*, which had just appeared. It was convenient to meet in Vassula's room, 712 in the Red Lion Hotel.

Those present besides Vassula, Fr Rupcic and myself, were Mr Pat Callahan of *Trinitas*, publisher of the original handwritten edition, Mrs Christine Lynch, publisher of the English printed edition, and Mr John Lynch, her representative in the United States. The meeting opened at 10am. Almost immediately Vassula turned to me and whispered, "I'm not feeling well." I mentioned this to the others, assuming that they would await the outcome and left the room for a few minutes. When I returned I saw that Vassula had collapsed into Pat Callahan's arms. Next she was lying on the floor.

I recognised the features I had seen previously: a searching look in the eyes with the whole face strained, the arms held upward though in cruciform pattern, occasional writhing motions of the whole body, accompanied by cries of anguish or moans. This time she was weeping occasionally. Pat Callahan knelt beside Vassula and wrote as she spoke. "Peace" was repeated several times. There was a message for Fr Rupcic and a message for the Conference. This may have fulfilled the word of Sister Lucy Astuto, the remarkable religious who had organised the event; she had confided to her intimate collaborators shortly before it that she had an intuition that there would be a singular grace. In fact it was the first time that a public communication had been made about such a mystical experience in Vassula's life - Pat Callahan and I decided to break the rule of silence we had until then maintained about such things. We spoke to the assembly on what we had witnessed.

As Vassula seemed to resume her normal behaviour, I suggested offering her some tea. She could not hold the cup and I am not sure whether she sipped some from a spoon offered to her. Then unexpectedly she told Pat that the experience would recommence. This happened. Pat and I moistened Vassula's lips with tea drops or water which she accepted.

With a view to lifting Vassula on to her bed, Pat and I singly, separately and both together tried to raise her from the floor. In the construction business Pat has had experience in lifting objects weighing several hundred pounds. We could not even stir Vassula's body, though she agreed to our efforts; she is very lightly built and could normally be easily carried. As our efforts failed she smiled humorously and I had the feeling that she was almost teasing me, as to imply, "Keep trying." When the experience was finished, Vassula, with little noticeable effort, raised herself to a sitting position, and reoccupied her chair. We persuaded her to take a little lunch. She was ready to give her hour long talk at 4pm. Before that Pat and I informed the audience, as I have said.

I PAT CALLAHAN'S TESTIMONY

We gathered in Vassula's room to discuss publishing procedures for the *True Life in God* messages. At the beginning of the meeting Vassula mentioned that she was not feeling well. Fr O'Carroll went to his room to pick up some papers. Vassula looked at me and asked me to come near, saying, "Pat, will you stay close, I am not feeling well." She slumped forward as if she were going to faint. I moved toward her to be of assistance. And, as I did, she began to fall forward. I reached out to break her fall, and lowered her to the floor. She was obviously in pain.

As we stood there by her, she began to moan and weep in a distressed, soft, pained way. Her pain became so severe, the great distress her body was experiencing became quite evident. It was as if she could hardly encompass or incorporate the intense pain. Her body writhed in the agony. I am not clear how long this lasted.

She began to twist from side to side in response to the pain, her movements became more violent, almost as if she was being handled in some way and trying to escape from it. Then, rather suddenly, her arms were slung back as if put upon the cross. With her hands and arms fixed, her head and her torso moved back and forth in great pain. Her torso from her hips up came off the floor six to eight inches and her head would bend over her left shoulder. She was raised to this position, with her hands, as it were, pinned to the floor. Her feet were together side by side, her left knee was bent a little, and her right knee bent and slightly raised.

It was unreal that we could be witnessing what seemed to have the qualities of the Lord's Passion. With the torso being off the floor, an image I saw was of one being on the cross. Her moans and cries of agony were interrupted at times with the words "peace... peace... peace" (repeated many times). I don't know how long this lasted, but her body quit moving and she hung there suspended off the floor as I described. At some point later her torso was again flat on the floor and she raised both hands. Her eyes opened and her face became radiant in a manner I had not seen before. She called out very softly 'Abba' with her hands raised. Her lips moved as if talking but I heard nothing. She became quiet again but I could tell she was still suffering. At one point she kind of hung her head to the left and became very still, almost as if dead.

She uttered, hardly audibly, the words 'I am thirsty.' Fr O'Carroll got her a glass of water to give her a drink, but she could not take it. I was kneeling behind her right shoulder. She was lying with her arms outstretched and appeared to be in less pain. She raised her hands in the form of a blessing, holding her fingers like Jesus is sometimes depicted giving a blessing. She then very slowly blessed each of us. Very agonizingly and determinedly, as she moved her right arm, she would point at each person, but never look at them. She did this with each one of us, Fr O'Carroll, John Lynch, Chris Lynch and myself. I had the awareness as though Jesus was blessing us from the Cross.

She became still, crossed her hands and laid them high on her stomach. She laid very still, with her eyes open. At this point one of the party had to leave.

I then moved to kneel below her feet on her right side. She continued to lay still for a while. She turned her head slightly to look at me as if to say something. I leaned over and bent down to hear her. She asked me to help her sit up. It appeared that her suffering was about over. I placed one hand under her left shoulder and the other under her right shoulder to lift her, but as I tried, I discovered I could not move her. This was a very strange sensation. It was like I was trying to lift a live force, not like lifting something heavy, which I have done before in the construction business. Vassula looked me in the eyes as if she knew I could not lift her and she could not assist me. Then a little amused smile came over her face, so I knelt back. I did not understand the meaning of the smile at the time.

I moved near her feet. Several times she asked me (softly and barely audibly) to help her sit up. Each time I tried and could not help her, and each time the little smile came momentarily over her face. I asked myself what this smile could mean. It was as though the Lord was telling me, 'How very little you can do without My help. You cannot even help one so small to sit up.' It was also an affirmation, as if the Lord wanted me to know 'It's okay. You don't have to do everything because I have everything in the palm of My hand. Relax and be at peace.'

As I knelt there after she had experienced severe pains, torment and body writhing, it came to me that we had just witnessed a crucifixion. The only things that were missing were actual nails and blood. How do you share what you have seen, what you feel, or your awareness? It seemed we witnessed something very, very profound, very dreadful, very holy, very sacred, very awful, extremely painful, and yet a great gift. It was like the crucifixion of Jesus re-enacted, relived.

At one point when trying to lift Vassula, I had put in maximum effort, to the point of straining my back. I was overwhelmed. I realized I was trying to lift the sins of the world placed on Jesus. Then even more personally, I felt the weight of my own sins on Him, that He has agreed to carry. With all my strength I could not even budge them. I don't know how many times I tried to lift her; it was three or four. Nor do I know how much time elapsed.

Fr O'Carroll moved to a bench nearby. She again asked for help to sit up. Even with both of us helping her we could not budge her. And again, it was a different sensation than trying to lift something very heavy in dead weight, but rather lifting a living force. Shortly after Fr O'Carroll and I tried to lift her, she, on her own accord, lifted one arm and sat up. It was as though the Lord was reminding us that 'Everything is on My time. You can do little until you receive My help, My assistance.'

As Vassula sat on the floor, she appeared to be very, very weak. We pulled a chair over and Fr O'Carroll offered her a cup of tea. He explained to me that sometimes she likes a little tea after this kind of experience. We assisted her to the chair by the table. She sat there, very quiet and still, slumped over in her chair. After the tea was ordered, I looked at my watch. It was about 12.15pm. When tea arrived we offered it to her, but she could not hold the cup. We offered her some with a spoon, but she did not take it. She appeared to be very weak.

Thinking that the Passion experience had ended Fr O'Carroll returned to his room. I believe John (Lynch) also left. I again tried to assist Vassula with her tea. She looked at me and said, 'Pat, I don't believe it is over yet,' or words similar to that.

And immediately she slumped forward a second time, as if she were about to fall off the chair. So again I reached out to break her fall and lowered her to the floor. She experienced much the same as the first time, but not as long and not as severe. There was moaning, crying, and deep, desperate weeping. She was stretched out again, like on the cross, in much agony and torment. After a while she looked at me. I knew she wanted to say something. Very softly, very gently, she said, 'I am thirsty.'

I remembered Fr O'Carroll's first efforts to give her a drink from a glass and then remembered nursing family members and how we would moisten a cotton swab and rub their lips. We had no swab so I took my finger and moistened her lips (Our Lord's lips). As I sat back on my heels and knelt there silent, words from the messages came to me, 'My lips are parched for lack of love.' I became overwhelmed with sorrow. My first awareness was how little love we give to Our Lord. Then it really came to me! How little love I give to my Lord. Yet how great is the love and tenderness that He has for me and for each of us. I became aware of the profound yet simple gift that He was giving to me to moisten His parched lips, such a small act of love and kindness. Still He let me be aware of how important it was to Him.

A great sense of comfort and joy came over me, knowing that the Lord would permit me, knowing my faults and my sins, in such a personal and intimate way, to serve Him as I served my 'sister'. I became keenly aware of what He wants from me - just a little love. He wants me to do what I do in love. I remembered how Mother Teresa loves and serves in little ways, and how she sees Jesus in each person she serves. Her words of 'Do what we do in love' kept going by me.

As I raised my eyes I realized Vassula was looking at me to tell me something else. I bent low to hear her. She gave me a message for Fr Rupcic. Speaking very softly and slowly she said, 'Tell Fr Rupcic that the Croatians will be delivered in the end.' When she started to say something else I reached for paper to record it. She began: 'All is not in vain. Everything hereto is for My glory.' She began speaking very softly and slowly, but gradually she spoke faster and faster. I became flustered trying to keep up with her. I started writing the fourth message: 'Blessed are the peacemakers.. (then I missed part of this..They shall see God).' The fifth message was 'Blessed are the pure in heart for they shall see God, too.' Then the sixth message: 'Blessed are..' (I missed the rest). The final message I did get down. It was: 'Rejoice for your King is on the road of return. Salvation is at hand!' She was still in great pain as she was speaking. I continued kneeling there.

As I handed the message to Fr O'Carroll he turned to answer a knock on the door. It was Fr Rupcic. The two priests visited in the hallway for a few minutes while I stayed kneeling by Vassula. She said, 'Ask Fr Rupcic to come in.' Then she asked me to read this message to him: 'Tell Fr Rupcic that the Croatians will be delivered in the end.' He was off to the right of Vassula at an angle. She was looking straight ahead.

When she was in this state, her face took on a different appearance - radiant, ecstatic, a very beautiful appearance: a mixture of joy and pain, perhaps transfigured. Her eyes were wide open and looking straight ahead. Shortly after I read the message to Fr Rupcic, she raised her hand in his direction, and blessed him (Jesus blessed him) in the same, very slow, deliberate way as before, looking straight ahead, not at father.

A little while later, Fr Rupcic left the room with the papers the messages were on. He later returned and gave me the messages after removing the one that was for him.

Vassula's passion experience continued with what appeared to be excruciating pain and agony, first with arms outstretched, and then folded across her chest, her eyes looking straight ahead into the distance with that different appearance, a beautiful appearance - almost radiant, somehow a mixture of deep peace, joy, and yet apparent pain. I was standing a little above her right shoulder. Fr O'Carroll was trying to make her comfortable. Again I heard her say, "I am thirsty." Father reached for the water and gently, tenderly moistened her lips (Jesus' lips) with his finger. She seemed to be more at peace.

Father left the room. While I knelt, silent, a short distance from Vassula's feet, I prayed. I had prayed a lot during her passion. She stirred, looked at me and said, 'I am thirsty.' Overwhelmed, I again moistened her lips (Jesus' lips) with my finger. My heart was overflowing with the awareness of Jesus' desire for a little love. It was such a joy to serve Him in this way.

After awhile, she began to stir as if to sit up. I moved a little so that she could raise herself more easily. She reached out and held onto my arm to sit up. When she finally managed to raise up she was so weak she leaned back on me. I supported her there for a short time. I was still so filled with the reality of the sufferings of Jesus for my sins that I felt as if I were holding Our Lord in my arms after the crucifixion. I felt as if Mother Mary let me experience some of the great grief and the great tenderness She had for Her Son. For a brief moment, it was like I was Mary, holding my Son. I have no other way to express it.

Vassula gradually began to revive and I helped her sit in the chair by the table. I asked her if she would like to try again to have some tea. She did, so I prepared it. She was so weak she could not hold the cup. I gave her some tea with a spoon. This time she drank some. She seemed to "come to" gradually.

Once again, I looked at my watch. It was about 1.45pm. Fr O'Carroll came back and waited on the edge of the bed. Her strength was gradually returning. She looked very tired. She finished drinking her tea and said that she was all right. Fr O'Carroll asked her if she would like something to eat before they went to give their presentations that afternoon. He was scheduled at 3pm. She thought she might have time for some soup.

Before we left the room, Vassula gave Fr O'Carroll a warm embrace - a very tender moment. We then went to the restaurant. At that time I showed Vassula the paper on which I had written the messages. She corrected some of what I had written and completed the unfinished: "Blessed are the peacemakers, for they shall be called the children of God." And "Blessed are the poor in spirit, for their's is the kingdom of Heaven." We visited briefly before Fr O'Carroll left for the conference.

Vassula had no time to rest between her passion experience and her presentation. It was miraculous that she could recover so quickly. After a brief lunch, the hospitality representative accompanied her to the conference where she spoke on the Messages of Jesus at 4pm.

Reflections

During her passion, the position of her head was opposite that of the crucifixes I have seen of Jesus. His head turns to the right; Vassula's head turned to the left. I have noted also that Jesus' left knee is the knee that is slightly raised; it was Vassula's right knee that was slightly raised.

The following day at the Franciscan Prayer Centre in Independence, where Vassula spoke at the Corpus Christi celebration, I spent some time in the Presence of the Blessed Sacrament. Vassula's passion kept running before me like I needed to do something - maybe to recall it and write it down! At first I ignored it, but I finally moved into it and began making a few notes. I then thought back to the Mass of the previous late Friday evening which Fr O'Carroll and Fr Rupcic concelebrated in Vassula's room. At Communion Fr Rupcic distributed the Precious Blood. When I received it, I looked in the chalice and saw an irregular Host with a couple of broken pieces. The Host was floating in a slight wave-like way, like it was thin and not rigid, but flexible. I was surprised and questioned what I saw. I did not see father put a Host in the Chalice, but I thought perhaps I had just missed it.

Saturday morning I asked Sue, who received ahead of me on Friday night, if she had seen father put a Host in the chalice. She had not. She saw no Host in the chalice when she received. She mentioned it could have been the Lord's Body and maybe a special gift for me. It suddenly came to me that it was the broken Body of Christ which I had seen, and this experience connected with witnessing the Passion of Vassula, in that they were both the unbloody sacrifice of the cross. Every Mass, Jesus offers Himself, His Body, His Blood, to the Father for each of us. Witnessing

Vassula I became aware of the agony our Lord suffers. We saw the unbloody sacrifice of the cross... relived... re-enacted through Vassula.

My awareness of the presence of Our Lord in Vassula during her passion was so strong and real that she seemed to disappear in Him. I had lost complete awareness of her.

II TESTIMONY OF CHRISTINE LYNCH

JMJ Publications
PO Box 385
Belfast
Northern Ireland

Since March 1991 I have been responsible for the editing, publishing and distributing world-wide the printed version of 'True Life in God' and books by Fr Michael O'Carroll CSSp relating to the spiritual writings of Vassula.

In June 1993 there was a Marian Conference in Omaha, which I attended - accompanied by John Lynch, from New York (my main agent in the USA for the True Life in God Books), and Moira Smith, helper from Toronto; both Fr O'Carroll and Vassula were speaking at the Conference.

We had met to discuss the distribution of the books in the States.

The Event

I was at my bookstand at the Omaha Conference Centre on Saturday June 12th 1993 at 9.40am when I had a message to go to Vassula's room at the Red Lion Hotel where our meeting would be held.

Vassula, Fr O'Carroll, John Lynch, Pat Callahan and myself were discussing the three new books I had just published and some problems I was having; after about twenty minutes I saw Vassula whisper to Fr O'Carroll. Fr O'Carroll stood up saying Vassula was not feeling well and we would have to continue the discussion in his room. John and I stood up and father moved towards the door - Pat Callahan sat beside Vassula and she leaned her head on his shoulder as if feeling very weak.

Then a very strange thing happened.

One minute the scene was just as described, the next minute Vassula was lying fully stretched out in the centre of the room, some feet from where she had been sitting with Pat.

Although I was watching her at the time, I did not see her fall, or slump down - she seemed to just suddenly be there on the floor, her eyes looking upwards - hands by her side - legs straight out, neatly together.

I think all of us realised something out of the ordinary was happening as none of us moved or went to assist her. We just stood; after a short time Pat went to kneel on the floor on her left side.

The next ninety minutes for me were so special and so strange yet very beautiful - time literally stood still.

We all watched this slim figure with long blonde hair lying on the floor of that hotel room, slowly take on the position of Christ on the Cross. Her arms slowly went backwards and upwards (flat against the floor) until they reached an angle of approximately 45°, both knees together slightly bent to the left. After a few moments her shoulders and head literally rose into the air in a most unnatural position - hands and wrists still on the ground, and then her head fell down against her left shoulder (identical to figures of Christ nailed against the cross when the weight of His body sagged and His head fell forward onto His shoulder) - slight moans could be heard. She held this position for a short time - whether it was thirty seconds or three minutes I will never know - one felt outside time and space. After an indefinite space of time, her shoulders and head relaxed back against the floor.

This happened again and again over the next 90 minutes that I was present.

In the quiet periods between these 'crucifixion' positions, father first of all offered her a drink but she declined. The next time he tried to give her a sip of iced water but she was unable to raise her head. After the third time she attempted to speak, and very slowly, painfully, as if her mouth were dry and in great pain, the words "PEACE, PEACE, PEACE" were slowly forced from her lips five times.

At this point two things were very clear to me - that Jesus was showing Himself on His Cross and that he wanted the four of us present to bring about peace and take Him from the cross.

I was in tears most of this time, very aware of my own sinfulness - in complete awe of what was happening - Our Lord and God answering our prayers and supplications in such a profound way.

Before I left the hotel room that unforgettable morning, Jesus showed us two things more. At one point, again after the crucifixion position had been relaxed, Vassula's arms came down to her sides - after a pause - her soft brown eyes, always until now looking at the ceiling, looked at the three of us at her feet. Her right arm began to rise gradually in the sign of peace - thumb holding back the two little fingers, the middle fingers raised in the sign of peace. This was repeated three times - three times to the front, where Pat, father and myself were and a very long sign of peace to John, who was standing all six foot five, three hundred pounds of him, to her right. He was looking at the floor and she seemed to will him to look at her.

The last thing Jesus showed us was completely different but completed the message He was giving us that day.

It was well over an hour after this extraordinary event started, just after a crucifixion position, when Vassula was asked if she would like to be lifted onto a chair or the bed. Vassula indicated with the closing of her eyes, that she did. I knelt on one side of her, Pat on the other, and we tried to put our hands beneath her in order to lift her slight frame from the floor. I was surprised and rather confused to find that it was impossible even to get my fingers beneath her head - she was like a stone carving - solid -immoveable. Father (who was standing behind me) whispered 'it is the <u>weight of the sin of the world</u>.'

It is some eight and a half weeks now since I had that strange, wonderful, extraordinary, powerful experience. Obviously I have thought about it a great deal. What <u>is</u> clear to me is that Jesus showed us He is on the Cross, that He is suffering and bearing the intolerable weight of the sins of the world. He has shown us through this powerful 'Hymn of Love' He is singing for us through True Life in God, that He wants us to be humble, kind, meek and to work for peace, love, unity through these messages.

He gave father, John, Pat and myself <u>His Peace</u>.

It was necessary for me to leave that room at 12 noon to return to my (Vassula) bookstand at the Conference Centre, which was opening again after 10.30 Mass. As I left, I looked back at that tableau, at the three people grouped around that small figure, lying so still; the crucifixion being re-enacted before our eyes. I was loathe to leave - my heart was with Our Blessed Lord and I felt sad to see Him so grieved and in such pain through sinfulness.

4

THE ORTHODOX

Orthodox Christians, in their different churches, are the heirs in our time of those who suffered what the Second Vatican Council calls "the first divisions" in the Church. These divisions the Council tells us occurred "in the East, either because of disputes over the dogmatic pronouncements of the Councils of Ephesus and Chalcedon or later by the breakdown of ecclesiastical communion between the Eastern Patriarchates and the Roman See."[1]

The Council provides a brief summary of the background which anyone interested in Christian unity should read and ponder. It is my contention that Vassula Rydén has given it immediate relevance. I shall first quote what the Council says and then explain why it is relevant through the mission of Vassula. "For many centuries" we read "the Churches of the East and of the West went their own ways, though a brotherly communion of faith and sacramental life bound them together. If disagreements in belief and discipline arose among them, the Roman See acted by common consent as moderator."[2]

The Council then gave a brief description of the Orthodox Church: "This most Sacred Synod gladly reminds all of one highly significant fact among others: in the East there flourish many particular or local churches; among them the Patriarchal churches hold first place; and of these many glory in taking their origins from the Apostles themselves. As a result there prevailed and still prevails among Orientals an eager desire to perpetuate in a communion of faith and charity those family ties which ought to thrive between local Churches, as between sisters."[3]

There is a word on the spiritual patrimony of the Orthodox, with acknowledgement of our debt to them in the West: "It is equally worthy of note that from their very origins the Churches of the East have had a treasury from which the Church of the West has amply drawn in its liturgy, spiritual traditions, and jurisprudence. Nor must we underestimate the fact that basic dogmas of the Christian faith concerning the Trinity and God's Word made flesh of the Virgin Mary were defined in Ecumenical Councils held in the East. To preserve this faith, these Churches have suffered much and still do so."[4]

The Council elaborates its praise on two matters of high interest to us: the Liturgy and Our Blessed Lady. On the Liturgy it speaks thus: "Everybody also knows with what love the Eastern Churches enact the sacred liturgy, especially in the celebration of the Eucharist, which is the source of the Church's life and the pledge of future glory. In this celebration the faithful, united with their bishop and endowed with an outpouring of the Holy Spirit, gain access to God the Father through the Son, the Word made flesh, who suffered and was glorified. And so, made 'partakers of the divine nature' (2 Pet 1:4), they enter into communion with the most Holy Trinity. Hence, through the celebration of the Eucharist of the Lord in each of these Churches, the Church of God is built up and grows in stature while through the rite of concelebration their bond with one another is made manifest."[5]

Thought of Our Lady reminds us of what we have in recent times lost through a one-sided understanding of ecumenism. It was seen by some entirely in terms of Protestants. Since some Protestants have difficulties in regard to Our Lady the facile conclusion was drawn by Catholics that there should be less in theory and practice about her; in places it was almost an assault on Marian theology and devotional practice. Combined with other tendencies not theologically justifiable, this gave us, in the words of Fr Ignace de la Potterie, SJ at the International Mariological Congress in Huelva last September, a "decade without Mary" - he would probably have placed it between 1965, the end of Vatican II and 1974, the publication of Paul VI's Apostolic Exhortation, *Marialis Cultus*: hyperbole, but a valid point.

Attention to these words of Vatican II would have given people pause: "In this liturgical worship, the Christians of the East pay high tribute, in very beautiful hymns, to Mary ever Virgin, whom the Ecumenical Synod of Ephesus solemnly proclaimed to be God's Holy Mother so that, in accord with the Scriptures, Christ may be truly and properly acknowledged the Son of God and Son of Man. They also give homage to the saints, including Fathers of the universal Church."[6]

In the Orthodox world the wealth of the ages surrounds the Theotokos and there the truths enshrined in the great traditions are not negotiable; this is not an area for bargaining. I may quote a great Orthodox theologian of the present century, Sergius Bulgakov. He was a dedicated ecumenist, a founder member of *Faith and Order*, which was to coalesce in 1948 with another movement, *Life and Work*, to make the *World Council of Churches*. In a commemorative volume prepared for the fifteenth centenary of the Council of Ephesus (431-1931) he wrote, "as long as there exists this mysterious antipathy against any Marian devotion on the part of Protestantism, a true reunion of the Churches is impossible - a correct doctrine of the Church is impossible without a Mariology. The Mother of God is the personal head of the Church (though certainly in a different sense from Jesus Christ himself), namely as head of mankind, as the creaturely centre."[7]

The Second Vatican Council did not aim at a full account of Orthodox theology or spirituality. Regrettably it did not delay on one theme wherein the Orthodox excel, the saving, dynamic presence of the Holy Spirit in the life of the Church and of the individual soul. I have given in the first book on Vassula's life and teaching some evidence of the reaction of one influential Orthodox theologian to conciliar doctrine in the making - the comment of Nikos Nissiotis on the need for a theology of the Holy Spirit. John Paul II in his Encyclical on the Holy Spirit acknowledges the contribution of the Orientals in this vital matter. It continues to the present time; an outstanding work on the subject, *Le Paraclet* was from Sergius Bulgakov some time before his death. A considerable contemporary literature testifies to awareness of a doctrinal need and resolve to meet it.

Nor did the Council Fathers feel obliged to attempt a description of the different Orthodox Churches, an analysis of the prevailing religious situation particularly as to practice, in the component bodies. We have no studies which would meet the criteria of the Sociology of Religion, a scientific discipline increasingly valued. Such reliable surveys are, for obvious reasons, not available. Much time, patience and compassion will be required to examine fully the conditions of those who have only recently emerged from oppression of one kind or another.

Statistics are difficult to obtain with certainty. A global figure of two hundred and twenty-five million has been given. The accuracy depends on one unknown, or largely unknown, area, Russia. The revival has begun and apart from those who had to conceal their membership of the Church, who can now without danger openly admit this affiliation, there is the daily increase in numbers through conversion: conversion from religious indifference, that is absence from the Church, or conversion from outright atheism.

One must allow for world-wide diffusion of Orthodox Christians. One must never forget that the faithful, consciously or unconsciously, bear a memory of ancient origins. They look to a past that touches the initial mysteries wherein our religion appeared as a public recognisable reality within the flow of history. Such a sense of continuity, such an intimate possession of roots, ancient but presently relevant, invests the whole Orthodox world with a dignity and value not to be overlooked or mistaken.

This sense of history and, among the erudite, the added enlightened reference to the Fathers of the Church and to the mighty theologians who have appeared within the Orthodox churches through the centuries impose on any outsider profound respect. This respect must be doubled by deep sympathy on the part of other Christians, on the part especially of Catholics. Tragically among many Catholics an awareness of such things is totally absent. Therein they are if not disobedient, at least disrespectful, towards formal recommendations emanating from their own Church authorities. We shall meet this defect again.

Available statistics have relevance. There are more than a quarter of a million

Orthodox in Great Britain. The United States has more than five million. France has provided an intellectual stronghold, though its teaching personnel, in the St Serge Institute, were mostly expatriate Russians. The St Serge Institute has great names in its history, Sergius Bulgakov, George Florovsky, Paul Evdokimov perhaps best known. Another Orthodox writer much associated with France is Vladimir Lossky.

If there is mention of neglect of the Orthodox in the ecumenical movement, a question mark must stand after the names of our great twentieth century theologians. Let us take three who would probably be universally accepted as at least among the greatest, the French Dominican, Yves M J Congar, the German Jesuit, Karl Rahner and the Swiss independent writer, Hans Urs von Balthasar. Fr Congar could not avoid treating certain Orthodox themes in his magnificent three volume work on the Holy Spirit; but in the whole corpus of his work one can scarcely say that Orthodox personalities, theologians or themes figure very prominently. Fr Rahner completely overlooked Orthodox thinking, past or present. Hans Urs von Balthasar came to realize towards the end of his life something of the importance of the eastern contribution, but it had no significant place in his gigantic, captivating synthesis.

I am not foolish enough to take a place beside these giants of contemporary Latin theology. But since I have published five theological encyclopedias I may be asked to submit to the test I have applied to others. My interest in the theology of Our Lady saved me. Anyone studying the history of Marian theology must be impressed by the contribution of the Palamite theologians. I gave them and other Orthodox personalities and themes due attention in my encyclopedia on Our Lady, *Theotokos*; in the subsequent volumes I gave full space to Orthodox theologians and themes.[8] It comes to this that I have possibly written more on the Orthodox than any Catholic writer in the English language, possibly more than any Catholic writer, with the exception of the giant in this domain, Fr Martin Jugie, AA.

What is the present inter-faith situation? Here we have three official documents to guide us: the Ecumenical Directory issued in two parts in 1967 and 1970, the revised Directory published in 1993 and the report of the joint commission of Catholic and Orthodox theologians made public after their meeting in Balamand, Lebanon, June 1993. Reading all three in the light of the conciliar Decree on Ecumenism must lead to an examination of conscience. The Directory points out that deciding ecumenical policy "is a pastoral care which will be the more effective as the faithful become more solidly and fully instructed in the teaching and authentic tradition both of the Catholic Church and of the Churches and communities separated from her."[9]

The Directory, to support its plea for spiritual ecumenism cites these words of the Decree on Ecumenism: "This change of heart and holiness of life, along with public and private prayer for the unity of Christians, should be regarded as the soul of the whole ecumenical movement, and merits the name 'spiritual ecumenism.'" "In these few words" comments the Directory, "the Decree defines spiritual ecumenism, and stresses its importance in order that Christians may, both in prayer and in celebration of the Eucharist and indeed in their entire way of life, carefully keep in view the aim of unity."

We are urged to practise sharing of spiritual activity and resources with our separated brethren. "Fraternal charity in the relations of daily life is not enough to foster the restoration of unity among all Christians. It is right and proper that there should also be a certain *communicatio in spiritualibus*, ie, that Christians should be able to share that spiritual heritage they have in common in a manner and to a degree permissible and appropriate in their present divided state."[10]

Finally we should recall an overall principle laid down in the Directory: "Since this (ecumenical) movement has been set on foot by the Holy Spirit, what follows here is put forward with the intention and in a manner to be of service to bishops in putting into effect the Decree on Ecumenism, 'without obstructing the ways of divine Providence, and without prejudging the future inspirations of the Holy Spirit.'"[11]

The revised Directory issued in 1993 is largely taken up with directives on the ecclesial structures and procedure required in the practice of ecumenism.[12] More relevant to the theme of this book is the report issued after the Balamand meeting. This derives special importance from the interest it had previously aroused in John Paul II. The Pope must be aware of a problem that will arise in the years ahead. The Catholic Church is dying in European countries. The decline may be arrested, and there are many centres of intense faith and fervour from which renewal may come. But the cold statistics of non-practising masses, the dried up fountain of priestly vocations, the spreading secularization are the present reality.

Meanwhile the Orthodox Church in Russia is awakening. On all sides there are signs of new life, and the revival will, on a reasonably reliable conjecture, be marked by the heroism which carried the Russian people through the ordeal of the Second World War, and the horrors of the Stalinist years.

We are told that John Paul II is currently studying Orthodox theology. What is certain is his interest in the practical problem of unity between the Catholic Church and the Orthodox Churches. In the Apostolic Letter, *Europae Orientalis*, establishing the Roman Commission for Eastern Europe he stated, among other things, "The Commission will be responsible for promoting the apostolic mission of the Catholic Church in all her activities and likewise for fostering ecumenical dialogue with the Orthodox and with other Churches of the eastern tradition."

This document was issued on 15 January, 1993. On Trinity Sunday 6 June the Pope addressed the faithful attending Mass in St Peter's as follows:

On this day when the Latin Church, following the Gregorian calendar, is celebrating the Solemnity of the Most Holy Trinity, our Eastern brothers and sisters, who follow the Julian calendar, are celebrating the great feast of Pentecost. Let us join in their joy and harmonious invocation of the Holy Spirit 'who is present in every place and fills everything,' according to the Byzantine liturgical prayer, that he may pour out an abundance of His gifts on us for a renewed Gospel flowering and a common growth in faith and in holiness of life.

Today's festive celebration of the Most Holy Trinity, mystery of communion and model of perfect unity for the Church and the observance of Pentecost by our Eastern brothers and sisters offers me the opportunity to entrust to God, the Father, the Son and the Holy Spirit, the forthcoming meeting of the Joint Commission for Theological Dialogue between the Catholic and Orthodox Churches, scheduled to be held from 18-24 June at Balamand, Lebanon, at the theological school of the Greek Orthodox Patriarchate of Antioch.

In December 1987, on the occasion of the visit to Rome of our venerable brother, Patriarch Dimitrios, we gave thanks together to the Lord for the firm progress made in our common dialogue. On the basis of those results and relying especially on the constant divine assistance, I now express my sincere wish that satisfactory solutions may be found for the question under examination today concerning the relations between the Oriental Catholic Churches and the Orthodox Churches. I invite you to pray with me that the Holy Spirit may enlighten hearts and move people sincerely to seek the paths of full unity which the Lord wants for His disciples. Thus the theological research, which has been so successful until now, can continue.

A loyal clarification of the historical controversies in a spirit of ecclesial fraternity and an attitude of obedience to the Lord's will alone, will further hasten the process of theological dialogue in view of full communion and will also point out the ways and means to offer henceforth a joint witness of unselfish co-operation in proclaiming the Gospel.

During this period of anxiety and tension, as tragic conflicts and fratricidal wars are spreading, the generous commitment of Catholics and Orthodox to intensify their search for full unity will certainly be a real contribution to reconciliation among peoples and to building new relationships of solidarity among the nations.

Dear brothers and sisters, I entrust this important meeting of dialogue and fraternal charity to your fervent prayer and that of all Catholics throughout the world. Let us now invoke Mary's motherly assistance upon it by reciting the Angelus.[13]

The meeting at Balamand began its work from a document drawn up in June, 1991 at Arricia near Rome. It was entitled: *Uniatism, the method of unity in the past, and the search for full communion.* The statement which was published in the name of those who met at Balamand constitutes a landmark in the quest for Christian unity. It is reproduced in full as an appendix to the present book. The reader must read it and reflect on the change which it calls for in the outlook of Catholics. Without attempting to summarize such an important text I would call attention to the following: the efforts made thus far have not achieved full communion, and have at times hardened oppositions; the break of certain communities with their Mother Churches in the east, which took place "not without the intervention of certain extra-ecclesial interests" has led to a situation "which has become a source of conflicts and of sufferings first for the Orthodox, but also for Catholics"; division persists "envenomed" by these attempts; the situation thus created in effect caused tensions and oppositions; the Catholic and the Orthodox Churches see themselves as sister Churches; re-baptism is excluded in case of change; there is a specific call for respect for "the religious freedom of the faithful"; the pastoral action of the Catholic Church, whether Latin or Oriental, does not tend any longer to have the faithful pass from one Church to another; proselytism, especially when it is supported by financial inducements, is condemned; bishops and priests have the duty before God of respecting the authority which the Holy Spirit has given to bishops and priests of the other Church, and to this end, to avoid interfering in the spiritual life of the faithful of this Church.

The ideas thus expressed and the entire contents of the document, could, if fully accepted and implemented, constitute a landmark in the quest for Christian unity. Never before has there been such a frank assessment and avowal of the position between the two Churches. There is an impression of total honesty and integrity. Cardinal Edward Idris Cassidy, president of the Council for Promoting Christian Unity commented: "I think what we've done is a very positive contribution to getting our dialogue back on track."

That much work remains to be done is still true. Cardinal Cassidy admitted that "tensions and difficulties" still existed between the two Churches. The meeting had been planned for a year earlier but was postponed after many Orthodox Churches declined to send delegates. Vatican officials thought the delay was due to tensions on these issues: property ownership by Churches; the Orthodox fear that Uniate Eastern Churches would try to convert Orthodox faithful; misunderstanding over the re-establishment of Latin-rite jurisdictions in some parts of Eastern Europe.

There were twenty-four Catholics at the meeting and representatives from nine Orthodox Churches. But there were notable absentees; there were no representatives from the Orthodox Churches in Serbia, Bulgaria, the Czech Republic, Georgia, Jerusalem and Greece. The absence of the Georgian delegate was explainable in terms of the "quasi-civil war" in his country. Absence of the others, Cardinal

Cassidy thought, could be taken as a "gesture of protest."

The setting of the encounter was marked by hospitality to the members when they visited local Orthodox leaders; and by a malicious deed. A bomb exploded on a mountain side where a bus carrying the Catholic participants was due to pass. Two men, apparently preparing the blast, were killed and a third wounded. The Catholics heard of the attempt after it had taken place. The meeting was not affected. Lebanese police quickly rounded up suspects, thought to be members of a radical Islamic group with ties to Iran.

Here I am desirous to relate to the theory and practice of ecumenism in this Orthodox context the mission of Vassula and the message she has so far given to the faithful. We may deal quickly with one question often put to her, during meetings or otherwise: "Why do you not become a Catholic?" She can now say, not only that God does not ask her to do this, but that as the joint commission stated, the Catholic Church does not tend to do this.

We are asked not "to obstruct the ways of divine Providence" and not to prejudge "the future inspirations of the Holy Spirit." Vassula certainly enters into the ways of divine Providence. Her contribution to the immense task of Christian unity has all the marks of providential intervention. She has a lucid message, totally acceptable in the light of the Christian mystery, and she has been heard by thousands of Catholics drawn solely by a desire to know and love Jesus Christ, Saviour of mankind. Is it far-fetched to see in her one inspired by the Holy Spirit?

We are in a very sensitive area. Here spiritual ecumenism is sought by the official directives. We shall follow in the next chapter Vassula's meetings in different countries. We shall see how her influence has been growing among the Orthodox. What needs to be stressed is her intuition on the importance of prayer at her meetings. It fully meets the directive of the Roman documents for she very frequently leads her audience in the Rosary - this from a member of Greek Orthodox Church is quite exceptional, most praiseworthy.

The reader also would do well to ponder this aspect of her mission: at a time when there is so much tension between Catholics and Orthodox is it not providential that we should have one who can fill the role of bridge-builder, a true mediatress? Is this not an example of the inspirations of the Holy Spirit which we are asked not to prejudge? He remains the God of surprises. What he does is not always what we would plan. We too easily assume our own certainty on things divine, what is entirely beyond our comprehension and assessment.

Vassula is within the Orthodox world, totally loyal to its teaching and precepts. But God has so ordered her life that she should have her first world-wide constituency among Catholics. There have been points of discord raised by individuals in one area and the other, but they have easily been settled. She stands between East and West, a symbol and bearer of hope.

Notes:

1. Decree on Ecumenism, n.13;
2. Op. cit., n.14;
3. Ibid.,
4. Ibid.,
5. Op. cit., n.15;
6. Ibid;
7. Die Hochkirche, ed. Friedrich Heiler, 1931, p.244;
8. In the five theological encyclopedias which I have published, there are fifty articles on Orthodox personalities and themes; cf. also my book, John Paul II, Apostle of the Holy Spirit, A Dictionary of his Life and Teaching, Belfast, 1994, article Orthodox, The;
9. Directory I, 14 May, 1967, n.2, ed. A Flannery, Vatican II, p.434;
10. Decree on Ecumenism, n.8, Directory n.21, A Flannery, p.490;
11. Decree on Ecumenism, n.24, Directory, n.2, A Flannery, p.434;
12. The new Directory is more than twice the size of the first. It benefitted by experience and by the publication of the new Code of Canon Law, 1983, which itself, as the Pope says in his introductory essay, assimilated into legal terms the teaching of Vatican II, especially that contained in the Constitution on the Church and that on the Church in the Modern World. In particular the directives about sharing in the Sacraments, that is Confession, the Eucharist and the Anointing of the Sick, are all important.
13. OR, 7 June, 1993; for further information on John Paul II's increasing interest in the Orthodox cf. article j.cit. in my book on the Pope. He has seized every possible opportunity to manifest his interest and sympathy in their regard. He has been represented frequently at the annual celebration of the feast of St Andrew at Istanbul, with a personal message to the Patriarch; he has welcomed in Rome delegations headed by a representative of this prelate, speaking words of warmth to Orthodox seminarists. There were Orthodox speakers at the International Conference organised at his instigation by the rectors of the Roman universities for the sixteenth centenary of the Council of Constantinople. In the annual Stations of the Cross on Good Friday he read the prayers composed by the Patriarch, was followed in procession by the latter's representative.

5

WORLDWIDE APOSTOLATE

I shall break the chronological sequence to write of a highlight in Vassula's apostolic career, her meeting with Pope John Paul II in the Hall of Benediction in Vatican City on 6 November 1993. I must single out certain features of the encounter before attempting an overall evaluation. I asked an experienced Roman priest his opinion of this aspect of the visit: did he think that any author had ever presented to the Pope his or her works in five languages (original in one, translations in four, including a volume in Russian, three volumes in Polish, four volumes in Italian and the French translation of my book about Vassula, *Vassula de la Passion du Sacre Coeur*)? The immediate answer of the venerable Salesian priest, Don Aldo Gregori, was "This is a first."

There was a protocol that those received in private audience by the Pope would immediately call on his Secretary of State. It seems to have lapsed save possibly for high dignitaries. Normally the Secretary of State is not present at the general audiences of the kind within which our meeting with John Paul II took place. He would be absent from his desk every day of the week if he had this duty. But on 6 November the Secretary of State, Cardinal Sodano, was present. He was identified with the diocese of Asti, which was being honoured, as this was a thanksgiving assembly for the fact that the Pope had beatified Giuseppe Marello, founder of the *Oblati di San Giuseppe*, a native of the same diocese.

The Cardinal's presence was important. We met him after the audience and he said something important. I or someone else mentioned that Vassula had presented several volumes of her writings to the Pope. The Cardinal assured us that he had seen them, adding "I am sure the Pope will read them with great interest." We were photographed with his Eminence. All doubts about the books being safely lodged for the Pope's attention were thus removed. We both perceived that the Secretary of State knew about Vassula and her mission. It would be very strange if he did not. He has surely information sources which would cover a mission which is now so far-reaching socially and geographically.

I have heard it said that a photograph showing Vassula with the Pope would be an asset. I have not been convinced. There are thousands of people with such photographs; I have a number myself with the present Pope and his predecessors.

What does it mean?   "That's me and that's the Pope."   But to offer him a multilingual gift of your work for the Church, fruit of both four years' labour and yet so diverse, and to have this on record and endorsed by the Secretary of State, is, I submit, something totally different: very meaningful.

In presenting the books to the Holy Father, Vassula was obeying a command given to her some years back: Jesus instructed her to place the message in the Pope's hands. She was thus emphasizing a unique aspect of her writing. Not only is she the Orthodox writer nearest to Catholic thinking and practice, not only has she anticipated the directive of an important recent decision of Orthodox and Catholic theologians in dialogue by remaining an Orthodox: she is the only member of the Orthodox Church who publicly supports the universal primacy of the Roman Pontiff. She has addressed Catholic audiences world-wide. She has spoken to Orthodox in Geneva at the World Council of Churches headquarters, in Jerusalem, Athens, Moscow and St Petersburg. She is a unique bridge-builder, go-between. And some Catholic priests are doing their best to destroy her. May God have mercy on us all.

How did the meeting with John Paul II take place? Here a wonderful seminarist of the *Oblati di San Giuseppe*, Joseph Ianuzzi, was the instrument the Lord used. There was some idea, coming from our good friend Carlo Sami, Vassula's good friend and collaborator in all her works, that while in Rome we might have a chance to see the Pope. This young man is a fervent reader of the messages; he is Italian American. We simply went to the Bronze Door with him, and without tickets were ushered in. We had a vantage point to offer the Pope our gifts. Modesty apart, I think that this may have been the first occasion in history when an apostle of Jesus Christ stood before the Pope with her biographer, who presented to the Holy Father a copy of his book in French translation. The book is dedicated to John Paul II to mark the striking similarity between papal teaching during this pontificate and the messages received by Vassula.

The year marked by this very important event was a crowded one for Vassula. The geographical range of this apostolate is impressive. It comprehends North and Central America, the Far East, the Middle East, the Scandinavian countries, Russia, Europe to the Mediterranean. For most of these journeys I speak as a witness.

In the month of January Vassula was in Los Angeles and in Sacramento. In Los Angeles the only hall which would be booked for her meeting was inadequate to the local demand. For security reasons only seating accommodation was allowed. This meant that thousands were turned away. The response of those present was enthusiastic. A question session afterwards yielded very good results.

The Los Angeles meeting was organised by a remarkable couple, Lebanese, Antoine Mansour, a very distinguished surgeon, Fellow of the American and Canadian Colleges of Surgeons, and his wife Claire, a dynamic lady with Lebanese humour and, like her husband, Lebanese courage. I had a natural kinship with them, having travelled together on the 1992 Pilgrimage of Peace through Fatima, Prague, Moscow, St Petersburg, Warsaw and Rome, and I was told by a South African Lebanese lady that the "Irish are the Lebanese of the North." What a compliment!

Because of her great love for the Mansours Vassula reverted to a former practice, painting. They had constructed an oratory which they dedicated to God the Father, the first with this title in the United States. On the wall behind the altar Vassula painted the face of Christ. This is the first time she has chosen this theme; she had already done a line drawing of Christ's head in profile, as she sees Him. Why, one may ask, the face of Christ, in an oratory dedicated to God the Father. The answer is in the Johannine text, lettered by Vassula around the image, "He who has seen me has seen the Father." (Jn 14:9).

For the meeting in Sacramento a large crowd assembled in the church. Bishop Montrose of Stockton had come for the Mass. Outside the church a small group demonstrated against Vassula. Her address was very well received by those who packed the building. The event was taken as the occasion of a nasty article in a Catholic weekly. Speaking from over fifty years experience of the Catholic press in many countries, as a Catholic journalist who worked for twenty-four years altogether on two papers I can say that it was the most disgraceful item I have ever read. I shall deal with it when I come to criticism of Vassula. As the ancient Romans said, "see how these Christians love one another!"

In the month of February Vassula went back again to the World Council of Churches in Geneva, where she had been invited during the Octave of Prayer for Christian Unity in the previous year. As then she was now received and heard with sympathy.

It is probably exact to say that no member of an Orthodox Church has so often visited Marian shrines as Vassula. In the month of February she was in Mexico, received again by good friends who are deeply committed to the Catholic revival which continues apace in the country, Fathers Massi and Chavariat, and Senora Olga Ascarraga, a lay apostle chosen to participate in the national synod, a lady with personal memories of one of the great events in the religious history of her country. This was the foundation of the *Missioneros del Espiritu Sancto*, by a French Marist, Fr Rozier acting on the private revelations of one of the great mystics of modern times, Maria Concepción Cabrera de Armida. Olga was also a close friend of a remarkable Irish priest, Fr Thomas Fallon, an intimate associate of Frank Duff, founder of the Legion of Mary, who resigned an important position in government service at the age of fifty to join the *Missioneros*. It was in the early twenties, when persecution had not yet waned. He was ordained at four o'clock in the morning behind closed doors by a bishop driven from his diocese.

The principal meeting place on this visit to Mexico, one marked by a fervent visit to the national shrine at Guadalupe, was in the cathedral of Guadaljara. Vassula had been personally invited by the Cardinal, he who was the victim of a mysterious assassination some months later. It would be difficult to exaggerate in describing the religious atmosphere of the assembly, which occupied every available space in the large building - the estimate of numbers was a minimum of five thousand. As was now Vassula's custom, questions in writing were invited after her address. Large sacks were needed to hold all the paper slips sent to the rostrum; it was thought that they numbered over five thousand!

Vassula was in Portugal later in the month and early in March went to speak in St Gall in the country where she resides. Later in the month she crossed the Atlantic again and spoke to audiences in California. In Santa Clara she had the great joy of meeting a Filipino community. They support her everywhere she goes, for they are everywhere, or almost! The Philippines and their emigrants are a hope of the Catholic Church.

An intriguing incident occurred in a church where Vassula had spoken. She was offered some roses by one of those present. Characteristically she went to give the roses to the Sacred Heart of Jesus, to his statue. She placed the rose in his hand, as she thought. But photographs show the flower beside the hand of Jesus, not held by him, existing in the air by itself.

For the last six days of April there were four speaking appointments in Great Britain. Jack Rice, an Anglican who died recently, a fervent believer in the writings of Vassula, desirous to promote Christian unity - it was the great cause of his life - propagated strong devotion to the Two Hearts. He had compiled an index to all the published volumes of *True Life in God*. He had organised a meeting, ecumenical in intention and attendance in the grounds of his own residence, Exhurst Manor in Kent; a special marquee was erected for the purpose. Jack, as he preferred to be known, hoped this was but the starting point in the vast plans and hopes which filled him. As I have mentioned the "miracle of the sun" was witnessed above the marquee.

In Manchester, Tony Hickey is widely known for a varied apostolate which he directs and sustains from the Manchester Medjugorje Centre. The excellent review which he edits, *Mir* magazine, goes into forty-seven languages; it is admirable. With his friend Peter Rooney he accompanied Vassula to St Augustine's church in Manchester, where she had spoken on a previous occasion, to St Dominick's in Newcastle and to University Hall in Glasgow.

I make two comments here. It is clear from the summary account I have given so far that those who support Vassula in different countries are people with proved quality in their service of the Church, committed and trusted. Secondly, Medjugorje Centres of Peace do figure much in the record. The suggestion has been made by one, who should know better, that Vassula exploits, in some way, the world-wide

Medjugorje network. I can testify that the initiative invariably comes from the Medjugorje supporters, as it should be abundantly clear that many who benefit by reading *True Life in God* and hearing Vassula speak have no connection with the Medjugorje movement. Readers will know that all genuine graces are from the same divine source, that if there is a "variety of gifts" it is the "same Spirit" (1 Cor 12:4). That there should be rivalry over divine favours, that the faithful devoted to one shrine should quarrel with or oppose, in any way, those with another piety would be unthinkable if we did not know that it happens. At a time when all those who bear the Christian name should unite, when Catholics seek unity with the Orthodox and Protestants, it is, at the least illogical to see them divided on their essential meaning.

Apart from a fleeting visit to Gex in France Vassula's next speaking engagement was with a French Canadian group on pilgrimage to Israel. Her meetings were enlivened by the presence of some thirty young friends from European countries, Greece and the islands, all of them led to a changed life-style by reading her books. One meeting was addressed by Rabbi David Rosen, former Rabbi in South Africa, Chief Rabbi in Ireland, now teaching in Jerusalem, responsible for inter-religious affairs in Israel, member of the joint Jewish-Roman Catholic commission on diplomatic relations between the Vatican and Israel; the Fundamental Agreement signed on 30 December, 1993 crowned their labours.

Of considerable interest also was the fact that the Archbishop of the Orthodox Armenians invited Vassula to address a meeting of his priests and theologians. She was received with respectful attention. Vassula's mystical gift did not abandon her in the homeland of Jesus. She had many direct signs of his love.

June of 1993 imposed a heavy schedule on her. She was in Canada from the 5th to the 10th, fulfilling speaking engagements in Winnipeg, Edmonton, Quebec and Chicoutimi, everywhere received with keen interest. From June 11th to 15th the venues were in Omaha, USA and Independence, Missouri. Omaha was memorable. Vassula was due to speak at a congress in honour of Mary, Mother of God and the Eucharist. The principal personality in the organisation of this event was Sister Lucy Astuto, a lady of lucid mind and strong character. She had been under pressure, on the telephone, not to allow Vassula to participate. She was staunch. A woman with a decided mystical endowment she had confided to her intimate associates on the eve of the congress that there would be a special grace during it. She may have felt that her prayer was answered when we informed her about Vassula's experience of the Passion.

From Independence, Missouri, via California Vassula set out for the Philippines, where she has a devoted following and assured audiences.

In September attention turns to three very different areas: the Scandinavian countries and Holland, France and Russia. The groundwork was thoroughly done in all these countries. An official of the American Embassy in Stockholm, Bob Carroll, has been active in making Vassula's mission and message known and he had evidence of the beneficial effects in many lives. He could report many instances of people touched by grace among those who came to hear the testimony. One person I shall mention again. Copenhagen was similarly rewarding. Here too there was a committed apostle of the message, Nils Christian Huidt.

France is in many ways a test case for anyone claiming to have a special supernatural message. Through the ages the French have known of God's accredited messengers chosen from among their own. How would they react to an outsider, one, moreover, who is not a Catholic, hoping for a response from this country with such strong Catholic traditions? Vassula had stood the test successfully on more than one occasion. But this time she was to face a challenge; she was asked to speak in a large hall, Les Pyramides in the parish of Le Pecq outside Paris, and in the Mutualité, a prestigious meeting place in the city, to where she would come from the heart of Catholic Brittany, Lorient.

Again there was a devoted, fully convinced supporter on the spot, Patrick Beneston. He was of course fully backed by the publisher of Vassula's books in French, Francois Xavier de Guibert. The publisher had accomplished a tour de force. My book on Vassula, *Vassula of the Sacred Heart's Passion* had appeared, through the immense industry and dedication of Mrs Christine Lynch, some time before this. Lucien Lombard, the expert translator of the different volumes of *True Life in God*, working as so many others without any remuneration, had the French text in M. De Guibert's hands in the shortest time possible. However, we had decided that three chapters should be added, on the chastisement, on extraordinary signs, and on Vassula's experience of the Passion. These I composed during my stay in France in the month of July, writing directly in French. M. de Guibert came to Chantilly, where I was based, and took the manuscripts. Within three weeks or less he had the whole work ready. It was available during the meetings.

Besides Fr Flichy who had invited Vassula to Le Pecq, she could count on the presence, and very much more than the presence of the doyen of French, indeed of Catholic Marian theologians, Fr René Laurentin. He was the first important Catholic theologian to study Vassula's personality and writings. He interviewed her searchingly but, as is his manner, sympathetically and the text of the interview widely diffused, was for many enlightening and reassuring. With the taped interview of Vassula by Dom Ian Petit, OSB, it was a decisive factor in the recognition and acceptance of Vassula by Catholics in many countries.

Fr René Laurentin, who is known to me as a fellow member of the French Society for Marian Studies, for many years, and increasingly admired, was with Vassula when she spoke in the Mutualité. With her he dealt with the questions which were submitted after her talk. In such matters he has exceptional experience. I heard him say at the International Mariological Congres in Huelva in September, 1992, that his daily correspondence abounds in queries of every kind. He has learned to cope.

Russia

Vassula, Greek Orthodox, had previously met her brothers and sisters of the Russian Orthodox Church. She was with a large party of pilgrims (940) in October 1992, all but two Catholic; she had come with them from Catholic shrines or cities. But she was Orthodox. She took an active part in the ceremonial presentation of an icon to the Patriarch's representative, one of his assistant bishops. She joined hands with a Protestant and Catholic, myself, to offer him chalice and paten. All through he was gracious and genuinely thankful. The moment chosen was at the conclusion of the Divine Liturgy. The Russian prelate spoke to the whole congregation present, explaining the significance of the event, recalling with gratitude the prayers offered for the Russian people over the years to Our Lady of Fatima. To end the ceremony he presented to each member of the Peace Pilgrimage, a miniature icon representing a very famous one, Our Lady of Khazan. The original is in Fatima awaiting its return to a worthy home in Russia.

On the next evening Vassula was invited to attend an Orthodox discussion group, the members of which on that occasion were dealing with the concept of tradition. She was allowed to speak, after some hesitation on the part of the chairperson. Jesus told her that she was as yet a pilgrim in Russia; she would come later to fulfil her mission.

A further phase was opened when Vassula went to Russia as guest of the society *Pro Deo et fratribus*. The society was founded by Bishop Hlnilica, the Pope's confidant and adviser on Russian and Eastern European affairs. It has an inspiring membership. I shall let Vassula tell the story herself:

> The journey to Russia was foreseen for a long time (October, 1992) for 13 to 19 September, 1993. I had retained this date in my calendar and I awaited signs from the Lord to confirm it. The time was approaching and I had no signs indicating that I should go. Then a month before the agreed date I sent a fax message to the contact in Moscow, a Swiss German priest, Fr Rolf (who also works in Rome with Bishop Hlnilica) that I would not come as I had not received the necessary signs from the Lord.

> On the morning of the 13th September I had a telephone call from Fr Rolf in Moscow, asking me the time of my arrival there. I got a shock and called to ask him if he had received my fax cancelling the journey. Yes, he said he had received the fax and had understood that I was coming. He told me that

he had arranged the meetings and that the Orthodox priests were expecting me... yet I had been quite clear in my fax.

In distress Vassula cried out to the Lord and she received an answer that she should go; she also thought that I should go with her. As it happened tickets and visas were obtained in record time. She arrived in Moscow on 14 September. I take up her narrative:

On the evening of the 14th September, the day of my arrival, there was a meeting in Dom Maria. Here there is a charitable organisation for those suffering in Russia. The director of the organisation is Russian, of Jewish origin, converted through his wife Antonia, to the Catholic religion. Antonia was Russian Orthodox, but felt the call to become Catholic, so now she is a Russian Catholic. Her husband is Micha (Michael), a man who has suffered several years in prison for his Catholic faith: 'priests and prophets were made prisoners and were forced to dwell in darkness.' (Volume II, p.352 - 3.9.91)

In the house of charity there were several young people, volunteers from different distant countries, helping Micha; so was Fr Rolf. They help those who suffer, in hospitals and elsewhere. The strongest of them are helping to build a church. There are many Catholics in the house, and also Russian Orthodox.

For the meeting I had an excellent translator. I spoke about my conversion, I presented an idea, a portrait of the Eternal Father; I explained my mission which is unity of the Churches, and I dwelt on the prophecies I had received about Russia. They were so attentive, visibly moved. Several people were weeping ceaselessly.

'With a loud cry she will manifest her joy, beholding her Saviour at her side. I will lift her to Me and My flame of love will inflame her heart, purifying her and leaving her in total rapture for Me her God.' (Volume I, p.291 - 11.3.88)

A lady who did not miss a single meeting came to me and gave me a very old golden wedding ring; inside it was engraved the date, 1890. She also gave me a golden coin with the portrait of Czar Nicholas II, saying: 'I give you this present. It marks the covenant of peace and love between Russia and God.' This inspired phrase confirmed for me very specially the message of Christ dated 13-14 November, 1989 (Volume II, p.108): 'Hence a covenant of peace and love shall be signed and sealed between Me and her.'

On the following day, 15 September Fr O'Carroll arrived. The evening meeting took place in the same room in Dom Maria; it was a different group.

These knew the little book in Russian, *True Life in God*, and they spread the message zealously; they are mostly Russian Orthodox.

Fr Rolf had also invited Russian television. They had agreed to make one half hour broadcast for their channel, which covers all Russia. In reality they did not know exactly who I was, or what it was all about. I made a protest when they told me that they would only register a half hour. For, since I had a translator, this would cut my contribution to a quarter of an hour. They refused to change.

We then began recording and I noticed that while I was speaking they were listening attentively and were quite interested in what I was saying. I saw from their countenances that emotion was growing; they wanted me to continue longer than the half hour planned. We did an hour and a half. Besides, they all wanted the Russian book and asked for my autograph.

On the last two days, that is the 18 and 19 September, I was the guest of two Russian Orthodox priests, very open on the question of unity. Thus far, of the two hundred churches open for worship three are committed to unity. I was informed of this by one of the priests who lives for unity, as I do.

When we reached the first church, on 18 September, where I was to give witness, the evening service was being celebrated. What struck me was the appearance of things. One had to watch where one walked, for there were planks, buckets, sand, a pile of things needed for rebuilding. We were beneath the scaffolding. Once again Christ's prophetic words about Russia came to my mind: 'When I will resurrect Russia she will restore My gifts, she will embellish My house again with love and I will unite her again to Me. I will offer her My bread and My wine, and she will not refuse My food. She will accept My offer, and she will eat My bread and drink My wine, renewing herself, praising Me.' (Volume I, p.277 - 1.2.88)

And on the 30 January 1992 Christ had said to me as I wept at the sight of her poverty: 'I shall embellish her.' (Volume II, p.416). Before my eyes these prophecies were being realised. The title of the church was 'Church of all Saints' and the priest's name was Martiri. He invited us to have tea with him and some friends in the corridor off the church. He told us that the communists had massacred forty people in the church - in the crypt. The KGB had their office there. 'Priests and prophets were made prisoners and were forced to dwell in darkness. Many of them were slaughtered pitilessly before My very eyes.' (Volume II, p.352 - 3.9.91)

Vassula, in her brief narrative, does not deal with the restoration work already accomplished - much remains to be done. The murals and frescoes have been done

by the greatest painter in Moscow. They are breathtakingly beautiful. When all is
completed this will be one of the most beautiful churches, as to interior decoration,
in the world. An image of St Michael, freshly painted is hauntingly beautiful.

"Next evening" Vassula continues, "my meeting was in the church of St
Comas and Damian. The priest, Alexander Borisov, had invited three other
priests, and as with the first church, this one was also in process of
reconstruction. Fr Alexander told us that the KGB had used it as a printing
house. When we arrived they were at the end of Mass. I heard their
melodious hymns which please Jesus and Mary so much. 'Her hymns and
chants that are so sweet in our ears, with her graceful movements, will rise
up to heaven like incense. Love will resurrect her as He resurrected her a
thousand years ago.' (Volume I, p.277 - 1.2.88)

Fr Alexander wished me to come back next day. I was already booked to fly
out. I shall return in the Lord's good time.

Africa - A Return

As wife of a highly placed official of a relief organisation in Third World countries
Vassula spent seventeen years in Africa. Those were the years of her religious
indifference; her only church-going was social, for weddings or funerals. I once
asked her if she had known our missionaries in Sierra Leone, my friends. "At that
time," was her reply "my interest was not in missionaries, but in the Casino."

Now Vassula is sought, requested by those who have read her books and who, as a
result of reading them, have the consciousness of a divine call to a more intimate life
with Jesus. Strengthened by this experience, which is part of her life since her
conversion in 1985, Vassula returned to the continent where she was born; at the
time her family, Greek as is known, lived in Egypt.

From 23 November to 3 December she undertook an apostolate in four African
states, Zambia, Malawi, Zimbabwe and South Africa - all in less than a fortnight.
Everywhere she was warmly welcomed. Priests and laity came to hear her. With
one exception all the meetings ended with Mass, for which, on two occasions, the
principal celebrant was a Bishop.

Vassula began with Zambia. After descending from the plane at Lusaka airport at
daybreak, we were met by Fr Tomazin - a Jesuit - Croatian by birth. After
completion of the introductions he signalled to a group of circa 100 Africans of all
ages - men, women and children, colourfully attired carrying gifts of flowers, who
proceeded to walk across the tarmac from the terminal building singing

harmoniously, their voices carrying clearly in the still morning air. As they surrounded Vassula's party at the foot of the plane, which had brought us from Paris, they proceeded to shake hands, present flowers, bob a curtsey or greet us with a kiss. What a welcome to begin the African tour! In the packed Church the congregation was lively and radiant with joy, most attentive to Vassula's message. The two Jesuit priests in charge, entirely committed to the cause of Jesus, eager to hear the witness of his love. There were other priests concelebrating.

Throughout the whole African tour Vassula was given hospitality by nuns - many Irish, who have such an important role in the young vibrant African churches. Sometimes they came from a distance to be in their convents; one sister in Lusaka had travelled for eleven hours for the meeting.

From Zambia Vassula left for Malawi, where Gay Russell and Sr Margaret, a blue nun, Matron of St Annes Hospital, Harare were awaiting her at the airport. Gay, an exceptional personality, deeply committed to the Medjugorje apostolate, is herself a senior air-line pilot. She is self-effacing but very well known, with very great influence in the Catholic life of Malawi. With an active committee she had prepared meetings in Lilongwe and Limbe. The Bishop of Lilongwe is recovering from a serious illness. He could not come to the Mass, but he sent his Auxiliary Mgr Zyayi, who had over twenty concelebrants - the entire seminary were present too. The church was full and the welcome was enthusiastic, hymns and dancing, manifest fervour. Next day we went to see the Bishop, Matteus Chimol. He said with a delightful blend of meekness and humour, "You've come to the wounded captain." As I gave him a blessing with a relic of the True Cross, I ventured to add, "This is from the Commander-in-Chief."

From Lilongwe Gay took us in her own plane to Blantyre. Travelling with her were Vassula, myself, Sr Margaret and Christine Lynch, directress of the publishing house of *True Life in God*, the English printed edition (Pat Callahan, of *Trinitas*, Independence, Missouri, puts out an edition reproducing exactly the original handwritten text). In the small plane we could admire Gay's skill, especially in landing.

The meeting took place in the cathedral of Limbe with a thousand present in the building and many more outside. Holy Mass was concelebrated by twenty-five priests. The Bishop, because of another engagement, was unable to be present. He received us next day in his residence. He gave us Rosaries which he himself makes, glistening stones with handsome chain, which he fashions from plain wire. His secretary was to drive us to the airport. But there was a change. The Bishop insisted on taking the wheel himself and drove us.

Gay was also our pilot for the journey to Harare. There we paid a short visit to the Sisters of St Clare. Like all cloistered nuns they find Vassula's writings very helpful; the Carmelites are particularly attuned to the message. It does bear a resemblance to that of their holy mother, Teresa of Avila.

About one thousand people had come to the Church where Vassula spoke. We were both introduced by a Redemptorist, Fr Webster. Next morning in a smaller church we had Mass and then open easy dialogue, and exchange of opinions in question and answer format.

It was then the plane to Johannesburg. A very sympathetic group awaited us at the airport. Fr Vincent Pienaar, a highly intelligent and deeply spiritual person took charge of transport during the entire stay; he shared with us his experience in a country at a great turning-point in its history. Like so many others whom we met, his confidence in the Lord's goodness and mercy is unshaken. A talking point, which also made front page news in the secular press, was a strange phenomenon seen some days previously in the sky, a rainbow forming a gigantic complete circle around the sun.

On arrival we were invited to meet friends in the home of Winnie Williams, a key personality in the whole African apostolate of Vassula. Next day, 28 November, came the big moment, a meeting followed by Mass in the Cathedral of Christ the King with seventeen priests concelebrating. More than 2,500 people were present, including a large number of young people, many of whom had been waiting up to four hours and through two Holy Masses, in order to be certain of a seat. Space was so packed that some were seated around the altar, on the floor! The Bishops had made it known in writing that they approved fully of everything. A radio programme a week before had given word of what would take place, a radio link between Johannesburg, Switzerland and Dublin.

Next morning there was another meeting, this time an informal question and answer programme with priests and religious, relaxed with much humour and marked sympathy. That evening our friends took us to a game park where almost all the animals living there came to greet us, or viewed us with curiosity from a safe distance. We lodged in the private bungalow as guests of Margaret Faris, who works with Winnie; she is Lebanese. I must add a personal note: in my teaching days I had several Lebanese students, none better.

Durban was the only African city where we did not have Mass at our meeting. The venue was the large hall of a secondary school. Few priests, but two who were with us were delightful and strongly supportive, Fathers Flanagan and Clancy. We stayed with the Oblate Fathers, who were most hospitable. I naturally inquired about their colleague, Archbishop Hurley, OMI, a leonine figure in South African church history. He is retired, writing his memoirs, which will be interesting. He made his name at the Second Vatican Council, a one time rugby player I seem to have heard, no disadvantage in that part of the world.

The Redemptorist Fathers were our hosts in Cape Town. Mass was celebrated by Bishop Cancutt, with twenty-five concelebrants. It was midnight when the entire ceremony ended. Not unusually one of those present came to tell me that during Vassula's talk she had seen the change in her countenance, Christ himself appearing instead of his faithful witness.

So ended a year's programme, arduous, demanding. The year 1994 was to see continuity with the same generosity on Vassula's part, the same deep effect of the message she bears. Something like an interlude was a visit to Vienna, where her hosts were the monks of the Holy Trinity; she spoke in a large city hall to a highly respectful crowded audience. Then later in the month it would be a new field of evangelization, Latin America.

Latin America

The young vibrant churches of Africa are one thing. How would the messenger of Jesus fare in the vast world of Latin America. Here are countries evangelised five hundred years ago, linked to ancient respected European traditions, proud to occupy such space on the world map of the Catholic Church. How many people were astonished to see so many Brazilian bishops at the Second Vatican Council; one would have to add those of Mexico and Colombia, and of the other countries of the vast continent.

One does not lightly enter on a domain whose theologians often make front page news in our Catholic papers. Let the reader recall all that theology of liberation and base communities prompt by way of reflection among Catholic intellectuals. At times everything seems in ferment. Could a messenger like Vassula have anything to give people, already enriched with creative intuitions, who claim to offer models of evangelization to the whole Church, whose theologians have the ambition to renew even Christology in the light of their own lived experience?

The answer is quite simple. Vassula goes only where she has been invited. She undertook long, tiring journeys through South and Central America because those who have read her writings are athirst for her message, and for her personal testimony. One may say that the welcome she received is evidence of an idea, theologically sound, brought to prominence by the great Newman, the *sensus fidei*, the sure intuition of the supernatural given to the faithful, the People of God. God speaks to his people through the voice of his prophets, taking the word in the biblical sense.

Portugal was the starting point of the journey - that is after Vassula had kept a speaking appointment in Gex, just inside the French border, not far from where she lives. The visit to Porto she owed to a faithful, discerning friend, Fr Millheiro, director of a new religious institute, dedicated to Christ the Youth. Fr Millheiro translated the writings of Vassula into Portuguese, opening the way to Brazil. In Porto, Vassula spoke twice before large audiences, mostly in Portuguese, which she had learned in Mozambique.

I accompanied Vassula and we set out immediately via Lisbon for Recife. We were there in the morning of 29 January, and were met by the one who had planned and organised the visit, Mauricio Fernandez. That afternoon we went to a sports stadium where thousands were waiting for us. I had, with the aid of friends who had been missionaries in Angola and Brazil, prepared a Portuguese text, listening carefully to a cassette. I was assured that people would appreciate my goodwill!

It is the unexpected that makes the headlines. We were certainly given something to arrest the attention and provoke reflection. On a balcony to the right we suddenly, in the course of Vassula's talk, saw a strong, sturdily built man rising from his place in agitation, screaming aloud, pointing to Vassula who, he said, gave him a headache, made him sick; he was foaming at the mouth. People tried to overcome him and it took ten men to hold him down. Then all those present rose in a collective prayer, which was deeply moving. Pointing with outstretched hands towards him, they joined in a moment of fervour. They vanquished the demon; for it was a clear case of diabolical possession. The fever suddenly subsided. Then the victim went through a kind of purification. He wept - tears of repentance. He raised his arms on high to praise God. Then suddenly he fell down, slain in the Spirit. At the end of the whole ceremony he joined in the act of consecration to the Sacred Heart of Jesus. To end what was a rather exciting meeting we had Mass concelebrated by twenty-six priests, with two bishops, Mgr Joao Martins Terra, SJ, Auxiliary to the Bishop of Recife, and Mgr Marcelu Carvacheira, Bishop of Guarolier. If I may add a personal footnote it would be under the saying, "It's a small world." Mgr Martins Terra, in the course of conversation before the meeting told me that he was leaving shortly to take part in the inter-religious assembly in Jerusalem: Cardinal Ratzinger and Cardinal Martini were participants. The organiser, who had been in contact with him was Rabbi David Rosen.

Next day it was Sao Paolo, where Maria Theresa had prepared everything. We were to meet a crowded audience in the principal hall of a college maintained by the Institute of the Virgin Mary, founded by Mary Ward, a prestigious name in the history of education. Two bishops were there, Mgr Fernando Antonio Figueredo of the diocese of Santo Amaro, and a friend, Mgr Victor Joannes Tielbeek, a Dutch Benedictine; we had met him in his homeland and he had promised us a warm welcome in Brazil, where, as he said, Vassula's writings are known and valued.

Before the meeting Mgr Figueredo, a Franciscan and French-speaking - he had studied theology in Lyons - wished to meet us with his priests in what turned out to be a very heartening encounter. After the lectures more than twenty priests concelebrated with the bishops. Vassula was deeply touched by the presence of an Orthodox priest, who gave her icons and a calendar on behalf of the Orthodox community. They would have wished to meet her, but this is for another time. While Holy Communion was being given to the faithful some of the priests came to ask a blessing from Vassula. When she touched one of them he was at once slain in the Spirit. I should add that all who came could not be given place in the hall. There was an overflow audience in the basement, who followed everything on close-circuit television; they were more numerous than those in the hall.

On 1 February we reached Joinville, still in Brazil. Here everything was in the hands of a remarkable lay apostle, José Beneval. Supported by his whole family he works the whole time in the diffusion of Vassula's message throughout Brazil; it is largely due to his interest and activity that fifty-seven thousand copies of her books have been distributed in the country - he worked in close collaboration with Fr Millheiro. I was very happy to learn that Jesus, in a message to Vassula at the time, had named José Beneval. The Bishop of the diocese has some reservations about Vassula's messages. But he so respects José that he allowed the meeting with Vassula to take place in the cathedral.

There were about 3,000 people present, with fifteen priests concelebrating. We learned that among those present were some who had travelled over one thousand kilometres.

The next stop was Quito in Ecuador. Already at the airport we made acquaintance with a great personality in the world of Catholic higher education, Fr Jukio Teran Dutari SJ, rector of the Pontifical University of Quito, first non-European to be appointed president of the International Federation of Catholic Universities, a graduate of Innsbruck and Munich Universities. He covers with his enormous prestige the message of Vassula throughout Ecuador. He presided at the meeting which took place in the large University Hall. In the evening there was an agape with our friends and with members of prayer groups who had come from Peru and from Panama; they invited us to their countries. Next day we met Patricia Talbot, the visionary of Cuenca. She had wished to have more time with us, but her plane was delayed. I found her a very impressive personality for a reason that the reader may not see at once. She is very unspoiled, truly simple in the correct meaning of that word, unselfaware. She reminded me of the first impression I had of Vassula Rydén, "Thank God, she's normal." Patricia, who was accompanied by her supporters, wanted us to spend some days with her. It was impossible. A member of the organising committee for Vassula's visit had arranged a Mass in her house, at which Fr Teran Dutari presided. Among those present was an archbishop retired but head of the Marian Movement for Priests, Mgr Bernardino Eccheveria OFM.

It's a small world. From Quito we flew to Bogota. Here, on 4 February, the Director of the *Foyer de Charité* at Zipaquira, Fr Fernando Umana met us at the airport. His brother was with him and he drove us all to the Foyer, where we were honoured to stay. Out of simple curiosity I asked Fr Umana if he had known a Colombian priest, Camillo Torriz, who had become very well known for his decision to leave the ministry and join the guerilla forces - he thought that talking about social justice led nowhere. "But we were together in the seminary" was the reply, "I knew him very well." Camillo, whose courage and good intentions were unquestionable, had chosen the way of violence which led to his death; his friend took another path. What wonderful work he has done; the Foyer is something splendid. Fr Umana is also a writer, with a particular interest in Marian theology and the theology of St Joseph.

The priest and his co-workers had succeeded in assembling over 3,500 people in the Coliseo of Nabia, not very far from the Foyer. We were some forty miles or more from Bogota, but many of its citizens were with us for the meeting. There were others who came from far distant places, some travelling over four hundred kilometers. The atmosphere was decidedly charismatic, with an abundance of hymn singing. There was also a special meeting of priests with Vassula. It was marked by a very frank exchange of views. A good deal of the talk turned on the destiny, the proximate future of the present Pope. I find that this topic recurs very often where people totally committed to the Church and the Pope come together. John Paul II may have his critics but he evokes in some hearts a loyalty, a concern, a sense of identity with him which is heartening, for it clearly comes from the Holy Spirit.

Fr Umana led us to a special sanctuary on a hilltop within the property of the Foyer. He showed us the Cross they had erected facing it. They learned that this had been done on the day Marthe Robin died. We were overjoyed to learn that the same anniversary occurred while we were still there: 6 February, the day of our departure.

Next we were to meet our Mexican friends. At the airport awaiting us was Fr Massi, with members of the families whom we had come to know on our previous visits, Carmen Bastiada and others. Mme Olga Ascgarraga came to greet us; she had to leave at once to be with her sister-in-law in the United States, gravely ill. But before leaving she had rendered us an important service; she had arranged a meeting with the Cardinal.

Vassula gave her testimony at a morning ceremony in the church of St Juan de Lagos. The building was packed to the walls, and she was heard with great attention. There would be another assembly in the afternoon. But, we were assured, it would be much smaller, just some hundreds. In fact the building was once again packed to the walls.

I note two surprising events - and I do not count as such the fact that at Mass at Guadalupe, the evening of our arrival, one of those present saw the face of Vassula change into that of Jesus - this has happened already so often. At the airport in the VIP room a special ceremony took place. The secretary of the Mexican Academy of Sciences, Maurice Porraz Jimenez Labora, having first as a courtesy spoken to me about his function there, informed Vassula that the Academy had, on 2 February, elected her an Honourary Corresponding Member, "with all the rights and privileges" accruing thereto. She was given a diploma signed by the president, vice-president and secretary, and a medal symbolic of her status.

The second surprise: We were very happy to have an opportunity to meet and converse with His Eminence Ernesto Corripio Uhamada. What was our astonishment to see him enter the room accompanied by Mgr Samuel Ruiz, the most talked of Mexican bishop at the present time, his doings and statements reported across the world. Background to his notoriety is the protest by Indians of the state of Chiapas against neglect. He has been their champion, not an advocate of violence, as has wrongly been said.

We guessed afterwards that the Cardinal had planned our encounter with the Bishop, whom he defends. Interestingly, no sooner had they both come into the room than the Bishop began to talk and he went on for quite a while. Eventually the Cardinal raised a point that he would like to see clarified: was this another movement, that is involving Vassula? No, we assured him, she is a witness, it is testimony she seeks to offer. He asked Fr Massi to make her known in Mexico city, his diocese, or since he lived at a distance, perhaps another priest locally based would do this.

We were accompanied by an Orthodox priest, Fr Vassilios Penteridis, who had become our friend. He was quite frankly interested in meeting a personality so much in the news, Mgr Ruiz. As we left the residence we noticed that the security officers, or so they appeared to us, had departed. The Bishop probably needs protection: he deserves it.

In Port au Prince, Haiti we experienced a people sorely tried, greatly suffering, but those whom we met were seeking comfort and strength in the Lord. Sister Claire Gagne, French-Canadian, directress of a large girls's secondary school, had seen the main hall quickly filled to overflowing. With marvellous ingenuity she set up loud-speakers for as many more outside: 4,000 in all. Judge of her problems; there is no public electricity supply on the island. The whole session was presided over by the Nuncio Apostolic, Mgr Ballesteros. He spoke encouragingly to Vassula and myself. Among the clergy celebrating Mass there were two bishops, one principal celebrant, Mgr Louis Kebreau and Mgr Louis Lafontan.

There were two meetings in Puerto Rico, one in a large hall in San Juan, the other on the Holy Mountain. The key personality in this beautiful island is Dr Gregorio ("Gogui") Merced, a University professor, first woman in the island to obtain a doctorate in accountancy and fiscal studies, dynamic, colourful, a gifted organiser.

Thanks to her and to the other members of her group, the "Golden Angels", everything went off very well.

Vassula endured the passion twice, first in Gogui's home, though it began in a restaurant, where we were at table looking at the menu, then while she was speaking on the Holy Mountain, this time without any visible sign. She was for a while puzzled by the behaviour of her audience on the Holy Mountain; they seemed to lose attention to her talk and were excitedly looking up in the sky. They reported afterwards that they saw the "miracle of the sun." On this sacred spot hallowed by legend there is a holy well. Cures took place there that day.

One testimony was singular. Among those present was a doctor friend of Gogui, until then slightly sceptical on the subject of Vassula. She looked in the sky in the moment of excitement and saw a figure which she took for that of Christ. She came to see Vassula later in the adjoining convent to relate her experience. While doing so she began to stammer, as she saw the face of Christ in Vassula herself.

We owe a special word of thanks to Bishop Hernandez, who welcomed us, advised us and was truly edifying, a priest essentially. He spent eight hours in the confessional and was principal celebrant at the Mass which closed a memorable day.

Poland

I beg to begin with a personal note. As a priest journalist, working simultaneously for two papers, *The Catholic Standard* and *The Leader*, and as a teacher of history I welcomed the opportunity to visit Poland. I first went there in 1966, the year of the Millennium, and had the privilege of interviewing the Cardinal Primate, Stefan Wysznski, the only foreign journalist to do so. How to describe such a moment? I felt that I was speaking to St Ignatius of Antioch or St Polycarp. He was under terrible pressure for the Gomulka regime who had needed him ten years previously in a moment of crisis now dreaded his prestige and launched a bitter campaign against him incessantly orchestrated in all the media. The pretext: he had fraternised with the enemy, for, with all the bishops, he had invited the German hierarchy to the Millennium ceremonies. He triumphed over his enemies, lived on to see his fellow bishop elected Pope.

Like most of my generation I came under the influence of the great Hilaire Belloc. He gave me some of his great love for Poland and I recall his words that a "sacred flame" burns ever in the land. Any time I have gone to Poland I have the feeling of magic. With such a mentality I took to the airways with Vassula for Warsaw on 24 March, 1994. Her writings have been translated into Polish and I have mentioned the fact that on 6 November, 1993 she offered three volumes of the translation to the Pope. My book on Vassula has this dedication: "To Pope John Paul II to mark the similarity between the message of Vassula and his teaching, and her defence of his universal primacy." Those who follow the Pope's addresses closely and who know the messages of *True Life in God* will readily believe that he has taken cognisance of these messages. For the first time he expresses ideas and even phrases which occur striking in Vassula's writings. He has spoke of the "anti-Christ", of the "Cains." On Good Friday 1994, the Holy Father did the traditional Way of the Cross followed by an Orthodox prelate, delegate of the Patriarch; he recited prayers which had been composed by the Patriarch. Jesus has spoken to Vassula of this union of prayer.

With my innate admiration for Polish Catholics and joy at having defended the rights and honour of their country, I heard with astonishment alarming news from Poland about systematic opposition to Vassula's mission. I did not understand it; I still do not understand it. Apparently it all came from one theologian. Critical articles appeared, even in the review which is under the patronage of the great St Maximilian Kolbe. I can say that I replied to the objections raised, and the summary text which I drew up, in haste unfortunately, was widely distributed. I also wrote to the authorities whose names I had been given, for we could count on good friends, lay and clerical, people of intelligence and courage. I name one priest, Michael Kaszowski; a tribute is also due to a young woman, intelligent, humble, free from fear, Eva Bromboszcz. She and the other members of the group, in my eyes, saved the honour of a country which has had so often to fight for freedom of speech!

Our friends could rejoice in the way things turned out. In Warsaw, where Vassula was welcomed by priests of a Marian Congregation, the church was packed; several priests concelebrated the Mass of the Annunciation - it was the vigil of the feast. A large number of written questions were sent up, and of these, as is her custom, she selected a number and replied to them. Understandably many people ask her questions related to their personal lives; for all these she can only promise prayers. It is not her charism to deal with personal problems. Some of those present, on that first night, had come a long way, over 400 kilometers.

We travelled by car to Katowice. Here Vassula was forbidden to speak in a church. Mass of the Annunciation was being celebrated in the Franciscan church in the early afternoon. We assisted from some distance, high above the altar in a kind of annex; through windows we could follow the liturgy. Soon our attention was deflected to what was happening beside us. Vassula began to suffer the Passion. We first thought that it would be invisible, as has occasionally happened - on the Holy Mountain in Puerto Rico for example; but we soon recognised that it would be fully visible. We had to allow her lie on the floor. Words came from her lips, "See the thorns that are piercing my Body; I shall extirpate them myself," "I shall take out the lance which is transpiercing me."

We had to think of the lecture which would take place in a hall elsewhere in the city;

it turned out to be small, but it was the best the organisers could find at short notice, the church being forbidden. Momentarily Vassula seemed to recover sufficiently to go there. We had to assist her in walking along a lengthy corridor; it was noticed that she fell three times! At Omaha, Nebraska, on 12 June 1993 she had a similar experience and recovered sufficiently to speak in public. Now she tried to take a little drink and we set out. It was understood that I would read her text if she were to suffer from fatigue. But this would be impossible as things turned out, for she collapsed into the visible Passion and lay outstretched before the entire audience.

Since cameras were in position with a view to videos, this whole unforeseen event was photographed. When Vassula was asked later if Jesus had given her a message for Poland, as he has previously done for other countries, she rightly replied that this public manifestation of the Passion was his message. With no sentiment of bitterness I venture to hope that those who forbade her to speak in a church - which she has done in many countries accompanied by priests and sometimes encouraged by the presence of bishops, will take the time to study this video recording. It will give them food for thought, possibly prompt regret at the decision taken.

Vassula was borne to a waiting car which brought her to a friend's apartment where she spent the night. Eva was in an adjoining room. The Passion had lasted eight hours, in its different phases.

Next day it was a journey, again by road, to Poznan. The meeting took place in a large hall, before some six thousand people, in an atmosphere of deep recollection. What made it singular, if not unique, was the presence of a group of Orthodox seminarists, in full religious dress, with their superior, Father Eugeniusz. They were members of the choir and they gave us all immense joy with the rendering of their beautiful hymns; they had come from Wroclaw. The superior is a reader of *True Life in God*; he showed Vassula the passages he had underlined. I was very flattered by his gracious thanks for my introductory remarks. Again there were very many questions - sign of the interest and attention; Vassula answered them with the help of Eva, now, as at the other meetings, a faithful, brilliant translator. We had chosen French as our medium throughout and in this she excels.

I cannot conceal the immense sadness I felt at the absence of the Archbishop of Poznan. Had he been there he would have presided over an event great enough to be a landmark in ecumenical history in his country. He must know of the constant efforts made by John Paul II to promote good relations between Catholics and Orthodox. The Pope has an almost divine obsession on this subject, coming back to it so often. What joy he would have to learn that his fellow-countrymen, brothers in the episcopate, share his ardent desire and are willing to translate it in practice.

6

CHASTISEMENT OR PURIFICATION

The threat of punishment, chastisement, occurs frequently in records of private revelations; a warning which should weigh on the Christian conscience. It is possible that with insistence in certain writings on future chastisement, the essential content and the richness of Christian teaching are forgotten; it is all reduced to doom and gloom. It is also true that in certain circles one may meet with success in talking about terrible things to come. This stirs a sentiment of fear, even terror, which, for psychological reasons, is pleasing to people of a certain temperament.

Then there are those who believe so strongly that God is a sovereign judge that they think themselves justified in interpreting the action of the divine judge in the tragic events of life; they claim to speak in His name. They may at times appear right; but they are often wrong, for God who is the sovereign judge is infinitely merciful, and He is influenced by prayer. Especially He keeps His secrets; He is master of time and of the future, for eternity is His lifetime. In the perspective of eternity all our problems will be solved, all wrongs will be redressed, all the sins not pardoned because there was no repentance, will be punished, all acts of virtue rewarded. God alone is lord of eternity.

It is in a perspective of this kind, which is revealed by fundamental theological truth that I put forward some reflections, with the relevant texts, on the idea of chastisement or purification in the writings of Vassula. I would not think of treating this theme which recurs in the messages if I had not first shown at sufficient length and with the necessary clarity, the positive, encouraging aspect of the teaching put forward in the writings.

Faithful to the deepest sense of the Gospel and to the most authentic spirituality of the Church, Vassula's gaze is fixed on Jesus Christ, the 'unique Mediator' (1 Tim 2:5), the 'Light of the world' (Jn 9:5), the 'Way and the Truth and the Life' (Jn 14:6). The personality of Jesus is at the centre of her spiritual quest - this is clear on every page of her books. Jesus is there revealed through His Sacred Heart, and from this source flow all the doctrinal riches which I have sought to analyze in the preceding chapters.

But we cannot stop there. One cannot deny that Jesus shows Vassula the effects of the apostasy, of the hardness of heart in which so many people are lost; they are lost because they do not answer the call of merciful love.

Let us then follow the thought of Jesus on this subject, in the hope of attaining an all-round view. Already on 1 September, 1987 Jesus dictated these words, a serious warning, to Vassula:

> Creature, since the beginning of times, I have shown My love to mankind, but I have also shown My justice. Each time My creation rebelled against Me and My law, I hardened My Heart, My Heart grieved by their iniquities. I came to remind them that I am Spirit of Love and that they too are spirit. I came to remind them that they are but a passing shadow on earth, made out of dust, and that My first drops of rain upon them will wash them away, leaving nothing behind. I have breathed into them My breath, giving them life. The world has incessantly been offending Me, and I, for My part, have incessantly been reminding them of My existence and of how I love them. My chalice of justice is full, creation! My justice lies heavily upon you! Unite and return to Me; honour Me, creation. When you will, then I too will lift My justice.[1]

Jesus was now dealing with a disciple increasingly strong, capable of assimilating a stern message without fear or shock or anxiety. He went on:

> My cries resound and shake the entire heavens, leaving all My angels trembling for what has to come. I am a God of justice, and My eyes have grown weary watching hypocrisy, atheism, immorality. My creation has become in its decadence, a replica of what Sodom was. I will thunder you with My justice as I have thundered the Sodomites. Repent, creation, before I come. I have indeed forewarned you many a time, but you have not followed My instructions. I have raised up saints to warn you, but, daughter they have closed their hearts. My creation would rather live in lust and ignore Me. I have given them signs to awaken them.[2]

We have studied this message in dealing with the apostasy. It may be well to read the entire dialogue that passed at the time between Jesus and Vassula:

V: My God, Your children are only sleeping; please, come and wake them up; they are only sleeping.

J: They are sleeping hour after hour, year after year.

V: But Lord, who is to blame if they have not been taught; they are almost innocent if they know nothing about You.

J: I have raised servants and teachers on earth to teach them.

V: But Lord, Your teachers and servants do work, but what can they do more when multitudes are negative; they are helpless.

J: Helpless? They should repent; they should come to Me and repent. I have, through times, given them signs, but they have rejected them as not from Me. I have given them warnings through weak and wretched souls, but they doubted My word. They have rejected all My blessings, grieving Me. O men with hearts out of rock! Men of little faith! Had they more heart, and had they even now even more heart, I would have helped them. I stirred them from their sleep, but how many times have they closed their eyes, falling back into sleep?

V: But why don't they make it known to the world when You give Your signs?

J: Some do, but the majority of My sacerdotal souls have closed their hearts, doubting, fearing; many of them fear. Vassula, do you remember the Pharisees?

V: Yes, Lord.

J: Let Me tell you that many of them are replicas of the Pharisees, doubting, fearing, blinded by vanity and with hypocrisy. Do you remember how many times I have given them signs? I have given them signs hundreds of times, and what have they done? Times have not changed; many of My sacerdotal souls are just the same replicas of the Pharisees! I have given them signs but they want signs which could be explained by proofs; they want proofs.

V: Will you give them of Your past signs a proof, and of this revelation any proof?

J: All that I give them is you yourself, child.

V: But Lord, it's not convincing; I am not convincing; I'm nothing to convince! They'll laugh outright in my face.

J: I have blessed you.

V: But Lord, I know that it's you, and a few others too, but many will disagree, since there is no solid proof it's from You. I am nothing, and you know it.

J: Daughter, let Me be everything; remain nothing, and let Me be everything. The least you are, the more I am. I have now laid My justice on mankind; upon them is what they have reaped.

V: Isn't there a solution, I mean that somehow everything becomes like You want, and so your justice can be lifted?

J: Vassula, when I will be received and not denied by My sacerdotal souls now I will lift My justice. I have warned them, but they keep My warnings hidden.

V: Please tell me the reason why they do this.

J: They seem to forget My omnipotence and My wealth; they tend to amass everything into one thing, they will believe only if they see, grieving Me, counting not My blessings. Creature! Creature! Revive My Church. Vassula, honour Me; the hour is near, beloved, the hour is at hand. Love will come again as love. Vassula, set My wisdom

revelations in order; I will help you; all will be in time; I am preparing
you.

V: Thank you, Lord. I bless You.

Vassula's final comment to this conversation was: "These last three days, I felt in my
soul an inexplicable agony between the first and fourth of September."[3]

That was just six years and one week ago, as I write. In the intervening years
Vassula would learn of the punishment but she would always have the reassurance
that Jesus is near her, thoughtful about every response that she would make, His very
presence an inexhaustible source of peace and joy. On 10 September she writes as
follows: "Suddenly Jesus reminded me of a dream I had last night and had forgotten.
It was the vision I saw lately, but it appeared worse in my dream." "Listen" said
Jesus "I have let you see the vision in your sleep to make you feel it. No, there is
no escape."[4]

"I remember" comments Vassula "when I saw it coming like a giant wave, I tried
to run and hide, knowing it's impossible." She went on, "But why do this if You
love us? Why?" When Jesus replied, "I am known as a God of love as well as a
God of justice," she asked "What can we do to stop this?" Jesus answered:
"Tremendous amendments are required now from all of you: uniting and being one,
loving one another, believing in Me, believing in My heavenly works, for I am
among you always."[4]

There was an interval between this explanatory message and the next warning. It is
important to bear this in mind, to remember that such intervals are filled with
positive, encouraging, consoling teaching. On 26 October Jesus spoke thus:

> Rejoice and exult all you who are faithful to Me! Woe for the unfaithful, for
> My Word will come upon them like a sword, striking them, destroying all
> their false wisdom, wisdom which inspired My creation to fall into Satan's
> nets, transforming My lambs into godless, fearless, immoral people. I have,
> Vassula, given you a vision of warning, an allusion to what I have done to
> Sodom and Gomorrah. Let them take heed of My warning, for I the Lord
> have foretold to My creation that unless they repent and accept Me as their
> Creator, My sword will strike them. It is out of My boundless mercy that
> I descend on earth to warn you. I am the Spirit of truth who speaks; listen
> to what I have to tell to My Churches. Creation, do not stand still, forward
> My warning.[5]

This is severe. Yet to the severity Jesus adds, "I am standing at the door knocking;
if anyone hears My voice and opens the door, I the Lord will enter to share his meal
side by side with him. Do not fear, I am fulfilling My Word. Before you I stand."

It was over eight months later that Jesus took up the theme again. This time He prepared Vassula to understand His message: "Peace be with you, child. My Ecclesia will revive but before this renewal she will suffer even more (Vassula adds in a note 'Than she is suffering now'). She is in the beginning of her tribulations. Here, take a look at My cup of justice."

"I looked" Vassula says "at a beautiful cup decorated with precious stones; it was full to the brim; if one would move it, it would surely spill." Then Jesus spoke:

See how full it is? It is very near to spill over - beware! For once My justice will spill over, it will pour out on you creation, revealing the anathema prophesied long ago. You will be plunged into darkness. I will come to you like a thief, unexpected. I have been giving you warnings; I have been giving you signs to stay alert but you are rejecting them; you are unwilling to acknowledge the End of Times, no matter how much I try to warn you. Your disbelief in Me is total. My warning will be like a purge to convert you and this will be done out of great pity. Alas for you creation! Alas for you disbelievers, who will intensify your disbelief and turn even more against Me. Your spirit, enveloped by obscurity, will be pulled as in a current by obscurity himself (Vassula notes that 'while saying this God was in pain and was suffering'). Creation! How I pity you! How I suffer to see you lost forever! My children, in whom I breathed in you raising you to life, consecrating you before you were born, return to Me. My Heart lacerates to see how many will be drawn in this current into total obscurity and eternal damnation! Creation, although your sins are scarlet I am all so willing to forgive you. Come, come to Me; return to Me, your Father. I will welcome you and treat you a thousand times more lovingly than the 'Father of the prodigal son'; return to Me before My cup brims over; return before My justice blows on you, arousing limitless blisters upon you, scorching you and every other living thing around you. You would want to breathe but you will only inhale a scorching wind, burning you inwardly and leaving you as a living torch. Creation, understand how imminent this Hour has become - for today you see the trees still blooming, but tomorrow there will be none left; you will be covered by Satan's smoke - a deadly veil. O do understand that these disasters and calamities are drawn upon you by your evil doings - by your apostasy, and by rebelling against Me. Repent now that there is still time - convert now! I am ready to forgive you. Vassula allow Me to use you.

Yes, Lord, let everything be according to Your will.

Jesus concluded: "Please Me; obey Me your Lord; I will never abandon you. My Sacred Heart gives you My peace."[6]

The reader will see that this is not blank, hopeless condemnation. Cause and effect are clarified and the mystery of divine mercy made manifest - in so far as we can ever grasp this astounding attribute of God made accessible bounteously in Jesus Christ.

Mercy too is prominent some weeks later when Jesus speaks more of purification:

> I have come, through you, to give My message of universal peace and love and show to all My creation My Sacred Heart and how I love you. O Vassula! My mercy is great upon all of you! Dearest souls, the time for your purification is drawing near - what I will do is out of love; your purification will be to save you from the gates of hell. I will descend upon you like lightning and renew you with My fire. My Spirit of love will redeem you by drawing you into love and consume you into a living flame of love. I will let My Spirit pour out of heaven and purify your blemished souls into holy spotless souls - purifying you as gold is purified in fire. You will recognize the time of salvation, and when My Spirit of love will descend. Unless this happens, you will not see the new heavens and the new earth I foretold you. My child, by My fire, by My love, by My mercy and My justice, My seeds (Vassula notes 'us') will sprout and open like new lilies which face the sun - seeking My light and My dew; and I will pour from My heavens My light, embellishing you and My dew nourishing you to see a new era of love. By My power I will sweep away all iniquity, perversion and evil; I will descend upon you like a violent torrent of cleansing waters and wash away all your evil and leave you standing upright as columns of pure gold. With My torrents of fervent love I will sweep away all that is false and faked - just like clay is washed away with a few drops of rain, so will My Spirit of sublime love wash away your sins which blemished your soul. I, your Saviour, will renew you creation and offer you My Gift. My Gift will descend from heaven: **a glittering New Jerusalem: A Renovated Church** - pure and holy, because I who was, is, and is to come, will be living in her midst and in her very soul. You will all feel her, palpitating and alive, because My Sacred Heart will be throbbing within her. I, the Lord of Lords, am like the fire and My Sacred Heart is in ardent flames - so eager with desire to enwrap you all - thrusting you in the furnace of love and leaving you ablaze in total rapture and ecstasy of love for Me, your beloved God! Yes, I will make out of each one of you a living altar, ablaze with My fire. O creation! when My fire will enkindle your hearts you will finally cry out to Me: 'You are the One God and only, the just one - you are indeed the Lamb. You are our heavenly Father - how could we have been so blind? O Holy of Holies, be-in-us, live-in-us. Come, O Saviour?' and to this cry of yours I will not hesitate. I will descend upon you, as quick as lightning, and live among you; and you, beloved ones, will realize that from the beginning you were My own and My seed. I will then be among you and will reign

over you with an everlasting love. I will be your God and you My own. Dearest souls, treat Me as your King - crown Me with your love. We, us. Come.[7]

The reader will see that this is not "doom and gloom." I have quoted a lengthy passage to show two things: the overwhelming importance of personal reference to Jesus; and closely related to this, the emphasis on purification as a stage, a preparatory phase for a beatific fulfilment. Prophets of "doom and gloom" too often view punishment as an end in disaster with no hope. Jesus does not give Vassula that opinion. He holds out the prospect, shining and consoling, of better times when what is evil has been purged.

On 1 May in the following year Jesus spoke some words that certainly sound severe. But they are part of a lengthy communication which is replete with an existential doctrine of the Holy Spirit and centres all in the Sacred Heart of Jesus:

I do not come to you as a judge, not yet, I come to you as the Beggar, in rags and barefoot with parched lips, imploring and lamenting for some love, for a return of love. Today you have in your sight a lamenting Beggar with his hand constantly outstretched, begging you for a return of love. 'I beg you come back to Me and love Me; learn to love Me, learn to love Me; make peace with Me, make peace with Me. I will not reject you. I am love and I love you everlastingly.' Come to Me when the Hour has not yet come, do not wait for My justice to arrive, do not let My justice take you by surprise and unaware. Remember then that I shall be in this terrible, awesome hour, standing before you as a majestic severe Judge and My voice which was that of a lamenting beggar shall turn into a glare of a devouring fire, in cloudburst, downpour, hailstones. My breath will be like a stream of brimstone which will set fire everywhere, to purify you and renovate you all, uniting you into one holy people.[8]

Past midway in the following year Vassula records a mystical experience which was related to all that Jesus tells her by way of warning to those who are still hard-hearted:

I saw in a vision that I was looking from outside a window. It was daylight; suddenly the earth started to shake violently under my feet, the ground was going up and down, the earthquake was of point eight, it was not stopping. I looked from the window at the sky, because it was losing its luminosity. I was staring up at the heavens while they were becoming darker by the second until they reached to become full night. Then I saw the stars falling, or rather as though they were speeding away from the eastern horizon to the western horizon, it seemed they were leaving the heavens. Then the tremor stopped and there was a menacing darkness. I saw that I had a faint light in my room. I looked out of the window, but there were about three or four houses which had a light in the whole town.[9]

Again there was some time, a whole year, before Jesus took up the subject again. He did so in terms reminiscent of the Old Testament:

Keep praying for your brothers then. I said: it will not go as hard on Sodom as on this generation. Do you remember Nineveh? They were at the verge of a great disaster, but they listened to Jonah, My mouthpiece, and from the highest to the least...all fasted, repented and vowed to change their life and live holy. Put yourselves on the ways of long ago. Enquire about the ancient paths. Seek the truth. Daughter, happy the man who will follow My advice. Let Me tell you one more thing. I, the anointed one, will engulf you all with My fire and consume you to give your soul a new life. I have little time left now; these times of mercy and grace are almost over. I am not concealing My plans, nor am I hiding My Face. I am revealing, as never before My Face and you, My beloved ones, your duty is to go and spread these messages of the Second Pentecost and what the Spirit teaches.[10]

In the course of this year, 1991, Jesus seeks insistently to awaken our generation from what he calls its "deep sleep."

Come close to Me and listen carefully: today I come all the way to your doorstep holding the banner of peace. I am coming to save you Jerusalem. On it is written: **Faithful and True, the King of Kings and Lord of Lords** (Rev 19:11,16). Will I hear from you, Jerusalem, 'My King, it is You that I have to worship' or will you still be unaware of Him who offers you His peace...now? Will you in these last days before the Day of Retribution recognize My Holy Spirit who descended from above in all His glory to make house with you? During your whole lifetime generation, you flouted My law and turned away rebelling. Are you ever going to be prepared to meet Me, your God? I am going to pass through your city and it will be sooner than you think. These will be My last warnings.

We may select some details from the sombre, rather frightening pictures by which Jesus shows in three phases how the purification will take place. In the first phase it is thus:

Suddenly upon you will come a time of great distress, unparalleled since nations first came to existence. For I will allow your soul to perceive all the events of your lifetime, I will unfold them one after the other. To the great dismay of your soul you will realize how much innocent blood your sins shed from victim souls. I will then make your soul aware to see how you had never been following My Law. Like an unrolled scroll, I will open the Ark of the Covenant and make you conscious of your lawlessness.

Then the soul will find itself surrounded by a dazzling light,

> A light so pure and so bright that although myriads of angels would be standing nearby, in silence, you will not see them completely because this light will be covering them like a silverish, golden dust. Your soul will only perceive their form, not their face. Then, in the midst of this dazzling light your soul will see what they had once seen in that fraction of a second, that very moment of your creation...They will see: Him who held you first in His hands, the eyes that saw you first. They will see: the hands of Him who shaped you and blessed you...They will see the most tender Father, your Creator, all clothed in fearful splendour, the First and the Last, He who is, who was, and is to come, the Almighty, the Alpha and the Omega, the Ruler.

Jesus then describes the effect of this purification on the soul:

> Shrivelled with your awakening, your eyes will be transfixed in Mine which will be like two flames of fire. Your heart then will look back on its sins and will be seized with remorse. You will, in great distress and agony suffer your lawlessness, realizing how you were constantly profaning My Holy Name and how you were rejecting Me, your Father...Panic-stricken, you will tremble and shudder when you will see yourself as a decaying corpse, devastated by worm and by vulture.

The third phase in the purification is thus put forward by the Lord:

> And if your legs will still be holding you up, I will show you what your soul, My temple and My dwelling, was nursing all the years of your life. Instead of My Perpetual Sacrifice, you will see to your dismay that you were fondling the Viper and that you had erected this Disastrous Abomination of which the prophet Daniel spoke in the most profound domain of your soul: the blasphemy that cut off all your heavenly bonds linking you to Me and making a gulf between you and Me, your God. When this day comes, the scales of your eyes will fall so that you may perceive how naked you are and how within you, you are a land of drought...Unhappy creature, your denial of the Most Holy Trinity turned you into a renegade and a persecutor of My Word. Your laments and your wailing will be heard only by you then... As it was in Noah's time, so will it be when I open the heavens and show you the Ark of the Covenant: "for in those days before the Flood, people were eating, drinking, taking wives, taking husbands, right up to the day Noah went into the ark, and they suspected nothing till the Flood came and swept all away."

Then Jesus, who liked to recall to Vassula Old Testament figures who would help her understanding, also liked to remind her that Our Lady was her protectress:

> This is how it will be in this day too; and I tell you, if that time had not been shortened by the intercession of your Holy Mother, the martyr saints and the pool of blood shed on earth, from Abel the holy to the blood of all My prophets, not one of you would have survived.[11]

Jesus states that He is sending angel after angel to announce that His "time of Mercy is running short" and the time of His reign on earth is "close at hand." He relates the future change that He will effect to the reign of His Holy Spirit. Some days later when He spoke at some length of the Day of Purification He spoke thus:

> Let My Spirit of truth shine on you so that you, in your turn, reflect My image, reminding the world of My true face, since the world seems to have forgotten My true image. In a short time all of you will learn how to live a True Life in God and be one with Me as the Holy Trinity is one and the same, because all three of us agree.

Jesus becomes more specific speaking of the fact that He is on His way of return, and when this happens His voice over the years will be known to be authentic. "I am telling you this" He says,

> so that you may rejoice, because I too rejoice for this day when Satan's head will be crushed by My Mother's heel. Hear Me: I shall pour out My Spirit on this evil generation to entice hearts and lead everyone back to the complete truth, to live a perfect life in Me your God. But be brave, because there will still be a fire before My Day, so do not fear nor be sad, because without this fire the world's face cannot change...and when it comes, it will show the world how wrong it was. It will show its godlessness, its rationalism, materialism, selfishness, pride, greed and its wickedness, in short all those vices the world worships. No one can say that I have not been telling you the outset of My plans. No one can say that I have been hiding My plans from you.

Jesus then recalls all that He has done to enlighten people on what was to come. Then He says:

> Now, I solemnly tell you, that when that Day of Purification comes, many will be sorrowful to the point of death for not having allowed My Holy Spirit of truth to enter their house, but have welcomed in his place the viper, the abomination of the desolation and shared their meal side by side with My enemy. They welcomed inside their house the one who apes the Holy One, they worshipped the deceiver, who taught them to misconceive My Holy Spirit: My Holy Spirit, the Giver of Life and the inner power of their soul,

He who breathed an active soul into them and inspired a living spirit. I tell you solemnly, My fire will descend in this world quicker than you expect it to come, so that those without sight of their sins may suddenly see their guilt. It is in My power to bring this day forward and it is again in My power to shorten this hour, for this hour will bring so much distress that many would curse the hour of their birth. They would want the valleys to open and swallow them, the mountains to fall on them and cover them, the vulture to devastate them quickly. They would want to dash themselves to pieces but no one will escape from this hour, those that truly love Me will suffer only for not having done more for Me. They too will be cleansed...If you love Me you would be glad to know that My Holy Spirit will come upon you in all His force and in all His glory... No one has yet loved Me as much as I love you, but on the Day of Purification you will understand how little you have done because I will show My Holy Face in you. You hear those footsteps? They are mine. You have the sound of My breath already? It is the sweet sound of My Holy Spirit blowing through your wilderness and your aridity. You felt a breath slide over your face? Do not fear. Like the dove's wings My Holy Spirit touched you slightly while hovering above you. O come! Come to Me and as Moses lifted up the serpent in the desert, I too will lift your soul up to Me and revive you! ......My forbearance is great and although I know you are sinners and you have polluted the earth with innocent blood, if you come to Me repentant, I will forgive your guilt and your crime. I am an Abyss of Grace. Do not be afraid... do not fear Me. Fear rather the Hour if it finds you unaware and asleep. This is the voice of your Father; this is the voice of the sublime source of love; this is the voice of Him who once said, 'Let there be light.' Come to Me and I shall give you My Spirit without reserve. Do not be like the soldiers who shared out My clothing and cast lots for them at the foot of My Cross. Come to Me with John's spirit, come to Me out of love, come to Me to console Me and be with Me. The Hour is coming when the world will find itself only in distress and darkness, the blackness of anguish, and will see nothing but night. Bewildered, they will call out to Me, but I shall not reply, I shall not listen to their cry. Frenzied they will blaspheme My revelation, wisdom and truth. The whole world will be inundated by distress upon seeing the Ark of the Covenant, My Law. Many will fall and be broken, rocked and shaken because of their lawlessness. When the heavens will tear open, like a curtain ripped in half, showing them how they flung My Glory for a worthless imitation, like stars that fall from Heaven they shall fall, realizing then how folly led them astray, how by trying to climb up to the summit and rival Me was only folly. When that day comes, I will show the world how wicked it was, how they befriended the Rebel and dialogued with him, rather than with the Holy One. The hour has come when constancy and faith, prayer and sacrifice are vital, they have become an urgency.[12]

For months after this Jesus maintained His teaching on the great themes which Vassula has heard from Him, which I have attempted to analyze in my first book. It was ten months later that He took up again the subject of chastisement. On 20 July, 1992 He evoked the mighty theme of the general judgement, when the fallen angels will be included:

> I will judge everyone according to what he has done or not done. In front of My throne everyone will stand in silence and in awe, for the Day of this final judgement will be so dreadful that it will make everyone tremble with fright in front of the supreme Judge that I am. You will all see a huge number of fallen angels who were driven out of heaven and fought in bitterness and spite Michael the Archangel and his angels. Yes, your eyes will see My rivals, the rivals of the Holy One, of the Anointed One. You will all see those fallen angels, adepts of Lucifer, the primeval serpent who tried to lead My sons and daughters all astray. You will see multitudes of those who defiled My name and transgressed My law, those who refused to be reared and fostered by My holiness and preferred to be labelled on their forehead by the Deceiver (at this point Vassula was given a vision of this multitude of fallen angels standing in front of God's throne in the day of Judgement; it was awesome and sad to her). Yes, Vassula, a harsh vision has been shown you. I tell you: I will soon come with My saints to pronounce judgement on the world and to sentence the guilty. Today My grace is being revealed to all mankind to renew you all with My Holy Spirit before My Day and remind you of My law. I will in that day repay everyone according to what he deserves. I have said that I will severely punish anyone who insults the Spirit of Grace and treats My Spirit as foolish; that is why you should stay awake. Today, more than ever before I am asking you all to consecrate yourselves, your families and your nations to Our Two Hearts. Allow Me to seal your forehead with the seal of My Holy Spirit. **The time of sorting has come, the time of reckoning is here.**[13]

Jesus points forward more than once in the subsequent months to the day of final reckoning. He used such words as these: "I shall come suddenly upon you, in a pillar of blazing fire! A Fire that will change the face of this earth... Come, take courage, My child - every step you take I the Lord bless."

Jesus speaks of melting those hardened against him. One passage spoken in February, 1993 may conclude the quotations:

> The sixth seal is about to be broken (Rev 6:12) and you will all be plunged into darkness, and there will be no illumination for the smoke poured up out of the abyss will be like the smoke from a huge furnace so that the sun and the sky will be darkened by it; and out of My cup of Justice I will make you resemble snakes; vipers. I will make you crawl on your belly and eat dust

in these days of darkness; I will crush you to the ground to remind you that you are not better than vipers...you will suffocate and stifle in your sins; in My anger I will tread you down, trample you in My wrath! See? My four angels are standing anxiously now around My throne, waiting for My orders; when you will hear peals of thunder and flashes of lightning know that the hour of My Justice has come; the earth will shake and like a shooting star will reel from its place, extirpating mountains and islands out of their places; entire nations will be annihilated, the sky will disappear like a scroll rolling up, as you saw it in your vision, daughter. A great agony will befall on all the citizens, and woe to the unbeliever!

Jesus makes it clear that people will not wish to believe, expecting mercy, but they will have to learn that they spurned His messages.

When the hour of darkness comes I will show you your insides; I will turn your soul inside out and you will see your soul as black as coal; not only will you experience a distress like never before, but you will beat your breast with agony saying that your own darkness is far worse that the darkness surrounding you. As for you... (Here there was a message concerning only Vassula).

The concluding note is hopeful:

That is how I shall display My Justice to the nations and all nations will feel My sentence when this Hour comes - I will make human life scarcer than ever before; then when My wrath will be appeased, I will set My throne in each one of you, and together with one voice and one heart and one language you will praise Me, the Lamb.

Jesus speaks a consoling word to Vassula thereon:

This is enough for today My Vassula; do not be bitter with your own people, and do not, soul, trouble your heart either. I shall show you to the world as a sign of unity; you are contradicted and rejected but you know now why; because unity is unwelcomed, as love is unwelcomed in many hearts. Sincerity is missing... Come. We, us?[14]

On the next day Jesus, recalling that His severity is as great as His mercy, reverted to the root cause of all, the apostasy:

I have spoken to you of the apostasy, apostasy that bound the hands of My best friends, disarming them because of its velocity and its measure; have I not said that cardinals will oppose cardinals and how bishops will go against bishops and that many are on the road to perdition? They have in their endless battle, weakened My Church. Today this spirit of rebellion thrives inside My Holy Place. Do you recall the vision I had given you of the vipers crawling all over the Holy Sacraments of the Altar? Have I not revealed to you how many of them oppose My Pope? And how they push him aside. I have already given you a detailed account of the rebellion inside My Church. My faithful friend, allow Me to stop here - we shall continue later on. Stay near Me and please Me.[15]

Let the final word be from a communication made to Vassula by God the Father. He says, with regard to those who obstruct His Holy Spirit,

My compassion is great but My severity is as great. My wrath is as powerful as My forgiveness.

Deploring the decline in faith and religious practice, the Father goes on,

My Heart is broken within Me, My child, and My angels dread and tremble for the Hour I reserved to break out when My orders will be given. I cannot endure any more to see your Holy Mother's tears shed over and over again every time My Son is re-crucified; your generation's sins are leading My Son to Calvary every moment. Together, together in one voice the world is blaspheming My Holy Spirit and all the powers of heaven. Daily, the world is provoking Me: 'Look! Look what has become of the great Lord's House?' they say, while tearing it down. My soul cannot bear any longer the groans of My Son being re-crucified, although both My Son and your Holy Mother muffle as best they could their pain. My ears hear everything; My ears and My eyes are not human and nothing escapes Me. Since it is your generation that makes the choice, not I, the rebellion in My House will bring down on you My wrath and the deepest darkness is wrought on earth soon; it is not My choice but yours. I had chosen to lift you from your graves with mercy and love, compassion and peace, but look how so many of you are unmoved to My offer, nothing can touch you any longer.

Again there is consolation for Vassula, whom He asks to be His echo:

Hard as they may harass you, I shall not allow them to overcome you. On the contrary you will be like a sword when you will pronounce My words; remind them again that I take pleasure, not in the death of a wicked and rebellious man but in the turning back of a wicked and rebellious man who changes his ways to win life. This earth that you know will vanish soon. I have decided to hasten My plan because of the great sins your generation conceives. All will vanish, all will wear out like a garment. This will be My way of destroying the defilement of sin, and you will realize that from the beginning you were My sacred temples and that My Spirit was living in you. Ah! for this Baptism by fire. Pray and fast in these last days. I Am is near you.[16]

Notes:

1. True Life in God, Volume I, p.171f;

2. Ibid.,

3. 172, 173;

4. 180f;

5. 215;

6. 3 July, 1988, 343f;

7. 17 August, 1988, 360f;

8. *True Life in God*, Volume II, p.20;

9. 198;

10. 6 August, 1991, p.344;

11. 15 September, 1991, p.355-57;

12. 19 September, 1991, p.358-61;

13. True Life in God, Volume III, p.31;

14. 97f;

15. 99;

16. Communication from Vassula.

7

RUSSIA AGAIN

The reader will know from what appeared in my previous book and from what has been related so far in regard to Vassula's apostolate to Russia, how profoundly this whole subject enters into her life. It will be of interest then to reproduce textually the communication of Jesus to her on 13 December, 1993. Here is the text:

I Am is with you and I shall never fail you. You are bound to Me ...write My Vassula:

Your sister Russia will honour Me in the very end and one day will be called holy, for I shall be her ruler, once again integrity will live there...yes?

Vassula replied with these words: "Lord, corruption is penetrating in her now." Again she questioned the Lord when He replied, "I will lower her eyes," "I do not understand in which way, Lord, you will lower her eyes." The Lord replied: "Very well, I will tell you then. By the brilliance of My majesty.[1] Then I will come and rest in her heart."

"Lord" said Vassula "she still lives in the blackness of sin and anguish." Jesus went on:

Those who have taken the wrong turning will fall. I will destroy the luxurious forces with My fire and the proud will be brought low. I intend to rebuild My house and I shall adopt her sons and daughters to honour Me. Vassula, do not just stand there bewildered and uncomprehending. I tell you your sister Russia will be the head[2] of many nations and will glorify Me in the end. Listen carefully and understand:

Her shepherds will be gathering while treaties will be breaking elsewhere, and while rebellion will be working its way elsewhere to abolish the

---

[1] I understood by a purification, for when God reveals Himself and shines in a soul, the contrast of Light within darkness is so great that the soul sees vividly its imperfections and suffers a lot.
[2] Spiritually.

Perpetual Sacrifice. **Russia's shepherds will be gathering**, to restore My house, reverencing the Perpetual Sacrifice, worshipping and honouring Me. When in the last days, nation after nation will decline and pervert itself for having erected the disastrous abomination in the Holy Place, **Russia's shepherds will be gathering**, to sanctify her altars; and while others[1] will be reverencing a lifeless form, an invention of human skill, an unbreathing image. **Russia's shepherds will be gathering**, glorifying Me, for I, God, will preserve her Integrity. And while efforts very evilly are being spent elsewhere to shorten the days of My mouthpieces, since they are the **hope** of this world, **Russia's shepherds will be gathering**, to protect My Holy Sacrifice, and I, for My part, will be setting My Throne in her.

And I will assemble all those who bear My Name together for My Glory. I will repair her broken altars, for many who live under My Name will side up with her in the end. And her shepherds will, with one hand, and one spirit, re-erect My tottering House. What had once been twisted will now be straightened. And I will adorn Russia with impressive vestments because of her zeal in Me. I will place her shepherds at the head of innumerable nations. I have engraved her with the seal of Consecration to offer Me once more: incense and an appeasing fragrance; this is why I will overwhelm her shepherds with miracles.

Russia, My loyalty and My Gentleness will sanctify you. Russia, My daughter, **acknowledge Me entirely**, and I promise you on oath to exalt your descendants like stars and give them sacred vestments. **Acknowledge Me entirely**, Russia, and I will annihilate all your opponents. I will, **if** you **acknowledge Me wholly**, do fresh wonders in you to prove to everyone living under the sun, My Mercy and My Holiness.

I am ready to show My Compassion on her and I will not be slow if she welcomes Me eagerly. I will not delay to show her how, I, the Almighty can eliminate the arrogant and break their lawless sceptres. But,[2] if she will perverse the liberty I have now given her and will put Me out of her mind, even for just a while, I will allow an enemy to invade her...if Russia will not come back to Me with **all her heart and acknowledge Me with an undivided heart**, as her Saviour, I will send a vast and mighty host in her and from her to all nations, a host such as has never been before, such as will never be again to the remotest ages, and the sky will turn black and will tremble, and the stars will lose their brilliance...

---

[1] The apostates.
[2] Suddenly God's Voice dropped and became sad and very grave. It saddened me profoundly.

Today I am ready to make up to you, Russia, for the years you suffered and I can still snatch you all from the blaze, **were you to acknowledge Me fully.** Seek good and not evil. Have you already forgotten your famine and your drought?[1] ...I have pushed back the red dragon and destroyed the luxuriance of his empire. I have humbled the proud, I have opened the prison gates and freed your captives, I overthrew the kingdom of the red dragon that had coiled in your womb, that one that made the earth tremble turning your land into a wasteland. To honour My Name again in you, I have opened your Churches one after the other; I called you by your name that Day:

RUSSIA

to rejoice and be glad. And to celebrate the Feast of My Transfiguration,[2] I transfigured your image instantly. Your misery of oppression was your punishment for the crimes of the world; and now I am waiting to be gracious to you, Russia, for in the end you will glorify Me.

I tell you, while others will be destroying you will be building. While many will be falling, your shepherds will be rising, if you put your trust in Me. And, while some of My Own, sitting at table with Me, will be wickedly betraying Me, **you**, you will be the one who will stretch out your hand to defend My Name, My Honour and My Sacrifice. And so every one of your sins will have been paid. You will then step forward, loyally, and save your brother, your brother who was the prey of the evil one. You will resurrect the Church into One and Justice will come to live in Her. Justice will bring Peace and everlasting security.

Happy will you be, singing praises to Me; rich will you be, for the loyalty you showed towards your King. He will repay you a hundredfold, and there where treaties were broken, prophets despised and killed, there where much offense was sown and threats pronounced reaching the heavens with an uproar, there, My beloved, your shepherds' noble voices will call out:

SALVATION! Priests and ministers of the Most High, salvation will only be found in Love! PEACE! Shepherds of the Reflection-of-the-Father, peace will only be found in Forgiveness. UNITY, brothers of the Light Thrice Holy and Who is One in Three, Three in One Light, will only be found by intermarrying! May our Lord Almighty, the Irresistible One, render us worthy of His Name, may He grant us to be one in His Name. Eternal

---

[1]Spiritually.

[2]The Lord predicted to transfigure Russia in message 13.11.89 and the fall of the communism happened in the week of the Orthodox Feast of Transfiguration.

Father, let us be so completely one that the rest of the world will realize that it was You who sent the Sacrificial Lamb to glorify You and have Your Name known.

Thus, you will ravage the Divider and you will repair what had been undone.

Russia, your role is to honour Me and glorify Me. The Festivity has yet to come, but it depends from you in which manner that Day will come.

Do not let Me make you return to Me by fire, but with bonds of Peace.

Quite recently, President Yeltsin has restored two of the most famous icons in the world - Our Lady of Vladimir and Rublev's Trinity to the Church of the Assumption. Hitherto, they were museum pieces in the Tretirkov. The Church which will house the icon of Our Lady of Thazan is nearing completion.

8

AN ENLIGHTENING PARALLEL

Simeon the New Theologian (c.950-1022) is one of the greatest mystics in the history of the Church. Trained for the imperial service in Constantinople, living for a while a worldly life, he had a conversion through contact with Simeon the Devout (dc.987) and as a result of a singular mystical experience. He entered the monastery of Studios in Constantinople. He vowed a special cult through life to his spiritual master. This may have been his downfall, for the community refused his admission to vows. He was, however, accepted in the monastery of St Mammas at Xirokerke by the *hegumenos* (superior) Anthony. Ordained a priest he became *hegumenos* and revitalized the monastery, as well as giving it material stability. After twenty-five years the monks turned against him, complaining of his mystical tendencies - he had changed the monastic trend from mere asceticism to comtemplation; they also objected to the public cult given to Simeon the Devout. The ecclesiastical authority in the person of the *syncellus*, Nicholas of Nicomedia, deserted him and he was forced into exile on the other side of the Bosporus. He took up residence in the monastery of St Marina and soon this became a spiritual centre. He rejected attempts to recall and reinstate him, and died in St Marina in 1022. This was thirty-two years before the break between East and the West. Simeon arouses much recent interest among European theologians, foremost among his admirers the nonagenarian theological giant, YMJ Congar OP. He is understandbly valued by Orthodox theologians.[1]

He is of interest to readers of *True Life in God* for two reasons. Vassula has studied him assiduously. She has discovered in his precious writings striking parallels to messages which she received directly from Jesus. The results of her research are set forth in the following pages, with what I consider an appropriate theological commentary to follow each section. The references, which are incorporated in Vassula's text are to the works of *St Simeon: Catecheses, Theological Chapters* (Cap), *Hymns and Theological and Ethical Treatises* (Eth., ed. B Krivocheine). Reference to parallel passages are to the volumes of *True Life in God*.

---

[1]Cf. Article Simeon the New Theologian, in my <u>Veni Creator Spiritus</u>, Liturgical Press, Collegeville, A Michael Glazier Book, 1990, p.210-12; with bibl., MJ Congar OP., <u>I Believe in the Holy Spirit</u>, I, London, 1989, p.93-103.

1. Reticence of some Clergy and Theologians to accept Prophecy given by the Holy Spirit

Pray, that the Holy Church returns as in the beginning, when every Work of God was welcomed without disbelief and contempt, without doubt. Pray, that the Holy Church's faith will be renewed again, like in the past and believe in miracles, apparitions and visions, for this is one way of God speaking to you. Ask for a renewal. (Our Blessed Mother, on 24.3.88. Volume I, p.299)

One has often heard clergy and theologians say that private or prophetic revelations are not to be taken seriously nor any mystical experiences, that one should be led only by faith; they give themselves as examples. If it was as they say, not serious, and that revelations, (messages from above) must be taken lightly or not at all, why would God then bother to give urgent messages and ask those favoured to diffuse His messages? However, these people not only contradict Scriptures, but they also try to suppress the action of the Holy Spirit. They become "Théomachi," a Greek term meaning: "Fighters against God".

Let us hear the scriptures: "At all your meetings, each one has a hymn, a lesson, a revelation, a tongue, or an interpretation." (1 Cor 14:26)

And so, my dear brothers, by all means be ambitious to prophesy... (1 Cor 14:39)

In the Church, God has given the first place to apostles, the second to prophets, the third to teachers; after them, miracles, and after them the gift of healing;... (1 Cor 12:28)

And to some, His gift was that they should be apostles; to some, prophets; to some, evangelists; to some, pastors and teachers; so that the saints together make a unity in the work of service, building up the body of Christ. (Ep 4:11)

In *True Life in God*, God reminds us several times that a prophetic revelation is a gift from His Holy Spirit which builds up the Church. Therefore, to reject this gift from God is a sin and an offense towards God because His Holy Spirit is denied, suppressed and ridiculed.

Now consider St Simeon. These are his words:

I am in conflict once more with those who claim that they possess the Spirit of God in an insensible manner and who imagine that they possess Him inwardly from holy baptism; who are convinced that they undoubtedly own the treasure without feeling its weight in any way; and those who state that they have never felt anything during contemplation or revelation and have accepted this only "from hearing", through reasoning and faith, and not experientially. (Eth 5.1-12)

Many of Vassula's Greek Orthodox accusers mock her for having conversations with God daily and at all times. For them it is the impossible of impossibles!

She would hear almost word for word the same comments and remarks that St Simeon heard centuries back, coming from his own environment:

"Stop!" they would say to him, "you deluded, arrogant man! Who has become like the Holy Fathers? Who has seen God or is able to see Him in the least? Who has received the Holy Spirit to such a degree that he was honoured to see the Father and the Son? Stop, unless you want to be stoned." (Eth 9.364-375)

Vassula's mystical experiences and witnessing had aroused the hostility of certain monks. Not having had such experiences themselves, they denied its possibilities. St Simeon explains:

They do not believe that in our generation there can be someone who is moved and influenced by the divine Spirit, who perceptibly sees and apprehends Him (Cap 1.85). For every man judges others by his own condition, by what he is himself - in virtue or in vice. (Cap 1.85)

What, one may ask, is the relationship between Vassula's spirituality and the Tradition of the Church? The answer: nothing new or unique concerning herself, but only what is found in Sacred Scripture, the Holy Fathers and mystics.

One should know that if the teachers declare their agreement with the God-bearing Fathers of old, it is clear that, they in turn, speak with the same spirit, and those who do not believe them, or even accuse them, sin against the One who speaks through them. (Eth 5.431-435)

About knowledge of Scriptures, dogmas, devotions etc.., this is what St Simeon says:

The door of knowledge is opened by the fulfilment of the commandments or rather, by the One who said, "He who loves me will keep my commandments, and my Father will love him, and I will reveal myself to him." Therefore, when God lives in us and moves within us, and even reveals Himself perceptibly to us, then we consciously contemplate the divine mysteries that are hidden in divine Scripture. Otherwise it is impossible - let no one be deceived - for the chest of knowledge to be opened to us and for us to enjoy the blessings contained therein, to partake of them and contemplate them. (Cat 24.54-69)

The problem here, admirably stated by St Simeon and Vassula is that of the institution and the charismatic. The institution is necessary, but those who embody it have to recognise that their own sense of power and personality fulfilment may become so entwined with their official function that they overlook, or ignore or even reject and forcefully, unjustly combat the action of the Spirit in his many charisms bestowed on the faithful. Here too we must allow for clerical anti-lay prejudice. Priests accustomed to submission, obeisance from the laity, feeling themselves indispensable in the dispensation of Christ's saving mysteries, which according to the intention of the Master but only as his representatives, they certainly are, may think that any initiative coming from the laity is suspect automatically and should be suppressed. The classic instance of this kind of blunder is Joan of Arc. She was condemned to be burnt as a witch by Bishop Cauchon, who was no fool - he was a former rector of the Sorbonne and he had the misguided support of all the theologians of France at the time. I could fill a book with records of cases which I have personally studied in our time, genuine visionaries outlawed, harassed by ecclesiastical authorities. One whom I have met was a religious. If she did not sign a retraction of her reports of the visions and messages she had, she would be expelled from her convent. To her honour she refused to sign a falsehood. Five bishops, four of whom she had never met, signed a statement that she was bogus; one bitterly regretted this act and disavowed it as he lay dying. Another visionary was excommunicated because she foretold things which have come to pass, denial by priests of the mystery of the Eucharist - this was, at the time an attack on the Church! Others whom I have known or known of, have been refused Holy Communion in their parishes. Another has been denounced from the altar because of significant miraculous signs in her home about religious images. I add here that Pope John Paul II has repeatedly insisted on the fact of charisms bestowed on the laity. I give the texts in my book on the Pope, appearing simultaneously with the present work.

2. The Action of the Holy Spirit

...What is sealed and closed, invisible and unknowable to all men becomes disclosed, visible and knowable to us only through the Holy Spirit. How can those who have never experienced the presence of the Holy Spirit, His radiance and illumination, the visitation (He makes) in them, even possibly know, comprehend or understand even one iota of it? (Cat 24.102-108)

...Moved by the Spirit who guides us from above and enlightens our hearts, I bring these mysteries to light in these writings, since God desires unceasingly that His love for us be revealed, so that we may be led to love Him more by thinking about His immense goodness with reverence. (Eth 1 10.76-82)

God's message concerns a revelation of the mystery of salvation guided by the Holy Spirit; not new truths, but a way of interpreting and deepening them.

I have often said that Vassula did not need books and studies in theology as I did to obtain knowledge of theology and of scriptures. All she had to do was to listen to the Holy Spirit. She received knowledge by grace, directly moved by the Holy Spirit. Here is what St Simeon says:

> They no longer belong to themselves but to the Spirit who is in them. He moves them and is, in turn, moved by them. In them He becomes all the things you hear enumerated in divine Scripture concerning the Kingdom of Heaven: pearl, mustard seed, leaven, water, fire, drink of life, living spring of water that wells forth, stream of spiritual words, of utterances of divine life, lamp, wedding bed, nuptial chamber, bridegroom, friend, brother and father. But why multiply words, why endeavor to cover all (these titles): they are beyond numbering! Indeed, how can language fathom or express in words the things that no eye has seen and no ear has heard, things beyond the mind of man? How can it be expressed in words? Even if we have received all this within, as a gift of God, we are entirely powerless to measure it with our mind or express it in words. (Euch 1.223-237)

> A person who has consciously accepted the God who gives knowledge to men has carefully read all of Scripture. He no longer needs to read books, having harvested all of the fruit from his reading. How is this so? Whoever converses with the One who inspired the divine writings, and has been initiated by him into the secrets of the hidden mysteries becomes for others a book inspired by God. He bears within himself the old and new mysteries engraved there by the finger of God. He rests from all the labours, finding his repose in God, who is the highest perfection. (Cap 3.100)

Mgr Kvivocheine writes that St Simeon harshly criticizes the hierarchy and the clergy, with little subtlety. For example, in a long tirade in Hymn 58, he addresses the bishops on behalf of Christ. The majority are accused of every crime, but especially of lack of inner piety, of pharisaism, love of money and despising the poor: (Hymn 58.64-144) "And you, heads of dioceses," - it is Christ who speaks - "hear what I say! You, the imprint of my image; you, installed to converse with Me worthily; you, placed above all the just, since you assume the place of My Apostles and bear My divine countenance. You have received, however small your church-community may be, a power like the one I, the Word, received from my Father" (Hymn 58.64-72). "You bishops," - Simeon continues to record the words of Christ - "on account (of your high dignity), you haughtily view the lowly as weak, inferior beings. You, bishops, fail in your duty...I am not speaking of those whose life corresponds to their words and is a seal of their inspired teaching, but of those whose conduct contradicts their teaching, who remain ignorant of My awesome, divine (mysteries), who think they are holding bread which in reality is fire, who scorn me like ordinary bread, who believe they see mere morsel to be eaten, without detecting My invisible glory." (Hymn 58.78-96)

Christ had reproached them at that time, as He reproaches today certain clergy in His messages *True Life in God*: the clergy who have apostatized in both Churches, the Roman Catholic Church and the Orthodox Church. The reproaches are the same, hypocrisy, self-righteousness, pride, lack of love and an outward appearance of religion, but from within corrupt and spiritually dead, neglecting and lacking faith in the Eucharist. Here is a magnificent passage from Jesus:

It has been said that in the last days to come, people will keep up the outward appearance of religion but will have rejected the inner power of it... The inner power of My Church is My Holy Spirit in it, alive and active, like a heart in a body; My Holy Spirit is the Heart of My Body, which is the Church.... The inner power of My Church is My Holy Spirit, this Fire which enlivens you, purifies you and makes out of your spirit a column of fire, ardent braziers of love, living torches of light, to proclaim without fear My Word, becoming witnesses of the Most High and teaching others to look only for Heavenly things... The inner power of My Church is My Holy Spirit, the Life and the Breath that keeps you alive and makes your spirit desire Me, calling Me, "Abba". If you refuse, My child, and suppress the gifts of My Holy Spirit, what services will you be able to do and offer Me? Do not be like corpses that keep up the outward appearance of religion but reject the inner power of it with futile speculations thus limiting Me in My Divinity...for My Kingdom consists not in spoken words, nor of an outward appearance of religion, but an inner power that only I can give you through My Holy Spirit, if you seek it...

As in St Simeon's time, Christ does not reproach all the clergy, since in His messages of *True Life in God*, He separates them by calling the sincere ones His Abels and Jacobs, and the ones who displease Him, Cains and Essaus, and those who betray Him, Judas'.

Let us take the words of Simeon:

Outwardly, their body is adorned handsomely; to the onlooker they seem brilliant and pure, but their souls are mud and mire, even worse than the most deadly poison, the wicked perverts! Indeed, in those days Judas who betrayed Me unworthily received the Bread from my hands and ate it, as he would any ordinary bread. Satan thereby entered at once into him and made him betray Me shamelessly. Unbeknown to them, this is what happens to those who touch My divine mysteries unworthily, with audacity and presumption; to those who from their high throne dominate all the others, dominate the clerics, dominate the priests... and who trample my divine court! (Hymn 58.118-138)

Now compare this message of Jesus to Vassula:

> ...Daughter, Judas betrayed Me, but how many more like Judas are betraying Me still?   I knew instantly that his kiss would spread among many, and for generations to come, this same kiss will be given to Me over and over again, renewing My sorrow, rending My Heart... (Volume I, p.102 - May 16, 1987)

> ...Daughter, if souls only knew how wonderful it is to live in God, no one would be lost so easily, unless they chose to be lost like Judas who chose the way to perdition. Not that My Heart did not melt with sorrow every time I saw him take one further step away from Me; not that I had not prayed for him; not that I had not cried My Eyes out for him. I had opened so many ways for him to take, all leading to Me, but no sooner had he started one than he came out of it when he would realize I had laid it for him, for to sin he added rebellion, heaping abuses in his heart for Me His God. When he realized that My Kingdom was not an earthly kingdom in earthly glory he shut his heart and cut out our bonds and estranged himself **immediately** from Me...

This is what Christ said on 15 April 1991, (Volume II, p.307) regarding the outward appearance of religion of some clergy, but within, they are all dead men's bones.

> ...Justice, mercy, good faith!   These you should have practiced without neglecting the other parts of My Law.   And you, you who delight in your division and swear by My Throne and by Me, I, who sit on it, I tell you as I have said once: You are like whitewashed tombs that look handsome on the outside, but inside are full of dead men's bones and every kind of corruption. How can you **believe** you can escape damnation? You fail to please Me and your corpses litter this desert you are living in... (Volume II, p.436 - March 27, 1992)

> ...They are recrucifying Me. They are damaging My Church. Evil has blinded them. Love is missing among them. They are not sincere, they have distorted My Word, they have lamed even My Body... (Volume I, p.124 - June 6, 1987)

> ...They flout piety, they list bitter accusations against the works of My Holy Spirit and allow their mouth to condemn them!   ...Worse still, they have established a monopoly of ostentation and presumption... Why has the fragrance I have given you turned into a stench? I weep over your excessive pride...Your excessive pride made My Church resemble a gaping grave...wash your hearts clean and the heavens will shine on you...I am weary of seeing you preach spiritual things unspiritually...do not contradict what you teach on My Spirit... (Volume II, p.426-427 - February 2, 1992)

The point already made of misunderstanding of the Spirit by the ministers of the Church is here developed at length by St Simeon and by Vassula. In my previous book on Vassula I wrote of the neglect of the Spirit in the Latin Church; neglect is perhaps too strong a word, lack of full appreciation may be better. In the following chapter we shall see the special effect of the Spirit's action as a purifying force. But we should delay on the reality of the Spirit as the essential driving force in the Church to which we belong. The severe language about some of those who should be leaders in the spiritual life of the Church, those who move in the direction of apostasy instead of resisting it, should not shock the reader. The evocation of Judas should not alarm; it has a consoling aspect, when we see the care Jesus took of him, how he sorrowed to the point of tears for the moral and spiritual deterioration of the one who would betray him. Judas is a salutary reminder that only those given intimacy with Jesus - as are his ministers - can betray him.

3. The Love of the Divine Fire of the Holy Spirit - And the Holy Spirit as Cleansing Water

"Repentance works in a two-fold manner: it is like water because it extinguishes the flame of passion with tears and purifies the soul of its stains; it is like fire through the presence of the Holy Spirit who vivifies, kindles, sets aglow, and warms the heart and inflames it with love (erota) and desire for God." (Cap 3.12)

Mgr Kvivocheine adds to this: The love of God is produced by the fire of the Holy Spirit. This grace of the Spirit is the pledge of the mystic union with God.

St Simeon not only describes the Holy Spirit as a burning furnace, that gives you pain but fills you with joy which he calls: "fire of the spirit", saying:

Make no mistake about it! God is fire. He came as fire and has cast fire on the earth. It runs everywhere, seeking matter which it can seize and set aflame, that is, a good disposition, good-will. In those in whom it has been kindled, it rises to heaven with a great flame, leaving to the one who is ablaze neither respite nor rest. It does not consume the burning soul in an unconscious manner, for the soul is not insensible matter - but in full awareness and knowledge and with unbearable pain, since the soul is endowed with sensation and reason. Then, after we have been entirely purified from the defilement of the passions, this fire becomes in us food and drink, light and unceasing joy. Through participation it transforms us into light. (...) As in a mirror, the soul observes the blackness caused by the smoke and grieves. Then it feels that the thorns of thought and the dry wood of prejudice are being consumed and reduced entirely to ashes. After all this is finally destroyed, only the essence of the soul remains, freed from passions. Then the divine, immaterial fire is joined to it essentially. At once it is set on fire. It becomes translucent and, like the oven, partakes of this sensory fire. In this manner, even the body becomes a furnace that partakes of the divine, ineffable light. (Eth 7.509-537)

There are many passages in *True Life in God* about the Holy Spirit. In fact, today, there are more than 800 references to the Holy Spirit in Vassula's writings. A few excerpts about the Holy Spirit follows:

> Allow My Spirit in the inner room of your soul. Allow My Spirit to breathe and dwell in the depths of your soul. Leave Me free to shatter all impurities and imperfection that confront Me. My Vassula, although your soul will leap like on fire every time I will lift My Hand to shatter all that still keeps you captive, do not fear, do not run away in horror, allow Me to uproot in your soul all these infirmities. I shall come like a tempest inside you and carry out the decision of My Heart and that is your preparation for our perfect union. I had said in the beginning that you will be My Net and My Target but then you had not understood the latter, you had not understood that in order to prepare you for this perfect union, I need to purify you and adorn your soul. I would have to bend My bow and set you as a **target** for My arrow... Allow My Spirit to augment in you and My Divine Fire roar in your soul, you will be molten under the action of My Divine Fire. Do not lament then when I come to you like a hammer shattering your imperfections... I want to make out of you a docile instrument since My Presence will be felt inside you like a fire and like an arrow... Every little impurity will be seized by My Purity and annihilated and My Light shall continue to glow inside you and My Spirit shall flow in your spirit like a river... (Volume II, p.411-412 - January 20, 1992)

St Simeon explains how the Holy Spirit does not tolerate rivals:

> ...We cannot be the abode of Christ through the indwelling of the Holy Spirit if the heart is dominated by a single passion, no matter how small. (Eth 10.606-611)

> And He (God) will pour out His Spirit on you to invade your spirit and annihilate all that is you, never again shall you be "you"; your "you" shall be no more... I shall efface your "you" altogether if you allow Me... I shall make you dislike all that is contrary to My Holiness and to My Will. I shall sift you through to make sure that not one rival remains within you... I am only waiting now to consume your whole being with the Flames of My Heart and My Love. (Volume II, p.255 - December 10, 1990)

The Holy Spirit as cleansing water, purifying:

> And My Healing Water from My Breast, this stream that flows out of My Sanctuary, will fill you and make you Wholesome. No man shall be able to arrest this rivulet. The stream will keep on flowing profusely out of my Heart. I shall flow everywhere, breaking into several parts, separating into other and several rivulets going into all directions and wherever this healing water flows,

everyone, sick, lame, blind, will be healed. Even the dead shall come back to life again. No one will be able to stop me from purifying you. I shall demonstrate the power of My Spirit and make your lips open and your heart cry out to Me : Abba! (Volume II, p.320 - July 2, 1991)

One particular aspect of the Spirit's presence and action is forcefully expressed in these passages. These passages should afford food for meditation, for consolation and enlightenment to all those who hope for an Age of the Spirit in the Church. This will not be as Joachim of Fiore taught, a partitioning of history in a Trinitarian sequence, an Age of the Father, an Age of the Son and then an Age of the Holy Spirit, each exclusive and all-sufficient. It will be a phase of Church history wherein there will be a renewed consciousness of the third Person of the Holy Trinity, but a realization that he is the Gift par excellence, source of all divine giving, from the Father and the Son. The metaphor of fire in regard to the Holy Spirit derives ultimately from the descent of the Spirit in the form of tongues of fire at Pentecost. It is consecrated, as it were, in a principal hymn, in which he is addressed thus: "Thou who art called the Paraclete, Best Gift of God above, The living spring, the living Fire, Sweet unction and true love."

4. The Holy Trinity - The Oneness of the Trinity

O Immaculate nature, hidden essence, goodness unknowable to most men, mercy invisible to those who live like senseless men, essence unchangeable, indivisible, thrice-holy. (Hymn 13.37-40)

Vassula received this message:

Ah, My little pupil, I bless you; love Me and glorify Me, for I am three times holy. (Volume III, p.56 - September 28, 1992)

Let us again hear Simeon:

The ingathering of the powers of the soul in contemplation allows one to perceive God, One in the Trinity: "When all these blessings have filled man's desire, the excitable part becomes altogether fused with the thinking and the desiring. The Three are one in contemplation of the trinitarian Unity and begin to enjoy their own master. Indeed, their tripartite division is no longer recognized: they become absolutely one." (Eth 4.424-429)

He took pity on our ignorance and condescended to our weakness so that we might know that God is a perfect trinity and must be worshipped devoutly as Father, Son and Holy Spirit. But what is His form and where is it? How great is it? What is the manner of His oneness and unity? Not only did it never become possible for man to conceive of this; indeed, not even the powers above have access to His inaccessible, super-essential nature. (Theol 2.238-246)

For we do not believe that there is one being, then another, and another, one being of such and such a nature, thereby dividing the oneness of the invisible Godhead and having foolish recourse to distinctions that are alien to His nature. We know the three as one God, indivisibly divided in hypostases, unifies without confusion in the unity of a single essence. The same God must be "three" in the Persons and "one" in the unity of essence or of nature. (Theol 3.77-85)

For if you join them, they will be united. The three will be but one; if not, the unity escapes you. But you will never find the Father separated from the Son or the Spirit, nor the Son separated from the Father and the Spirit, nor the Spirit excluded from the union with the one from whom He proceeds. The Father and the Son are in the Spirit; likewise, the Son is in the Father with the Spirit. The Son is and remains co-eternal in the Father, with the Holy Spirit who shines with the same brilliance. Believe this! These persons are one God and not three. He is in three hypostases. He is eternally identical with Himself, praised by infinite powers in His unity of nature, of dominion, and of Godhead. Though aspects common to the One Godhead are found in each of the Persons, the three are nevertheless one. One by one, the three exist, which cannot be said about these suns. (Eth 9.80-103)

The Father is light, the Son is light, the Holy Spirit is light. Watch what you are going to say my brother, watch that you do not deceive yourself! Indeed, the three are one light, unique, undivided... God is seen completely as a simple light. (Hymn 33.1-8)

This is the vision Christ gave Vassula and she drew it. Three lights, then one, making the oneness of the Holy Trinity:

A vision of light. (There was just one light), then one light coming out then another one, making three. The Holy Trinity is One and the same (essence). They can be three (persons), but all three can be One, (the Oneness of God). Result, one God. (Volume I, p.233 - November 24, 1987)

St Simeon says this about the triple light:

...Nonetheless, the number is very small of those "who have received pure contemplation, of the One who was in the beginning, before all ages, begotten of the Father, and with the Spirit, God and Word, triple light in unity, but one light in the three." (Hymn 12.14-18)

Compare with this the message Vassula received on 11 April, 1988:

> ..."Be blessed My child. I your Holy Father, love you. I am the Holy Trinity - you have discerned well..." I discerned, while Jesus was saying I am your Holy Father, a "triple" Jesus, like those fancy pictures of one person but made as though they are three, one coming out of the other, all similar and all three the same. "I Am the Holy Trinity, all in one." [Unique, undivided, one essence, one substance]. (Volume I, p.310)

In this message, Jesus was trying to teach Vassula the Holy Trinity's Oneness, how the Three Persons are undivided and so completely one. And as St Simeon said in his Hymn 45. 7-21: "Three in one and one in three."

Mgr Krivocheine says (p.284) that St Simeon addresses the Trinity as if it were a Person, and he calls it "Spirit, God of the universe": "I saw Your Face and was afraid, however gentle and accessible it appeared to me. I fell into a trance before your beauty and was struck with amazement, O Trinity, my God. The traits in each of the three are the same, and the three are one countenance, my God, whose name is spirit, the God of the universe." (Hymn 21.491-499)

In another passage, later on, Christ taught Vassula how the Trinity is recognized in each of them as one and the same (substance):

> ...Have no fear, little ones, am I not Bountiful? Am I not the highest? So have confidence for you are in your Father's Arms. I, the Holy Trinity am One and the Same (substance)... (Volume II, p.48 - July 25, 1989)

And in another passage, Christ insists on Their Divine Oneness:

> I-Am-He-Who-Saves, I Am your Redeemer, I Am the Holy Trinity all in One, I Am the Spirit of Grace... (Volume II, p.51 - July 28, 1989)

And again:

> Daughter, I am the Holy One, the Most High, I am the Most Holy Trinity, please Me and hear Me as you heard Me today... (Volume II, p.105 - November 13/14, 1989)

Mgr Kvivocheine says on p.290: "On the mystical level, St Simeon sometimes addresses the Trinity as a single person. The divine essence even converses with Simeon in the first person. By contrast, the Three hypostases, Father, Son and Holy Spirit, also speak with him separately."

St Simeon confirms once more the oneness of God:

> ...You will never find the Father separated from the Son or the Spirit, nor the Son separated from the Father and the Spirit, nor the Spirit excluded from the union with the one from whom He proceeds. The Father and the Son are in the Spirit; likewise, the Son is in the Father with the Spirit. The Son is and remains co-eternal in the Father, with the Holy Spirit who shines with the same brilliance. Believe this! These Persons are one God and not three. (Eth 9.80-103)

Mgr Kvivocheine says that Simeon speaks of his vision of the Trinity in his hymns, while recognizing that it is beyond human capacity. Sometimes he sees the three Persons, but it is Christ who opens his mind by this vision in darkness:

> Even during the night, in the heart of darkness, I see Christ - O dread! - opening the heavens for me. Christ Himself who condescends and reveals himself to me with the Father and the Spirit, light thrice holy, one in three, three in one (light). Certainly, they are the light; the Three are the one light which, better than the sun, enlightens my soul and illumines my mind, that until then had been in darkness. This wonder perplexes me all the more when (Christ) somehow opens the eye of my mind, which was clouded before. For He appears to the one who contemplates Him, and it is in the light of the Spirit that those who contemplate Him see Him, and those who see in this light contemplate the Son. But the one who has been deemed worthy of seeing the Son sees the Father; assuredly, he contemplates the Father and beholds Him with the Son- This, I repeat, is what is happening in me. (Hymn 11.35-54)

And as St Simeon said :"God is a perfect Trinity and must be worshipped devotedly as Father, Son and Holy Spirit."

St Simeon confirms Vassula's vision of the Holy Trinity, when Christ was speaking to her from Him came out two other persons with similar traits as His, then went back with Him, leaving One Person. This is what He said:

> One Father, like the Son, with the divine Spirit. The three are one God, in an inexpressible manner. (Hymn 29.150-153)

Mgr Kvivocheine writes that: "God is beyond names. He is Trinity, yet the One and its Unity cannot be expressed." (p.284)

St Simeon clarifies this statement:

> Whatever multifarious names we call You, You are one being; but this one being is unknown to all nature. He is invisible, ineffable, the One who receives all the names when He appears. This one being is a nature in three hypostases, one

Godhead, one kingdom, one dominion. For the Trinity is a single being, since my God is a single Trinity, not three beings. And yet the One is three according to hypostases. They are conatural, the one to the other according to nature, entirely of the same power, the same essence, united without confusion in a manner that surpasses our understanding. In turn, they are distinct, separated without separation, three in one and one in three. (Hymn 45.7-21)

This is interesting, because the Father, the Son and the Holy Spirit have spoken to Vassula also separately but at times the Holy Trinity conversed with Vassula altogether in one voice.

...Your terrified cries pierced through the heavens, reaching the Holy Trinity's Ears... "My child!" The Father's Voice, full of joy resounded through all Heaven.

Then the Son said: "Ah... I shall now make her penetrate My Wounds and let her eat My Body and drink My Blood. I shall espouse her to Me and she will be Mine for eternity. I shall show her the Love I have for her and her lips from thereon shall thirst for Me and her heart shall be My Head-rest..."

Then the Holy Spirit said immediately after: "And I, the Holy Spirit, shall descend upon her to reveal to her the Truth and the depths of Us. I shall remind the world through her, that the greatest of all the gifts is LOVE."

And then the Holy Trinity spoke in one voice: "Let Us then celebrate! Let all Heaven celebrate!"... (Volume II, p.260-261 - December 22, 1990)

By taking passages and phrases in Vassula's writings out of context critics have tried to show that her Trinitarian theology is defective. This is a fundamentalist approach which would be like taking a word of Jesus so literally as to maintain that he said that the Father had become man; he declared "He who has seen me has seen the Father" (Jn 14:9). The words of Jesus have to be taken with the other Johannine passages wherein the separate existence of the Father is evident. Fr R Laurentin has shown that a misinterpretation of Vassula has been made by omitting a comma!

We should be grateful for a witness in our time to the Persons of the Most Holy Trinity. Fr Karl Rahner, as is fairly well known, thought that the Church had not succeeded in making belief in the Trinity, the very centrepiece of our Christian creed, relevant to the everyday life of Catholics. Theological debates have been necessary, but the abstract language which is their medium has not always been translated into the idiom of genuine piety, near to the needs of the faithful. Biblical study, which is not beyond the capacity of the faithful, should be encouraged.

In my first book on Vassula, I showed how the presence of the Father is so clearly affirmed in her mystical experience. At the present times there is, through many messages from mystics, a powerful urge towards profoundly rooted piety addressed directly to God the Father. St Thérèse of Lisieux achieved a new orientation towards the fatherhood of God. Her teaching has not always been interpreted in relation to God the Father personally. At the canonical inquiry preceding her beatification her sister Celine, Sister Geneviève of the Holy Face, spoke of her doctrine as necessary to offset fear of God as a master, almost a tyrant. But the emphasis, now so prevalent on the first Person of the Trinity was not evident. It comes through lucidly in the writings of Vassula.

5. Union with God - And the Teachings of the "We" and "Us"

Mgr Kvivocheine says: "The vision and the union with God begin here on earth. They are given their fullness, however, in the age to come, after the resurrection."

In *True Life in God*, God is teaching us that we carry Him within us as Light, and that the Kingdom of Heaven is within us. I quote a prayer from the messages:

> Lord, Holy and Faithful One, Your sound Teachings have given me Light. You are the Light of the world... Govern me, reign over me and build Your Kingdom in me so that my soul becomes the perfect dwelling of your Divinity and Your Holiness. (Volume IV - September 30, 1993)

St Simeon says in the same spirit: "...inheritors of the Kingdom of Heaven, since we carry the Kingdom within." (Eth 10.697-713)
"Wondrous! I see in me the One who I believed to be in heaven, I mean you, O Christ, my Creator, my King." (Euch 1.152-154)

Compare with these ideas what Vassula writes:

> Your Mercy, O Lord, has breathed in me and inspired a living Spirit within me, in the very core of where He dwells. It was your Word, Lord, who heals all things, that healed me. And the invisible God became suddenly visible to me. And the dimness of my eyes saw a Light, a pillar of Blazing Fire, to guide my steps to Heaven. And the Darkness that imprisoned me and terrified my soul was overpowered by The Morning Star, and gave my soul Hope, Love and Peace and a great consolation because I knew that Love and Compassion Himself was my Holy Companion for the journey of my life. (Volume II, p.381-382 - October 21, 1991).

St Simeon expressed the union of the divine fire and the soul:

> Then he mingles with the soul but does not blend with it. The One who is pure essence is entirely united with the essence of the soul... How, I cannot tell. The two become one. The soul is united with its Creator and the Creator is in the soul, totally with the soul alone. (Hymn 30 263-267.

On the 17 July 1993, Vassula asked in Greek: "Pou mas eblexess?" Where have you mingled us?" The Lord's spontaneous answer: "Sto Soma Mou!" "In My Body!"

Jesus told her on the 16 February, 1987:

> I will not part from you ever, but I have also made sure that neither will you. I made sure of our union... I desired us to be united for ever, you needing Me, loving Me, and bound for ever to Me; and I bound to you... You are now united with Me; you will work with Me; you will suffer with Me; you will help Me. Yes, I will share everything I have with you and for your part, you will do the same. Being united is being for ever together, because My bonds are eternal bonds, My elate love binds you forever to Me. (Volume I, p.37)

Again the Lord said:

> ...Remember, we are united and our bonds are bonds of Peace and Love. These cords which attach your wrists and feet to Mine are for eternity, for, beloved, you are Mine. I, Myself, have purified you, uniting you to Me; I have triumphed over you. (Volume I, p.38 - February 18, 1987)

And again:

> ...We have bonds together and being bound to each other, you will be unable to abandon Me. See! I have taken care of our union; we will stay united till the end, you needing Me and loving Me fervently and I, free, reigning over you and loving you without restraint... (Volume I, p.49 - March 4, 1987)

> I am the Source of your hope. I will always share with you till the end, so come and unburden your heart to Me, I and you, together... Remember My Presence at all times. Love loves you. (I suddenly remembered my household work.) Shall we share? (Volume II, p. 42 - July 8, 1989)

To emphasize His union, Christ taught Vassula to use the words "we" and "us". In Volume I, p.52 - March 7, 1987, Jesus said:

> ... Fill Me with joy and learn to say: "Let US go and work; let US do this or that." Use the word "us". We are united forever!

In Volume I, p.62 - March 20, 1987, Jesus taught Vassula how He can become one with the soul:

> ...Integrate your whole being in Me and I will dissolve you within Me." And the following day, (p.64): "Let your entire being penetrate in Me and dissolve within Me, completely..."

St Simeon says these words about this union with God:

> How can I explain who the One is who is joined to me and to whom I am joined, I who have become one? ...Nonetheless, having become one being, I and the One to whom I am joined, what name shall I give myself? The God who has two natures united in one person, has made a double being of me. Having made me double, He therefore has given me two names. The God, who has two natures united in one person, has made a double being of me. Having made me double, He therefore has given me two names. Behold the difference! By nature I am a man; by grace I am God... (Hymn 30.439-462)

In these extracts we meet the perennial problem of the mystic, how to translate into the language of the many what has been experienced by only one. Even with so gifted a writer and so authentic a mode of experiencing divine things as St Teresa of Jesus, the task is daunting. There is a parallel with the problem a believer has of communicating with one who does not share his belief. Ideally there should be an encounter on the same level, which is impossible. Likewise one with genuine mystical experience seeks some response that would come from similar communion with the divine. When St Teresa met and conversed with St John of the Cross the basis of complete mutual understanding was assured. It was not merely that like spoke to like, but that each found a true profound resonance in the spiritual endowment of the other.

6. Christ as Educator, Father and Intimate Companion

> ... He speaks and listens as friend to friend, face to face, invisibly. The One who is God by nature converses with the gods born of Him by grace. He loves his sons like a father and is loved by them... (Euch 1.196-211)

St Simeon says that those who are "taught by God" are in contrast to the ones who are "outside of the divine light," and who "cannot see the wonders that are in it. They believe that those who are visited by this light and see and learn what it contains, have gone astray, while it is they who are misguided, not having tasted the ineffable blessings of God." (Cap 3.85)

The Lord said to Vassula:

> Preach with accuracy all that My Spirit is giving you, proclaiming salvation and heralding Peace and Love... Drive in the sickle when you see Me driving in My sickle. Do not delay your step. Follow in time with My pace. If I delay, delay too. Speak up when I give you the signal and keep silent when I look at you... (Volume IV - December 23, 1993)

All that she has learnt has come directly from God:

> ...I am teaching you step by step, with the vocabulary that you understand... (Volume I, p.32 - February 12, 1987)

> Work for Me with untiring effort and with great earnestness of spirit. Work with love for Love. Worship Me, your God, and allow Me to educate you, even though it means through suffering... I am your teacher and from Me you will learn... (Volume II, p.72 - September 14, 1989)

St Simeon says:

> ...He is at the same time food and drink, and He provides them with sweetness such that they no longer experience or rather, such that they cannot detach themselves from Him. For those who have been weaned, he plays the role of a loving father who watches over his children's growth and development. (Eth 4.269-270)

Although Vassula knew that it was Jesus speaking to her in the passage cited below, she called Him "Father", because it was the manner in which He spoke to her. His approach was very fatherly. It was like those instances when fathers are explaining and teaching certain things to their children with patience and love, for their growth and development. Most of the time, when she is with Jesus, He makes her feel as His adoptive child, and He, her tender father and educator, educating her with His Wisdom. Here are a few quotations:

> ...Grow in spirit Vassula, grow, for your task is to deliver all Messages given by Me and My Father. Wisdom will instruct you.
> - Yes Father!
> How beautiful to hear you call Me "Father!" I longed to hear from your lips this word: "Father". (Volume I, p.38 - February 16, 1987)

The next day, she avoided calling Him "Father", thinking she should give Him more glorious names than just a simple "father". Jesus was not happy, and said:

> Vassula, why, why were you avoiding calling Me Father? Vassula, I love being
> called Father. I am Father of all humanity.
> - I love you Father.
> I love you. (Volume I, p.38 - February 17, 1987)

> He is the same, the One who speaks throughout the whole world, both then and
> now. For if He is indeed not the same who was of old and yet is now, who
> remains God in every respect and in everything, whether in His operations or in
> the rites, who is it that the Father always appears in the Son and the Son in the
> Father through the Spirit? (Cat 29.11-15)

Scriptures say:

> For there is a child born for us, a son given to us and dominion is laid on his
> shoulders; and this is the name they give him: Wonder-counsellor, Mighty-God,
> Eternal-Father, Prince-of-Peace. (Is 9:6)

Mgr Kvivocheine says that God reveals himself to St Simeon and adopts him as His
son. Here is how He addresses St Simeon in the Hymns:

> Tell Me, is there in the world any greater pleasure, joy or glory than seeing Me,
> Me alone, reflected as in an enigma, or contemplating the light of My glory and
> it alone... To know with certainty that I am God, the creator of the universe,
> and to understand that man, sitting in the deepest pit, has been reconciled with
> Me? He converses with me directly, as a friend to friend. After he passed from
> the rank of hireling, from the fear of servitude, he serves Me without contention,
> and knows Me with love. (Hymn 41.101-111)

Through the whole revelation, one cannot help noticing how God adapts Himself to
His creatures' level. He comes as a tender Father, as a best Friend or sometimes as
a loving Spouse. What God is asking from us is our intimacy towards Him, to
befriend Him, to share with Him, converse with Him, and confide in Him as best
friends do with each other.

The Eternal Father said to Vassula:

> Fear not, for I am your Heavenly Father and I love you beyond any human
> understanding. I am Yahweh, and if you have not heard before, I am telling you
> now that I am known to be Faithful and My Word stands secure... I want you
> to be intimate with me... (Volume I, p.37 - February 16, 1987)

On December 23, 1987 Jesus told Vassula:

> Vassula, talk to Me, treat Me as your holy companion. (Volume I, p.251)

St Simeon had formal instruction as we have seen. In his case the didactic or teaching role of the Lord was on a store of acquired theological knowledge. He certainly gained still more profound insights through the action of the Holy Spirit, to whom he was singularly devoted. His case is quite different from Vassula's in regard to previous theological instruction. With her this was totally nil; she knew nothing about theology, even about the elementary truths of religion. Jesus chose to work on a mind entirely blank, which makes the content of her writings a serious challenge to the theologian. There is no natural explanation of the theology and spirituality found in the series of works which bear her name; I have analysed this theology in the previous book.

From the extracts which she has given here it can be seen how under the divine action knowledge and love, intellectual conviction and intimacy, can be wonderfully intertwined, sustain and nourish each other. One thinks of the phrase of Hans Urs von Balthasar, "Theology on one's knees." He knew thoroughly how the mystical dimension may be recognised. He worked in partnership with Adrienne von Speyr and publicly asserted that he did not wish his theology and his achievement therein, which was mighty, in any way dissociated from her. He directed the circle of friends united in her memory.

7. Intimacy with God - Christ as Bridegroom - Mystical Marriage to Desire and Thirst for God - Pursuing Christ

> For now your Creator will be your husband, His name, Yahweh Sabaoth. (Is 54:5)

> I will betroth you to myself for ever, betroth you with integrity and justice, with tenderness and love; I will betroth you to myself with faithfulness, and you will come to know Yahweh. (Ho 2:21-23)

> Let him kiss me with the kisses of His mouth. Your love is more delightful than wine; delicate is the fragrance of your perfume, your name is an oil poured out, and that is why the maidens love you. (Sg 1:2-3)

There will always be those who will misinterpret what is purely spiritual and symbolic and interpret it as carnal. The spiritual marriage is a divine union with God. Everything therefore that is written by the inspiration of the Holy Spirit should be interpreted as purely spiritual. The language of human relationships is used symbolically.

Mgr Kvivocheine writes : Simeon's language in the Hymn 15 shocked many of his contemporaries, just as nowadays it still offends some people who are allergic to the speech of mystics.

Mgr Kvivocheine says that in St Simeon's Ethical Discourses, he retraces in detail the road of man towards God, the arduous path at the end of which men fall exhausted. It is then that the God, so desired by them, appears and leads them into the wedding chamber where they take part in the mystical marriage. After having encountered God by fulfilling the commandments:

> He loses sight of Him. Perplexed, he starts again from the point of departure and runs faster, more energetically and more assuredly. He watches his feet. He walks with care. His memory burns, desire flames and the hope of seeing Him lights up again. When a long journey has left him without strength far from the goal he could not attain, totally defeated and unable to move forward, it is then that he perceives the One (whom) he pursues. He becomes a total stranger to the world, and loses memory of it. He is reunited with the angels. He melts away into the light. He tastes of life and embraces immortality. He enters into a state of wonderful delight. He rises to the third heaven and is taken up to paradise. He hears words that cannot be uttered. He enters the wedding chamber. He comes near the marriage bed and sees the Bridegroom. He takes part of the spiritual marriage and is sated with the mystic cup, the fatted calf, the bread and water of life, the immaculate lamb, the intelligible manna. He is delighted with all these blessings on which the angelic posers dare not look directly. (Eth 6.110-129)

Mgr Kvivocheine explains how St Simeon craved to kiss Christ's hands, His feet, His face. "Allow me to kiss Your hands - these hands that created me by Your word, the hands that fashioned everything without effort. Let me be filled with these (graces) without being sated. Grant me the sight of Your face, O Word, and the enjoyment of Your ineffable beauty. Let me contemplate and delight in Your vision - the vision unutterable, the vision invisible, the awesome vision." (Hymn 24.1-10)

To become the bride of Christ would mean to share His Cross. This is what Christ said to Vassula in the very beginning:

> I love you as you are... be My bride, Vassula.
> - How could I!
> I will teach you to be My bride, beloved.
> - Do I carry a symbol for this, Lord?
> I will let you bear My Cross. My Cross cries out for Peace and Love.
> (Volume I, p. 16 - January 8, 1987)

St Simeon says:

> I am sitting on my couch, all the while beyond the world. Being in the middle of my cell, I see him present, the One who is beyond the world. I see Him and I speak with Him. I - dare I say it? - I ("filo", which means in Greek, "kiss") kiss Him and He, in turn, kisses me. I nourish this contemplation alone. Forming one with Him, I transcend the heavens... I know that the One who is separated from all creation takes me inside Himself and hides me in His arms, and then I find myself outside the whole world... (Hymn 13.63-)

One day Jesus asked to kiss Vassula, (it shocked certain people and made them turn wild), she felt immediately like a leper in front of His Perfect Beauty, she hesitated, she felt embarrassed by her utter wretchedness, she wanted to refuse, yet Jesus was trying to convince her that He loves us in spite of our spiritual leprosy and that marriage with Him will restore and heal her soul. Here is this passage:

> Allow Me to kiss you...
> -Jesus kissed my forehead. He left me in an ecstatic state of mind. How can I explain it? For the following two days I felt hollow, transparent, like clear glass. He gave such a tremendous feeling of peace of the soul. My breathing seemed to go through my lungs and fill into my entire body, thus having the feeling of being air. (Volume I, p.62 - March 19, 1987)

Now, compare what St Simeon says of Christ:

> For He becomes the Bridegroom each day, and all the souls to which the Creator is joined become brides. The souls, in turn, unite themselves to Him and a marriage takes place, when He is joined to them spiritually in a manner befitting God, without deflowering them in any way (let this thought be far from me!) Yet even when He possess them when thy are deflowered, He at once restores their integrity by joining Himself to them; and what was formerly soiled by corruption is now, in their view, only blessedness and incorruption, being perfectly healed. The souls glorify the Merciful One. They are enamoured of the most Beautiful One. They unite themselves fully to the fullness of His love. Or rather, as we have said, in receiving His holy seed they inwardly possess God in His fullness, God who has taken form. (Hymn 15.220-231)

> I wanted to say rather that Christ called me to repentance. At once I followed the Master who was calling me. When he ran, I ran behind Him. When He fled, I would pursue Him like a hound chasing a hare. When the Lord drew away from me and concealed Himself, I would not lose hope and would not go back as though I had lost Him. I sat and moaned in that very same spot; I cried and called out to the Master who was hidden from me. After drawing near, He

appeared. I advanced to seize Him, and He fled at once. I ran strenuously, and often in my impatience I would catch the fringe of His garment. He would stay awhile. I was overjoyed; and then He would start off, and once more I would hunt Him. Thus He would leave, then return; He would hide, then reappear. But I never ran away... (Hymn 29.50-93)

It pleases the Lord that we seek Him and pursue Him. This is why He withdraws his Light for just a while, but not entirely. It makes our soul more eager to look up in heaven in search of Him. By hiding for a while, Christ makes our soul thirstier and ever more languishing for Him. But when Christ withdraws a little His Light from us, the soul, moans after the One she loves but does not feel near as before.

This is what Vassula said to Christ, in one of these moments:

In the anguish of my spirit, I pray and ask You: Where are those Eyes so loving upon me? Where is my Abode, Your Sacred Heart? How is it I cannot hear Your Voice or feel Your Presence? Have I lost Your Friendship because of my insensitivity? Have I lost Your Companionship O Holy of Holies? (Volume II, p.400 - November 25, 1991)

At another time during Vassula's pilgrimage in Israel:

...You know how much my soul and heart are pining away with love for You and how I long, oh how I long to gaze on You incessantly to the point of insanity. Yeshuah, You know how my soul thirsts for You, so why have You turned Your back to me? Yeshuah, why do You take pleasure in breaking every fibre of my heart? You made out of me a Target for Your Archery, thrusting arrow after arrow, am I to cover myself from the rain of Your arrows? (Volume IV - May 19, 1993)

When thus I lost You, now, how am I to stand alone? Have You brought me all this way to desert me?

Yeshuah, I lost all the taste for life now that You have gone... but tell me the reason at least for Your abrupt decision! Is it right for You to carry me in Your homeland and ignore me? Would it be that You had second thoughts about me?

O my Faithful Yeshuah, I cry out to You but Silence is the only thing I hear. I stand in the heart of Your homeland but You take no notice of my wretched soul.

When I went at the gates of Jerusalem, when I took my seat in Your country, no sooner had I entered Your land, my praises echoed in every ear. You let me build my hopes upon entering Your city, but no sooner had I entered than You shut out my soul from Your Light. When one is deprived of Your Presence, does not Your Heart feel it?

By Your own initiative You traced a path for me to reach You and now You take pleasure in plunging me into darkness. Night is my sole route companion. Were You to pass me, I would not see You... Were You to touch me I would not feel You, nor would I detect Your Presence. So how am I to walk now without You, my Light? I am full of fear before this emptiness. Why do You do this to Your faithful friend?...

St Simeon speaks passionately, longing for God:

For I was searching Him, the One I desired, for whom I had passion, by whose splendid beauty I had been wounded. I was burning, my entire being was aflame. (Hymn 30.373-378)

The Lord delights in spontaneous outbursts of love to Him from our heart. Many times God showed Vassula His delight by very simple words she used, but that came out with a flame of love from her heart:

"You are my joy, my smile, my breath, my life and my bounce!" I had said to Him.

St Simeon too had the same outburst of joy:

"Come my breath and my life. Come consolation of my contemptible soul. Come, my joy, my glory and my delight forever." ..."Come, You who have become desire in me and have made me desire You, You the utterly inaccessible One. Come, my breath, my life. Come, consolation of my poor soul. My Joy, my glory, my unending gladness, come!" (Preface to the Hymn 1-23)

Vassula received these words too under divine dictation:

Emmanuel come, come my Beloved, come and revive my soul, come and endow my soul with life! O Beloved of the Father, I have opened the door of my heart, will I have to wait very long before You step in my chambers? Your mere passage in my heart will leave behind a trail of the most delicate fragrance of your perfume, because Your Love will remedy my pitiable soul. Spirit of Love, grant me only my share of Your Love. Emmanuel come, come my Perfect One, come and ravish my soul, or destitution shall overtake my miserable heart! O Beloved of the Father, how Beautiful You are! Son of the Most High, who is like unto You?... (Volume IV - November 11, 1993)

For seeing You wounds my heart inwardly. I do not have the strength to look at You, and yet I am unable not to do so. Your beauty is inaccessible, Your splendour has no equal. Your glory is beyond compare. Who has ever seen You or could see You completely, my God? (Hymn 42.74-78)

And finally Jeremiah's cry to God:

You have seduced me, Yahweh, and I have let myself be seduced... (Jr 20:7)

The prototype of all mystical writing on the spiritual marriage which is the consummation of love, is the Song of Songs. Among those who have written to describe their experience St Simeon excels in the Byzantine world. The language has generally become classic in spirituality, and the reader must consult the great exponents of the doctrine who wrote from personal experience. In some cases as with St Catherine of Siena and St Mary Magdalen of Pazzi, a physical sign of the espousal, a ring, was used; it could be visible or identified by a swelling on the finger. The accounts of St John of the Cross and St Teresa of Avila, who deals with the subject in her description of the seventh mansion, are illuminating since here we have the special grace and supreme gift of human communication combined. There is a fine distinction between the spiritual marriage and a degree of intimacy known as the transforming union. They are sometimes different aspects of the same spiritual reality. Certain effects may be analysed, such as adaptability to different human problems and situations, something like a notable increase in spiritual, even psychic energy, what St Thomas Aquinas received when he was visited by angels who girdled him with a band that caused both intense joy and pain, or St Teresa of Avila when she received the transverberation of the heart, or St Philip Neri when his heart was physically enlarged. In each case the soul was so bonded to God that divine power flowed through it without obstacle.

8. Sharing the Cross - Suffering as One's Daily Bread

...You the impassible one, wished to suffer unjustly for the unjust, in order to give me, a man condemned, impassibility in imitating Your sufferings, O my Christ. (Hymn 36.1-9)

Christ said to Vassula:

...Ah, one more thing, a simple reminder: I and you are united, anyone who is united with Me takes the same road I had taken, the road to Calvary. Anyone who follows the Supreme Victim becomes part of the Victim. You are part of Me, a remnant of My Body... (Volume IV - May 30, 1993)

St Simeon says under inspiration these words:

> ...Look at Him now as He is with you, sharing your existence, your life, He who is above all the heavens. Behold, both of you travel together. Someone meets you on the road of life and slaps your Master in the face: he also slaps you. The Master does not strike back, but will you resist? How then will you partake of his glory if you refuse to be a partaker of his disgraceful death? In truth it is in vain that you have abandoned your wealth if you do not take up the Cross as He himself has commanded... (Cat 27.335-370)

Jesus said to Vassula:

> I, as your Spouse too, offered you My most precious jewels - have I not entrusted you with My Cross, My nails and My Thorned Crown? (Volume II, p.69 - September 13, 1989)

Jesus inspired Vassula to say this prayer to him:

> Suffering has become my daily bread, but what an honour to share it with You. You come daily into my room to share my meal, side by side with me. You sup with me sharing my daily bread. You are my Sacrificer. Pitilessly You bend Your bow aiming at me and Your arrows are raining on the target You have chosen. You make my soul leap like on fire, from Your arrows. And yet, when I do not have this bread, I ask: "Where is the bread that burns up one's heart?" (Volume III, p.70 - October 21, 1992)

Jesus gives Vassula a long description of what it is like to share His Cross, reminding her of His saving love. This is what Christ revealed to her:

> ...Let your heart and soul rejoice! Your King came to you in your bareness and your poverty, your King has covered your nakedness with His Love and His Peace and in His Tenderness adorned you majestically with His most precious Jewels. Have I not adorned your head with My Thorned Crown? Have I not entrusted you with My Nails? Are we not sharing My Cross as our matrimonial bed? Have I not revealed to you My Beauty? Speak, daughter!

> - My Lord, whatever I say will never be enough! Have mercy on my misery, I trust in Your love, I will be glad to sacrifice more.

> Then open your ears and hear My wedding song. I know what you are made of: dust and ashes. Come out of your gloom by lifting your head, look at Me. I am He who has raised you and He who keeps your soul tranquil and quiet. Enveloped in My Arms I guard your soul. I have given you everything so that I raise your soul to Me. I have shown My Infinite Mercy and I have favoured

you, giving you to drink from My Cup, have I not? Seek to please Me daughter; seek My Ways, My Ways are Holy. So beware of complaining about nothing, I have always been near you guiding you.

Come always to Me in simplicity of heart, My Vassula, for your days on earth are but the passing of a shadow, a superficial passage that will fade away. Nothing on earth lasts forever; keep then My precepts and follow My Commandments. I have entrusted you with My most Precious Jewel, guard It, embrace It and hold fast on to It. My Cross of Peace and Love shall be the sweet torment of your soul. Your eagerness in sharing My Cross should be an ardent flame in you as it is in Me. Your thirst for My Cross should grow like Mine. By now you must have realized how I show My Love, yes, by allowing you to suffer.

Soul! I have turned your aridity into a flowing spring; your hostility towards Me into tenderness; your apathy into fervour for My Cross; your lethargy into nostalgia for your Home and your Father. Rejoice soul! Your King has unwrapped the shroud covering your body and has raised you as He has raised Lazarus, to possess you. (Volume II, p.81-82 - September 28, 1989)

Slowly but steadily, Vassula's soul started to understand Our Lord's Love and how eager He is that we become copies of Himself, living crucifixes. Vassula said to Him:

It is good for me to have to suffer, the better to learn Your statutes. I **know** that You make me suffer out of Love. You are **lavishing** Your love on me because You have made me Your offspring. I know that You train those You love, **You are, Lord, a consuming Fire!** (Volume II, p.83 - September 29, 1989)

The place of suffering in the Christian life, in the spiritual life, is understandable in terms of the Cross of Christ. The world is filled with suffering and it has been well said that the tragedy of many lives is wasted pain. For the illusion that people inevitably gain, improve through suffering is sometimes found. Many collapse into bitterness, hopelessness, despair; many end their lives as suffering becomes an intolerable burden. Wishing pain to others in the hope that it will do them good is a futile exercise.

Only pain transfigured by the Cross of Christ does good; it does so to those who suffer and others for whom they suffer. Only the Lord knows how much his disciples can endure without breaking or losing hope. When the soul is at the point of profound intimacy with Jesus all irregularities and deviation like sadism and masochism are eliminated. Pain is increasingly transfigured by love.

9. Calling Christ, "Spirit"

Vassula had been attacked because Christ told her on December 4, 1986:

Remember, you are spirit and I am also Spirit and Holy. I live in you and you in Me. (Volume I, p.10)

Before I quote St Simeon, let us see what Scriptures say:

"God is Spirit," (Jn 4:24) and "Now this Lord is the Spirit, and where the Spirit of the Lord is, there is freedom." (2 Cor 3:17) and "...this is the work of the Lord who is Spirit." (2 Cor 3:18)

St Simeon says:

In all other cases the same name or comparison attached to a specific person is attributed to all three. For example, when you say "light", each one is properly light and the three are one light; "eternal life,", each one of them is life, the Son, the Spirit, the Father, and the three are one life. Thus God the Father is spirit, Christ is spirit and the Holy Spirit is God. By Himself each one of them is God, and the three together are God. Each one is Lord and the three are Lord; the One God, Creator of all things, is pre-eminently what each one is by Himself. The three are the one Creator of the universe, and God. (Cat 33.193-202)

For God is uncreated; we are all creatures. He is Spirit above every spirit as the Creator of spirits and their Master. We are flesh taken from dust, mere earthly substance. (Hymn 42.113-117)

Anymore than Jesus means that the Father became man like him when he says, "Who has seen me has seen the Father" (Jn 14:9). He does not mean that he is the Holy Spirit when he says that he is spirit. As God he is a spiritual being, as human beings we have a spiritual element, our souls.

10. Christ and Traditions as Garments

We put Christ like a garment. St Simeon says:

...He is called garment because He surrounds us entirely with His radiance, because He shrouds and makes us warm with the glory of His divinity. Thus we say that we put on Christ... (Eth 7.356-369)

In the following passage, as in many others, Christ speaks to Vassula in metaphors. She did not understand and took every one of His words literally, but He reassured her that in the end she will understand Him. Here is what He said to her on the May 4, 1988:

> I desire that around your waists you wear a Belt, offered by Me, which will represent: Child-like-Faith, which delights Me. Yes, let this Belt be as a symbol; I desire you to be bare-footed - be like monks; I desire you to wear My Garments of Old. (Volume I, p.320)

Vassula took Christ's words literally and yet she knew He meant something else, and that they were symbolic, nevertheless, she asked Him:

> "Which are Lord?" Our Saviour responds, "My Garments are Simple." Vassula still did not understand, saying,"Beloved Lord, they might think we are a new sect!"
> The Lord said: "Ah Vassula! How little do you understand! Daughter, I will enlighten you and My sons and tell you what I mean by "wearing My Garments of Old." (Volume I, p.321)

Vassula took the above passage to mean that we should wear Christ's Traditions as He passed them on to us and not to change one iota - that Christ wants us to keep His Traditions and not go along with the extreme progressives wave.

This is an interesting example of how Jesus uses the same metaphor in talking to Vassula that his Spirit had inspired in St Simeon.

11.   Ezekiel's Vision of the Dry Bones - Comparisons

Christ was explaining that it is through the Holy Spirit, the Giver of Life that these dry bones (us) will come to life again. Christ compares these dry bones which are scattered as the separated members of the Churches. Christians are scattered and because of their division have become like the dry bones of Ezekiel's vision.

But one day, Christ will glorify His Body by joining all the scattered bones to make one body out of them, a body that will be transfigured into a divine body because the Holy Spirit's Breath will blow in it. It seems that after Christ brings unity among Christians, the Body (the Church) will be so radiant that others will be attracted too to join that Body.

> ...Offer your life in atonement and come with Me in the valley of Death, that is where I will pour out My Spirit, that is where I will pour out My Love to revive every dry bone.

Your work is in that valley, Vassula. I intend to overflow it with the River of Life. I, who am the Resurrection and the Life intend to flower these dry bones of that Valley, I will show My Compassion and My Love by raising the dead from their graves, leading them back into My House and with Me in My House, their table will be full, their cup I will fill and brim over, and My Sacred Heart will be their Holy Companion.

I shall make one single Body out of all those dry bones now lying scattered in the Valley of Death. Yes, like in the prophet Ezekiel's vision, I ask you the same question: "Can these bones live?"

- No. Not without Your intervention. Not without You putting life into them, my Lord, for they are quite dry and lifeless.

I am going to revive them; **I am the Resurrection.** I shall put sinews on them, thus the scattered bones will be joined together, then flesh will grow on them, I shall cover them with skin and give them breath so that they live. I shall make out of them one single Body... and bring them back to life again.

I shall send My Holy Spirit to blow through Its nostrils a most powerful Breath which will revive It and make It stand up once more on Its feet to glorify Me.

I shall pour crystal-clear Water over you from My Throne to cleanse you from all defilement, and I shall pour out My Holy Spirit to live in your midst. My Holy Spirit will be given to you to become your Heart. Then, I Myself will anoint this Body and the light I will give in your eyes will be My Own Divine Light, it will be from My radiant Glory, and like a warrior you shall walk fearless for I will be your Torch walking before you, showing you the way. You will need no lamplight, as I Myself will be your Light. **All the other nations** upon seeing your Beauty will follow your step, bringing their treasure and their wealth offering them together with themselves to you; and in your hand I will place an iron scepter dressing you in majesty and splendour... this is how My Spirit will unite every single one of you in the end and every one will believe it was the Father who sent Me. Every one will recognize Me as the Sacrificial Lamb. (Volume IV - May 30, 1993)

We also find that in St Simeon's writings, the Lord inspires him to take up Ezekiel's vision:

To put bone against bone and joint against joint - apply this, if you like, to the acquisition and working of virtue - serves no purpose in the absence of the One who is able to weave flesh and sinews on them. Even if one had admittedly succeeded in connecting the joints with sinews and in covering such dry bones with flesh and skin to form a complete body, even this would serve nothing if it lacks the breath that vivifies and quickens, that is, if it has no soul. Believe me, this happens to the dead soul. Put yourself inside its faculties and view all practices such as fasts and vigils, sleeping on the bare ground, poverty, the absence of baths and everything that ensues from all this, as dry bones and interconnected parts, one calling upon the other, the whole of which constituting somehow the body's entire soul. What good is it if such an entity remains without soul or breath, since the Holy Spirit is absent from it? Indeed, when He dwells in us, only He links these virtuous practices - which are as dead as lifeless members, disconnected from one another - with the sinews of spiritual strength. He unites them in the love of God. He renews and quickens us, who were old and dead. There is no other way for the soul to live. (Eth 7.311-333)

A famous passage in Ezekiel is here interpreted in similar fasion by two very different writers, that is different in background, though so similar in thinking. The "bones" which will be revivified stir a thought on the actual divisions of the Church and the action which Jesus will take to unite the members. The context is the doctrine of the Mystical Body, with an admirable synthesis of the doctrine of salvation through the death and Resurrection of Christ. Through all, penetrating all is the insistence of Jesus that he will bestow his graces, including that of compassion, through the working of his Holy Spirit.

12. Our Soul as a Paradise for the Lord

Many times the Lord said to Vassula: "Be my heaven". Our Lady also asks us to allow Jesus to transform our soul into a delightful garden where the King of kings can take His rest. The Holy Spirit transfigures our soul into a heaven for His Majesty. This is what St Simeon says about the Holy Spirit:

... The One whom You planted in my inmost being is, in truth, the one Tree of Life. Wherever He is planted, that is, in the soul, and wherever He takes root, he changes man at once into a splendid paradise with all manner of beautiful plants, trees and varied fruits. They are humility, joy, serenity, meekness, the rain of tears and the curious joy resulting from it. (Hymn 47.1-29)

And this is what Jesus told Vassula:

O come! I long to tell you something. My heaven is in you, because I feel glorified and rested... I delight in you. Love Me without restraint, making up for those who forget Me and are but multiplying My Wounds; love Me, Vassula, healing My beloved souls, be my heaven. (Volume I, p.40-41 - February 19, 1987)

Another time again the Lord said to Vassula: "Be my heaven." (Volume I, p.66 - March 22, 1987)

St Simeon says:

> Without the musician's breath the trumpet will never sound; without You, I remain as if lifeless. The body cannot do one thing without the soul. Likewise, without Your Spirit the soul cannot move or observe Your commandments, O Savior. (Hymn 47.1-9)

Jesus said to Vassula:

> I know you are helpless, I know you are weak. You see, you cannot do anything without Me... (Volume I, p.58 - March 17, 1987)

The parallel here is in the insistence on the soul's absolute need of Christ: "Without me you can do nothing" (Jn 15:3). One is reminded of the word of Jesus to St Catherine of Siena, "When I said nothing, I meant nothing."

13. Beatitudes and Prayers to the Shepherd

Like St Simeon, one day God asked Vassula to write Beatitudes, quite similar to the Beatitudes of the Gospel. But here are first some of the Beatitudes inspired by St Simeon where Mgr Kvivocheine says that one can certainly see the divine light that Christ unveils to us, a light which is His glory:

> Blessed are the ones who receive Christ who comes as a light into darkness, for they have become the children of the light and of the day. Blessed are those who have already put on Christ, they are already dressed in the wedding garment. Their hands and feet will not be bound to be cast into the eternal fire. (Eth 10.778-782) Blessed are those who at all times savour this ineffable light with the mouth of their mind, for they will walk upright in broad daylight and will pass their time in gladness. Blessed are those who here below have recognized the light of the Lord as the Lord Himself, for in the age to come they will not be ashamed to appear before Him. Blessed are those who always live in the light of Christ. For now, as in the time to come, they are and always will be His brothers, His co-heirs. Blessed are those in whose heart the light has been awakened and who have not let it go out, for at the end of this life they will precede the Spouse and will enter with Him into the nuptial chamber, carrying lamps... (Eth 10.794-807) etc.

On April 14, 1991 (Volume II, p.304-305), the Lord dictated these Beatitudes:

> Blessed are those who work for Peace, they shall prosper in My Peace and radiate My Light forever and ever. Blessed are the compassionate, they shall see Mercy in the Day of Judgement. Blessed are the generous souls who share My Cup, they will be called heirs of My Salvation. Blessed are those who espouse themselves to Me, this same joy I feel as a Bridegroom they too shall feel, the day they meet Me face to face. Blessed are you who have not accepted any other testimony but the One and only Truth I Myself have given you. I tell you: Come! come into My Kingdom and share **everything** I have, with Me. Blessed are those who do not differentiate themselves under My Holy Name, but show their unity through their humility and love, they shall be called Pillars and Foundation of God's Sanctuary. Blessed are **you** who believe without seeing, rejoice! for the Grace you received from My Father, and pray for those who have not yet received this Grace...

St Simeon offers a fervent prayer to the Shepherd:

> Yes, O compassionate Shepherd, good and gentle, who desires to save all those who believe in You: have mercy, hear my prayer. I beg of You, have mercy, You who are always compassionate. Do what is profitable for my wretched soul, because You alone are God, the Lover of mankind, uncreated, unending, all-powerful, the life and the light of all who love You and are so loved by You, O Lover of mankind. (Hymn 47.69-81)

God inspired Vassula one day to offer Him this prayer:

> My God, rationalism, modernism, the sects and atheism have invaded Your Glory. They have desecrated Your Holy Temple and defiled Your Sacred Name. They have reduced Your Sanctuary to a pile of ruins. They have left on their passage corpses of Your children, a prey for the vultures. How much longer will You be away, Lord? For long? Shepherd! Where are You? Apostasy is devouring Your sheep and rationalism is battering Your sheepfold. In tenderness quickly intervene, we can hardly be crushed lower; help us, God our Saviour, for the honour of Your Holy Name. We are Your people, are we not? The flock that You pasture. Shepherd? How much longer, Shepherd? Why hold back Your steps? O pick your steps over these endless ruins. Apostasy roared where Your Heart used to be, determined to destroy all that came out of Your Hand. My Shepherd, loudly I cry to You; our strength is running out, so tell me, how much longer have we to wait? The time has come to have Mercy on us, hear our sighs and let our cry reach You! (Volume III, p.9 - April 23, 1992)

The Christian message is simple, manifold, profound, accessible to those of every cultural level. There is a constant danger of misinterpreting, falsifying, diminishing its wondrous content. The sole safeguard is Jesus Christ himself, central to every aspiration, endeavour, reflection. He averts every danger, that, for instance, of conceptualizing his religion into a system of rigour, harsh injunctions, joyless frustration. Such an impression may be given by those who preach the Cross of Christ, omitting his beatitudes, as formerly there was at times so much emphasis on the Passion that the Resurrection was overlooked or treated as an event designed to the needs of Christian Apologetics, "He claimed to be God, he rose from the dead, therefore he was God." Now we have recovered the full intuition of the Paschal Mystery, the Passion and Resurrection enclosed in this one saving reality. In the same way we must, in considering Christ's code of conduct, take full account of the promises inherent in the Beatitudes. We must recognize that the saints have the secret of happiness, that suffering is overcome by Christian joy, that there is no keener satisfaction than the blessing of Jesus Christ on one who is intimate with him. In such a spiritual perspective, I suggest, one should read the programmes of bliss set forth in the passages here quoted from St Simeon. Incidentally it is comforting to see such a close similarity between the one and other author and the teaching of the Master himself given to us in the gospel narratives. The eight beatitudes have through the ages given inspiration to the disciples of Christ, a charter of happiness through rectitude. The words of St Simeon and Vassula may encourage us to deepen our response to them.

14. Total Detachment

Mgr Kvivocheine says:

> Simeon strongly insists on the conscious character of the spiritual experience. After mentioning "the fruits of the Holy Spirit: ...love, joy, peace, kindness... that bring with them divine knowledge, the wisdom of the Word and the abyss of the hidden plans and of the mystery of Christ," Simeon describes the change undergone by man - a change he calls "conceiving the Holy Spirit" - which occurs with indescribable joy when one reaches the abyss of humility: "The one who has finally come to this valley and steadfastly remains there undergoes the graceful change which turns man into an angel. With his body he moves among men, but his mind lives in heaven, sharing the life of the angels and growing in the love of God - a love no one is able to approach unless one first purifies the mind through repentance and flowing tears." (Eth 8.207-216)

On June 26, 1987 (Volume 1, p.140) Vassula had a similar experience:

> After my purification, I said: "So now I realize: I have been split. My body goes around, but without my soul in it. I feel like a carcass: detached totally. Has anybody experienced this: to think, as long as you are awake and conscious,

of God only? Has anyone experienced an awareness of God for twenty-four hours a day for every day, and more than one year? And the minute my mind would start to forget, my chin is taken by a hand to turn my head and face Jesus' smiling Face. I surprise myself how I cope still with other things!

"I am learning what God means by surrendering completely. To be detached (is) to leave everything and follow Him. His Words are symbolic, they are not material. **Surrender:** I have, by loving Him first and beyond everything else and feeling I would like Him to use me. **Being detached:** Yes, to the extent of being detached from my body, meaning that I realize I have a soul that desires to detach itself from the body to join him and follow him only. **Suffer:** Yes, suffering because of not being with Him, of being still material on earth, of having the feeling of being a widow here. Suffering to know that I have to follow a daily life, material life... still feeling dissolved in God." (Volume I, p.93 - May 6, 1987)

All great spiritual writers insist on total self-renunciation or detachment as a necessary condition of progress. It is the law laid down by the Lord himself. True, it has been misunderstood or misinterpreted. It has been taken for mortification, which has its place in the spiritual life, but is different. There have been wicked men who were mortified, capable that is of denying themselves certain things which give pleasure, and imposing this discipline on others. But they were monsters of egoism. The test is the capacity to yield the self entirely to God.

15. The Symbolic Tree of Virtues

Mgr Kvivocheine says that St Simeon gives us a symbolic image of a tree onto which charity is grafted. He says that the saint contemplates it together with the other virtues, especially faith and hope. These are his words:

It is in faith that hope was planted. On it hope was watered by tears and compunction, before being illumined by Your light, before becoming rooted and well-grown. Then You, the good Craftsman and Creator, came with the knife of ordeals or rather, of humility... Upon that hope alone, as upon the one root of a tree, You grafted Your holy love. By watching love grow day by day and hearing it speak to me - for it is through love that You taught and enlightened me - I live in gladness, as if I were already even beyond all faith and hope. (Euch 2.273-284)

Vassula quotes the parallel:

My Vassula, Love comes first. **I am a God of Love.** Remember how I taught you that **Love is the Root?** I have given you an example of a good tree bearing good fruits; this tree is The Perfect Tree - because its root is Love; its branches are all virtues and they are all good. Without the Root of Love, this tree will have no virtues and thus no fruit. When you see a tree which is barren, or its fruit rotten, know My child that its root is made out of the most vile evils existing. I tell you solemnly that the Root of all virtues is called love. I am Love. I am The Root who nourishes you - embellishing you. Come and be in Me and you will live forever! (Volume I, p.366 - August 26, 1988)

St Simeon in the same spirit says:

The first among all the virtues, the queen and mistress, is love. It is the head of all the others, both their raiment and their glory. (Hymn 17.483-490)

On November 13, 1991 Vassula received this message in which the Eternal Father compared us to trees:

I happened to be taking a walk nearby a river when I saw a driftwood drifting away with the worldly current. I leaned over and picked it out of the stream I brought it Home with Me and planted it in My Garden of Delights; from a dry piece of wood I made out of you a Tree. I said: "Grow! grow and take root in My Garden, in My Property, and from your blossoms exhale a perfume to appease My Justice." I said: "Crops of fruit shall sprout each month and your leaves will be the cure to many."

Now and then I amuse Myself in pruning you. My delight is to see flowers in blossom and constant a constant growth in your fruit. Alone the Water from My Sanctuary can give you growth and Life. I, Yahweh, will see to it that you prosper.

I take pleasure in picking now and then on My way pieces of driftwood. I can give life to anything I pick on My way. (Volume II, p.394)

Again a biblical metaphor sanctioned by the Master, who gave us the principle to judge the tree by its fruits. The corresponding phrases are very illuminating, even to the mention of the root, in the exposition of St Simeon and of Vassula.

16.   Mystical Experiences with God's Divine Hand

God's Hand touched St Simeon and immediately after he craved to kiss it:

I give You thanks with my whole heart, because You did not avert Your gaze from me when I was lying in darkness, down below. Your divine hand touched me. When I saw it I arose, rejoicing, for it was brighter than the sun. I, the miserable one, attempted to seize it. It vanished from my sight at once, and once more I found myself in darkness, I fell to the ground, mourning, weeping, in prostration, lamenting with all my strength in my desire to see Your divine hand once again. You stretched it out, I saw it more clearly, or so it seems. I clasped it, I pressed my lips to it. O loveliness! Excessive mercy! The Creator gave me his hand to kiss, the hand that sustains the universe with its strength... (Hymn 50.91-109)

Vassula had expressed one day how much she wanted to be near God, and He said to her:

..."Vassula, feel My Hand, My Hand is trying ever so hard to get hold of you and keep you near Me..." And I remember how I felt that His Hand was trying to get hold of me and how I was evading It.

Another time, in Greece, she had an experience of His close Presence and she remembers touching His Divine Hand that time. She remembers that His fingers were beautifully long. He had a handsome Hand. This is what happened:

...Before leaving for Panormiti (Greek island of Simi, called St Michael), that morning, at 8.00 am, Jesus came to me in a dream-vision. He did not allow me to look at Him. He allowed me only to touch Him and feel extensively His Presence. His Presence gave my soul such peace and consolation that at this moment I could have gone through the biggest ordeals without any hesitation. He stood at my right side and felt that He is my Defender. Just then, He put His left Arm around my shoulder, as if to show me that indeed He is near me and protecting me. Immediately I felt God's warm consoling love for me. My soul rejoiced! He allowed me to touch his left hand which held me and was posed on my left shoulder. I touched each one of His Fingers. Then He allowed me to touch with my left hand His Heart, my hand climbed to touch His Beard, then part of His Holy Face, all the time never allowing me to turn around and look at Him. Every one of those seconds put my soul in an indescribable consolation, peace, joy and reassurance. He did not utter a word, He did not need to, His Presence was enough. (Volume III, p.45)

When we speak of Jesus ascending to the right hand of the Father, we are using anthropomorphic language, which theologians justify within limits; it is applying to divine attributes and actions language which strictly apply to human realities. The early chapters of Genesis abound in this mode of expression, with God burning "hot with wrath" and such other human oriented idiom. But we have to take account of another factor in dealing with descriptive phrases about Jesus Christ, the Incarnate Word. For human language applies perfectly to Jesus Christ, and there is another way of speaking about him, what the theologians call "communication of idioms", the name given to the mental and linguistic process whereby human properties are attibuted to God in Jesus Christ and divine properties to man in him. The basis of the practice is the single divine Person, with two natures united in Christ. Fathers of the Church gave the doctrinal explanation. Where two persons are affirmed, as by the Nestorians and only one nature as by the Monophysites there is confusion, as there is when the divine or human properties are attributed, without the Person as the obvious reference. "Humanity is divinity" is unjustifiable; "Jesus is divine" is. In the extracts here aligned, again interestingly similar, it is sometimes the human hand of Christ, at others the hand of God, spoke of anthrophomorphically.

17. Mystical Vision of Spherical Light

St Simeon says:

> ...I often saw a light which appeared to me, sometimes inside (of me) when my soul was enjoying calm and peace, and sometimes it appeared far outside, or hid itself completely, and by hiding caused an intolerable affliction at the thought that it would never appear again. Yet as I fell into cries and lamentations once more, proving my total renunciation of the world, together with obedience and humility, it appeared again, like the SUN which tears away the covering of clouds and shows itself, little by little, gentle, spherical. (Euch 1.164-180)

Vassula also saw a spherical light, but much bigger than the one seen by St Simeon:

> God wanted to show me Heaven. I was with Him suddenly, walking in a beautiful garden...while walking I noticed an enormous ball of light, almost touching the horizon. It was like a big Sun, but one could look at it without having the eyes burnt. "What can you see?" God asked me. I replied: "This sort of "Sun." He said: "Yes, it is My Holy Abode, and what can you see around the Light?" etc... (Volume I, p.68-69 - March 26, 1987)

St Simeon says:

> "God is Light; we are the ones sitting in darkness. Perhaps it is more true to say that we are the darkness. Let us not delude ourselves; we are the darkness, and God will shine in no other place than in those souls who are united with Him before death." (Hymn 34.56-60). "Thus if He shines spiritually in a heart or mind, like lightning or like a great sun, what is He able to accomplish in such a soul immersed in light? Will he not enlighten such a soul? Will He not lead her to a precise understanding of who He is? (Hymn 34.78-82)

Contemplatives and mystics are consciously or unconsciously influenced by the Gospel of John, in which the concept of light is so important, Jesus' saying being sometimes taken as a key phrase of the Gospel, "I am the Light of the world" (Jn 9:5). Among mystical theologians St Simeon excells in relating all his intuitions to the vision of divine Light. Darkness as failure to meet God's plan is seen in its full meaning by one like the saint who had expeiential knowledge of God as Light. The vision of a spherical light given to Vassula, who at the time knew nothing of the close parallel with the saint's experience, is very remarkable.

18.   Mystical Language on the Totality and Completeness of God

A certain priest in the States criticized me publicly in print stating that in saying: "God is all," was heretic. Nevertheless, this priest did not complete or follow-up that sentence, so that it may appear to the reader, ambiguous. The sentence was thus: "I am Everything, I am the Alpha and the Omega. I am the Eternal. I am the Elixir..." (Volume I, p.126 - June 4, 1987). By adding the words Alpha and Omega, God was showing His utter completeness and totality.

Here is what St Simeon says to show the totality of all the good that Christ is:

It is Christ who will become ALL and will replace everything..(Cat 2.56-64)

Christ has become everything: understanding, wisdom, light, enlightenment, resemblance, contemplation, gratitude... (Eth 3.304-309)

In mystical writings it is often said "God is all, man is nothing." Among those who thus spoke was Venerable Francis Libermann on his deathbed. Libermann is thought to be one of the great mystics of the nineteenth century.

19.   Divinization

Here is what St Simeon says about divinization:

Imagine now that the body is a palace and that the soul of each of us is a royal treasure. God, who is joined to the soul thanks to the observance of the commandments, fills her entirely with divine light and transforms her into god as a result of His union, His grace. Anyone who follows the said road of virtues arrives at this condition which is truly worthy of God. To pass elsewhere, and to take a short cut somehow to reach the next mansion, is a manoeuver that is totally impossible. (Eth 11.82-89)

When Christ says in His messages that He will give us back our divinity, He means that by our conversion, our renewal and our union with Christ who acts together with the Father and the Holy Spirit, we will become His divine reflection, the "New Jerusalem". By repenting we will obtain the gift of deification for the fruit of repentance will bring us to become like Christ.

St Simeon says:

> ...Then the Creator... will send the divine Spirit; I do not say another soul like the one you had, but the Spirit, that is, the one coming from God. He will inspire and illumine you, He will make you shine and re-create you altogether. You who are corruptible, He will render incorruptible. He will renew the dilapidated home, I mean the house of your soul. Together with this, He will make your whole body incorruptible, entirely incorruptible. He will make you god by grace, similar to your Model. (Hymn 44.147-165)

Today God is pouring out His Holy Spirit more than any time to revive us, renew us and make us similar to His own Divine Image. This is God's first appeal in the messages to divinize us. On November 21, 1988 Vassula received this message:

> Come in your Saviour's Arms - give Me your faults and I will purify you and heal you. I will divinize you for I am Divinity - I will perfect you... (Volume I, p.401)

In the following passage, God shows us that His Heavenly Works are to attract us for our conversion and lead us to perfection:

> ...My Cross of Peace and Love cries out to the world for conversion, for love, for peace and for unity. My Works are to bring to divinity again this human race... (Volume II, p.104 - November 9, 1989)

Here is an announcement for the new heavens and the new earth, the new Jerusalem:

> I will not delay, only a little while now a very little while, and the ban will be lifted. I will renew you and I will give you back your divinity...
> (Volume IV - November 11, 1993)

Our Blessed Mother explains to us what God wants from us:

> The Lord wants your full abandonment to make out of you a perfect being reflecting His Divine Image, this Divine Image your era has lost. Jesus and I do not "descend" by means of Our messages to judge you. We do not come to judge you nor do We come to condemn you, We come to you with great Love and Mercy to bring you all back to Us and make out of you all divine beings... (Volume II, p.108 - 16.11.89)

Mgr Kvivocheine says:

> Such divinization is the fruit of repentance and reception of the deified Body of
> Christ. It involves the whole man, body and soul, and takes place in an ineffable
> manner by receiving the Body and Blood of Christ in communion. Man is
> changed entirely: immersed in the light, he acquires a divine mind. By making
> us incorruptible, the Holy Spirit deifies us, if we imitate Christ. (p.387)
> Divinization is the state of man's total transformation, effected by the Holy
> Spirit, when man observes the commandments of God, acquires the evangelical
> virtues and shares in the sufferings of Christ. The Holy Spirit then gives man
> a divine intelligence and incorruptibility. Man does not receive a new soul, but
> the Holy Spirit unites essentially with the whole man, body and soul. He makes
> of him a son of God, a god by adoption, though man does not cease being a man,
> a simple creature, even when he clearly sees the Father. He may be called man
> and god at the same time. It is the Incarnation which is the foundation of
> deification. Divinization has become possible ever since the Word took on flesh,
> assumed our humanity and gave us His divinity, and ever since man has taken
> on Christ in Baptism. Above all, deification is effected by partaking of the body
> and blood of Christ... (p.389)

One finds these words from Christ in *True Life in God*:

> Come and receive Me in My Sacrifice as an unblemished lamb, you must come
> pure to Me (meaning after confession). If you only realized How I am present
> in Body and in Blood in which I have won an eternal redemption for all of you,
> you would approach Me without blemish and with respect. I have out of My
> Infinite Love offered Myself as the perfect Sacrifice to purify you all from sin.
> I want you all to fully understand this Sacrifice, yes, I want to encourage you by
> understanding what I am offering you and thus stir in you a response of love.
> This sacrifice can lead you into sanctification and into divinity. It can achieve
> in you My purpose and bring you to eternal perfection... (Volume II, p.131 -
> December 29, 1989)

> I repeat that My Holy Spirit of Grace is being sent out to the four corners of the
> earth to teach you to be holy and raise you up into divine beings. The earth shall
> turn into a copy of heaven and thus My Will will be done, the prayer I have
> taught you to pray shall be fulfilled... Recognize the Times, recognize the gentle
> Breath of My Holy Spirit of Grace upon you, I am blowing now on your nations,
> raising up with My Breath your dead, turning them into a reflection of My
> Image. I am raising new disciples every single day to glorify My Name again
> and evangelize with love for Love... (Volume II, p.168-169 - April 22, 1990)

The great mystery of our Redemption is manifold, mysterious. It has been the object
of reflection in different phases of the Church's history, and within two great

traditions, that of the East and that of the West. Whereas in the West thinking was influenced by the mighty tradition of law inherited from Rome, in the East, in the great theological school of Alexandria, for long dominant in that area, the contemplative approach focussed on divinization.

A bold slightly hyperbolic statement by St Athanasius set the intellectual pattern, "God became man, so that men might become gods." How was this process of divinization explained? In the light of the divine image, a concept not often prominent in western thinking. Man was created in the image of God, but the image was defaced by original sin. The One to restore it was himself "the Image of the Invisible God" (Col 1:15). This was the theological outlook inherited by St Simeon. It was connatural to him as an eastern and a mystic. It is most heartening to see the elements of this doctrine set forth attractively and readably by Vassula.

20. The Mother of God, The Second Eve

Mgr Kvivocheine says that:

> According to the writings of Simeon as well as those of the Church, one cannot present Christ and His saving work without also speaking of the blessed Virgin Mary, the Theotokos, since these themes are woven together and constitute a whole.

Neither have the given messages of *True Life in God* been in any way omitting our blessed Mother. In fact, messages and instructions from Her were also given to us. After all, One is never away from the Other, (Christ from Mary). The messages teach us that wherever Mary is, so is Christ. Their Two Hearts are united and become one.

St Simeon clearly expresses how our Blessed Mother is the bride of the Son of God in this passage:

> It is the daughter (of David) Mary, I say, the pure and more than pure, the altogether irreproachable, whom He took as wife. Completely irreproachable and more than pure, it is thus that I describe her in comparison to us and to men of that time, comparing her to them and to us, her servant. In relation to her Bridegroom and to the Father of the Bridegroom, I recognize that she remains human. Yet she is also holy and more than holy, of an immaculate purity, greater than that of humans of all generations. She is the one whom God chose for His Son's wedding. (Eth 1.9.42-51)

In a message given to Vassula by the Eternal Father, He Himself instructs us with great joy of that moment of His choice:

> I, the Creator of the heavens and earth tell you, My Holy Spirit is the Spouse of the Bride, of her who held the Infant Who was to save you and redeem you and in Whom through His Blood you would gain freedom and forgiveness of your sins. He is the Spouse of the One Whom He found like a garden enclosed, holding the rarest essences of virtues, a sealed fountain, the loveliest of women, bathed in purity because of her unique perfection. My Spirit came upon Her and covered Her with His shadow and glorified Me making Her the Mother of God, the Mother of all humanity and the Queen of Heaven... (Volume III, p.60 - October 5, 1992).

Sometimes St Simeon uses the name for our blessed Mother "the Ark", or the "vessel" that sheltered Noah and his kin. Whereas in *True Life in God*, She is given also the name as Ark, but it is of the ark of alliance where the Israelites kept inside it the ten commandments and a small portion of the manna that God had fed them while crossing the desert, that these messages are speaking of. Nevertheless both are carriers, containing manna. St Simeon says:

> The ark was the figure of the Mother of God, and Noah, the figure of Christ. Noah's kinsmen were the first fruits of the part reserved from among the Jews, taken from those who in the future would believe in Christ, whereas the wild and tame animals with the birds and reptiles, were figures of the nations. Consequently, if the ark contained Noah after the Flood began, then Mary, the Mother of God, contained the Incarnate One, God and man. But the ark saved only one man and his family, while the Incarnate One kept His ark and the entire world from the flood of sin and from the slavery of law and death. (Eth 2.4.9-19)

In a message Vassula received which Christ called "Emmanuel's Song" Christ gives several beautiful names regarding our Blessed Mother. He tells us:

> She is the Queen of heaven, She is My Mother and your Mother, the loveliest of Women, beautiful as Heaven, radiant as My Glory, unique in Her Perfection, the Delight of My Soul, She is the Woman with the twelve stars on Her Head for a crown, the vessel of my glory, a Reflection of My Eternal Light; She is the One whose Presence in My Courts outshines all the constellations put together; she is the vessel of the true Light, the Word, made flesh and who lived among you. She is Grace in Grace and the Sweetest Song of the psalmists. She is My Theme of Joy, My Honour and My Boast. She is the Gate to Heaven the One who shows Her children how to enter into My Kingdom, She is My Masterpiece, She is the Consoler of your Consoler, co-redemptress of your redeemer, the Bride of My Holy Spirit... I will take no rest, not until I take you too into My

Mother's House into the Room of Her who conceived Me, to reveal to you too Her Beauty.. (Volume IV - November 11, 1993).

As Mgr Kvivocheine commented: "The Mother of God is both the promised land and the vessel of manna," and further on he says that She is "the role of His (Christ's) Mother in the work of salvation", in other words: Co-Redemptress of our Redeemer.   He continues to explain why the Virgin Mary is at the same time the Queen of the saints and their Mother, in what St Simeon wrote:

According to this, the Mother of all the saints. The saints are, on the one hand, her servants in that She is the Mother of God... (Eth 1 10.166-171)

St Simeon says that:

...The Word of God took on flesh from the all pure Mother of God, and in exchange He gave not flesh but essentially the Holy Spirit. Above all, He vivifies the precious and immaculate soul (of the Virgin) by raising her from death, because the first Eve had died from the death of the soul. (Eth 2 7.210-215)

In one of our Lord's messages given to Vassula, He explains the reason why He is in our days sending our Blessed Mother everywhere before His Second Coming. At the same time, Christ introduces Her with several Names He has given Her:

This is why before My Return, I am sending you before Me, the Ark of Alliance, I am sending you the Woman of the Apocalypse, the second Eve, who will crush the serpent's head with her heel. I am sending you before Me My Mother, to open a broad highway and level it in this desert. I am sending you the Queen of Heaven, the Door to Heaven to prepare you and to school all you who still lie in the dust, to come forward and make your peace with Me, your King, before My Great Return. I am sending you the Queen of Peace... (Volume II, p.235 - October 10, 1990).

St Simeon says:

Let us observe then the parallelism of the ancient facts, and how they were placed according to a precise parallelism through the plan and covenant of God. Thus, first of all God introduced Adam into paradise and then created Eve. In the first place, likewise, the Son of God, the creator of Adam, came to earth and entered the Virgin's immaculate womb. Only then did He assume from her Adam's rib, this, the immaculate flesh, and He became man. Instead of an Eve deceived by the serpent, a new Adam, who must destroy the serpent that deceived Eve, presented Himself to the world. In the first place, it was Eve who was fooled by the words of the serpent. She ate (the fruit) of the tree, disobeyed the commandments and suffered death in her soul. Mary, the new Eve, the Mother of God, receives the good news from the angel. She adds faith to God's plan which is announced and gives her consent by saying, "Behold the handmaid of the Lord; be it done unto me according to Your word." She, the first, then received within herself essentially the Word of God, which in truth redeemed her soul from the earlier (sentence) of eternal death. At that moment the Word Incarnate recreated Adam's body, into which He breathed the breath of a living soul; for He took the already living rib and made it into a woman and did not have to create the breath. (Eth 2 7.114-136)

Here is Vassula's conclusion:

I shall close these chapters by saying that while I was on the Greek island of St Michael called Panormitis (Simi), on a retreat with some friends, I received the following message after having asked loudly the Lord in front of them: "O Lord, where are You leading us!" The Lord's immediate response came to me: "to the truth!"

An important point in regard to these readings from St Simeon and Vassula is the powerful stimulus that the Marian revival in the Catholic Church has received from her writings. It is interesting to note that this has come from a member of the Orthodox Church, though one utterly devoid, as has been made clear, of previous instruction in Orthodox theology or spirituality. The Orthodox have mighty traditions of doctrine and devotion centred on Our Lady; they will not lessen or abandon them. St Simeon illustrates the general truth.

The saint raises a question about the sponsal relationship of Mary to the divine Persons. He sees her motherhood in a bridal context. A powerful advocate of this thesis was the German theologian, MJ Scheeben, in the last century. It has not gained universal support. Nor has the view found among eastern Fathers of the Church, notably St John of Damascus (d.c. 749) that Mary was the Spouse of the Father - the idea also occurs in a great age of French spirituality, the seventeenth century. Since Jesus Christ was the etneral Son of God and the Son of the Virgin Mary, it seemed logical to see this relationship between the divine Father and the human Mother. Again widespread support is lacking.

Vassula expresses a truth which saints like Louis Marie Grignion de Montfort and Maximilian Kolbe have defended and three Popes have accepted, Leo XIII, Pius XII and John Paul II: Mary's sponsal bond is with the Holy Spirit. Vatican II simply declared that she was the "sanctuary" of the Spirit, which is true of all Christians.

Jesus in his beautiful eulogy of his Blessed Mother reminds us of the biblical foundation so often discussed by Marian theologians, the "Woman of the Apocalpyse", the "new Eve." St Simeon who adapts the story of Noah's Ark figuratively, is true to the great patristic tradition, what Newman called the rudimental idea: Mary the new Eve, a core concept from the second century writers to Vatican II. There is a widespread movement at the present time to petition from John Paul II a solemn definition of Mary's role as Co-Redemptress, Mediatress, Advocate. Vatican II kept away from the word Co-Redemptress, with difficulty admitted Mediatress - a misguided gesture to Protestants. Some of the opponents apparently thought that "Co" implied equality; it means "along with", as St Paul speaks of all Christians as "co-workers with God."

9

TESTIMONIES

I give here some examples of the testimony I have received on the subjects mentioned in the book under the heading *Extraordinary Signs* and the *Passion*. Sometimes testimony has been oral, with no opportunity to collect a written statement. Thus in Rome where Vassula spoke in a theatre a passer-by seeing that entry was free, went in; it was a Saturday evening. To his astonishment he saw a man in a long robe come out through the curtain on to the stage. He was naturally perplexed. Still more so when he saw the robed, bearded figure disappear and Vassula take his place. Likewise in Stockholm, a young woman who had read *True Life in God* was coming to the meeting which Vassula would address. But her mother, very ill, who knew nothing about Vassula, had to accompany her, as she could not remain alone. She was surprised at what she took to be a "woman preacher." Then, suddenly, in place of Vassula she saw a figure which she took to be Jesus Christ. She was astounded. When the meeting was ended her daughter rejoined her. Thereon another wonder occurred. The elderly woman felt a rush of water through her body. She knew that she was healed and so told to her daughter. From hardly being able to keep up with her daughter on the way to the meeting, she astonished the daughter by running before her, all the way home. Next day the latter wrote a brief note for me confirming the event. The lady herself I did not meet. Occasionally word has been sent after a meeting about such events, with no means of securing a record. After Vassula's address in Athens, two people, members of the Orthodox Church, telephoned to say that they had this experience, but gave no personal particulars. There may have been occurrences not at all reported.

I begin with two touching testimonies: from prisoners in Muntinlupa Prison - Renato Pastores and Francisco Natan. They each signed a very brief statement: "I saw Jesus and Mama Mary in the face of Vassula." In the Philippines I also received this statement:

To Whom it May Concern:

This is my testimony of various incidents that I have personally witnessed involving Vassula Rydén for whatever purpose it may serve.
    During Vassula's first visit to the Philippines in December 1991, while she was giving a talk at the Sanctuario de San Antonio Parish, I was sitting in one

of the front pews when I witnessed a change in Vassula's face. I saw her face change to what looked like Jesus with a beard. Several other ladies who were sitting with me saw the same thing I did.

I witnessed the same thing happen when she spoke to the Congressional Ladies in the Lobby of the Congress Building (Batasang Pambansa). I was sitting in one of the front rows, behind Mrs Aurora Aquino, the mother of the late Benigno S Aquino when I noticed Mrs Aquino rubbing her eyes several times with both her hands. After the talk, I had the chance to tell Mrs Aquino that I saw her rubbing her eyes during Vassula's talk, and that was when Mrs Aquino told me that she saw Vassula's face look like the face of Jesus with a beard, which is exactly the way I saw her too. Mrs Aquino said she could not believe what she saw, so she kept on rubbing her eyes. The lady beside her told her that she also saw Vassula's face change, and that is the only time she found out that she really saw what she did.

I affirm that all these events took place and that I was a witness to them.
In Jesus and Mary.

Mercedes Tuason,
7 McKinley Road,
Forbes Park,
Makati,
Metro Manila, Philippines.

Another document from the Philippines reads thus:

I am Margarita L Bernado of 816 Miguelin Sampaloc, Manila, Philippines. I saw Jesus Christ in (the) person of Vassula Rydén when she and the prayer group pray 'Our Father.' Her face changed to a man, and this is Jesus Christ, Our Lord. I'm so happy and I'm praising the Lord. Thank you very much, oh Lord. Thank you Vassula. M L Bernado.

A "PS" is added:

This (a drawing of the head of Christ) is .Vassula look when we pray 'Our Father' that evening at Mandaluyong City Hall Library.

A letter I received from another lady in the same country, I quote in full:

The first time I saw and heard Vassula speak was last Thursday 6/18/93 at the Stella Maris Chapel, Cubao, Philippines from 9 o'clock to 11.30 am. Vassula transformed before my eyes (I was sitting at the first row) with Jesus, Mother Mary and other spirits, who - I'm not sure who they were.

Especially at the part wherein Jesus talks to Vassula about the "REBEL" I saw Vassula transform into a man in a silver metal warrior costume. I saw different kings, queens, Jesus at 10 years old, Jesus at around 13 years old - different ages. Different women, I think one was Mary Magdalen with long clothes. There was constant light around her, engulfed in clouds also. Vassula's height stayed the same.

I think it is important to note that this day was Sister Angelina Lim's birthday and she is the first underline activist nun in the Philippines. Jesus' messages to me were very clear, stressing that he was the King, the King of all nations. Vassula's eyes turned into Jesus's eyes also; her eyes turned brown and other colours depending on the impact of the message for me.

The next morning Vassula came to our church, Santuario de San Jose in Greenhills. She arrived at 9.30 or so for the Mass. I was preparing to introduce her in the sacristy, and from where I was I started to see Vassula transform into Jesus with beard, moustache and all. This lasted on and off till 12 o'clock when Vassula ended her speech.

6/20/93 Sunday morning, Araneta Colesium, Cubao. Again as Vassula spoke after the Mass I saw her transform into Jesus, and God the Father and Our Lady. This is Fathers' Day.

Please note that I, Maria Antonia Rodriguez am a designer and a member of the PAGIBIG (means love in the Philippine language) contemplative prayer group. Many other people witnessed the same as I did.

I praise God for these miracles and am grateful to be of any assistance in the work Our Lord has paved for you and Vassula, dear Father Michael. So sorry for the delay of this. You made me promise you this at the Manila Pavilion yesterday and you said you'll be leaving on tomorrow Monday - 6/21/93. My heart is always with you...always.

An account from Mrs Pat McCaffrey, Fountainebleau, South Africa:

When Vassula was at the Cathedral in Johannesburg I was really listening intently to her when somehow I started to see another face 'emerging' from hers. It seemed a man's face with a short beard. It was like a super-imposing of one face over the other. I immediately became afraid as I did not know what to expect, so I tried to blink, and blink it all away, thinking that my eyes were blurred, but the face kept coming and going. Then suddenly, and all in one gradual movement Vassula's face shrank to a little blot in the centre of where her face was. The blot stayed a second and in the next second it was gone leaving only her hairline behind which immediately framed the man's face, which had now reappeared clearly and fully this time. This took me by surprise and I was to see a fatherly and wise face, yet as soon as I saw it, I quickly turned away so that I could not see it change to something else in case it did. After a few seconds when I looked again, the face was gone and Vassula was herself. I do not recall colour as it seemed to be neutral or flesh colour. I also cannot recall what Vassula was saying at the time. As I worked out later, this may have all happened in under 30 seconds.

I now give a French testimony, that of Patrick Beneston, who has helped very much in the organisation of Vassula's meetings in France, and in the diffusion of her message. He recounts to Vassula what he saw on the last Saturday of October, 1992 in the church of St Joan of Arc in Versailles:

> The church was full. I was on the side and I saw you therefore in profile. Geneviève had asked me to take some photos. While I was taking them I felt a very strong perfume of roses, which lasted during the photos, a few minutes. Then I went back to my place, with joy in my heart. Towards the end of the lecture while you were reading the messages of Christ, you face was transformed. First it became smaller, it was round, white as porcelain with a fine little nose...then it disappeared and I saw another face, with thick moustaches, a beard, a nose straight and long; your bodily outline was changed, your shoulders became wider and rounded, becoming more developed, slightly arched. The garment was of one piece like a robe or monk's chasuble... I had, at that precise moment, the conviction of seeing Christ in person.. Jesus, with a countenance identical with that of the Holy Shroud, preaching to his disciples. This vision lasted while the messages were being read; at first I dared not look, thinking myself the victim of hallucination; but my eyes were irresistibly drawn towards this countenance; it was really him; this nose long and as it were broken, these moustaches, this beard, this bodily outline; it was really him, Our Lord, who was there.

The next witness is very different from Patrick Beneston. I have mentioned Jack Rice in the course of the narrative of Vassula's journeys. He deserves a special tribute for his tireless zeal in the cause of Christian unity. An Anglican with deep Christian commitment he not only read and took to heart Vassula's books, but really espoused her cause. He longed especially to inter-communion. He willingly received Holy Communion in Catholic churches. He had taken initiatives at every ecclesiastical level possible to further this cause. I have mentioned the index which he painstakingly made of the volumes of *True Life in God*; this he was seeking to improve. He had a great moment on 25 April, 1993 when an ecumenical gathering in his own property at Exhurst Manor, Kent, listened to Vassula's message. She was his guest, as was I, and I was deeply touched by his request to consecrate his home to Our Lady - to her he had the most tender, enlightened devotion. Still more striking was his special regard and practical commitment to the Two Hearts, not often found among Anglicans. A true knight of Our Lady, a true soldier of Christ! Here is his testimony on the change of countenance:

> On the occasion of my first visit to speak with Vassula in Switzerland on 18-20 May, 1992, we discussed for three hours various theological matters as well as the revelations of eschatology in the writings of *True Life in God*. On four or five occasions as we spoke on that first day I was amazed to see the Lord's face take the place of her face as we spoke. I mentioned this to Vassula and she

acknowledged that a few others had said the same. I was very much aware of Jesus' presence, especially when, on the following day, I consecrated my life to the Lord as per the Consecration of Book 57/25-30, 26 June '92.

The letter to me is dated 26 July, 1993 and characteristically ends with the phrase, "Yours in our Two Hearts."

Now a testimony from one of a different background:

I, Brother Aloysius, a member of the Congregation of the Holy Ghost and the Immaculate Heart of Mary, have a ministry of the Eucharist in Blackrock College. I also make preparations for all Masses celebrated in the Fathers' Oratory and the College Chapel. This work engages me especially for Sunday and Feastday Masses and all ceremonial occasions. I also make all altar and liturgical preparations for assembly Masses in large halls in the city of Dublin, as for the monthly Masses for the Medjugorje group and for the Messengers of Mary Immaculate, Queen of the Universe. I therefore undertook to make all ready for the Holy Mass celebrated in the College Jubilee Hall on 12 March, 1991 when Vassula first addressed a large Dublin audience. I did likewise when she spoke in the National Stadium in the following year.

Vassula came to Dublin for a meeting to be held in the same Stadium on 15 October, 1993. I undertook the same task and she was always most gracious in thanking me. What I now relate took place as I encountered Vassula in the Fathers' Dining Room during her brief stay. I entered by a side door and my gaze fell upon her as she was seated at table for her meal. Her head was turned sideways looking at a picture on the wall of the Last Supper, our Lord with his Apostles. Suddenly the face of Christ seemed to pass across her face. As she looked at me, the face of Christ remained on her face. It looked like that on the cover of her book. Then slowly the face disappeared. Vassula smiled at me. I kissed her hand. I told her that I was leaving to get everything ready for the meeting and Mass in the National Stadium.

I honestly relate what happened to me. Joy and peace were running through my mind. That evening I was on the altar with the priests and Vassula. I could see Vassula, and I could not get the face of Christ out of my mind. I said to myself that the following morning I would see her and tell her what had happened. I was disappointed. Vassula left Blackrock College at 7 o'clock in the morning.

Father O'Carroll told me that in the course of the afternoon Vassula had suffered the Passion in her room in his presence and that of her Austrian friend Erwin Schlacher, who is following a course in *Mater Dei* Institute for Catechetics in Dublin.

I should perhaps add to these records a word from a member of the Greek Orthodox Church, Despina Faka, who knew of Vassula from a television interview. Then some time later she saw the interview once again. This time things were different:

> Suddenly while I looked at her interview her face began to change, and the face of Christ appeared there before my eyes. In my soul I recognised Jesus and I truly felt his presence there. It was very beautiful to see and it lasted for two minutes.

I end with an expatriate Philippine lady:

> I saw a vision of you transformed into Jesus, as the image seen on the cover of your book, with a halo. (Milo Comiso, Winnipeg, May 1993)

So we pass to witness accounts of Vassula suffering the Passion. They centre on Puerto Rico and the Holy Mountain. First, however, I may recall the miracle of the sun. It has been reported three times: at Notre Dame, South Bend, Indiana; at Kent, England and in Puerto Rico. It is oral testimony in the first case. For the second we have this account which represents the experience of two people:

> Yesterday I received Jack Rice's letter asking me to tell you of my experience at Exhurst while Vassula was addressing the meeting. I was sitting just outside the marquee, as the sun was shining through the poplar trees. As I listened and as I watched, the sun began to spin, throwing off a rosy glow. I drew Pat McCaffrey's attention to the phenomenon, and he also witnessed it, as I believe it was Pat who told you. I wrote to Mr Rice thanking him for all he did to make Vassula's visit possible, and mentioned to him that I had seen the spinning sun and he presumed I was the person who had spoken to you.

The signatory is Mrs Elsie Brown, at one time a Methodist, now an Anglo-Catholic. I quote from Pat McCaffrey's letter to Jack Rice dated July 26, 1993:

> You have recently been speaking to Mrs Elsie Brown of Bedford about the phenomenon of the "spinning sun." Well she has asked me to put pen to paper as a witness of that event. I was the man who spoke to Dr Michael about the event after Vassula's talk had ended. I can confirm what Mrs Brown has requested - that we were both seated together immediately <u>outside</u> the tent in which Vassula spoke, fairly close to the front row and to the left of the audience as it faced the rostrum. I think it was about the time that Dr Michael had finished his introduction and we prepared to hear Vassula talk. The rain was stopped by then and the sun was shining warmly so we had decided not to be inside, as it was stuffy, the sides of the tent were detached although the rear behind Vassula was down so the people on the Rostrum were unaware of the sun behind them. Vassula Rydén was about the speak when Elsie Brown nudged me and said, 'look at the sun.' The sun was just visible at the edge of the tent and still quite high in a clear sky of blue that had recently been washed by the rain.

The sun was brilliant as I looked up but was dazzling until I then realized that it was in fact dancing and apparently spinning. The 'spin' is apparent because the sun seems to be hidden behind a white disc which eclipsed it and leaves a brilliant flashing edge around it which makes it seem to dance and spin. The centre disc was pale white and suggested the Eucharist. This continued to dance while Vassula spoke. It eventually disappeared from sight as the talk went on and the sun moved behind the tent. After the talk I mentioned it to Dr Michael as he walked back to the house with Vassula. We all walked back to our coach up the driveway and I mentioned the phenomena to the Bedford ladies who hadn't seen it, as they were inside the tent at the time. We turned to have a last look at the sun which was now getting low in the sky and found that it was still spinning to the delight of the ladies and myself. This time there were many colours involved with reds and yellows spinning around the outside of the sun. We have all witnessed the phenomena before in Medjugorje. I have witnessed it several times since at special times. These times I consider when I sense the pleasure of joy of the Lord.

Now follow a number of letters from people who experienced supernatural events in the presence of Vassula in Puerto Rico:

Dra Norma E Agosto Maury
Centro Psico Neurologico
65th Infanteria #567
Lodi A2, Villa Luarca
Rio Piedras, P.R. 00924

I am a doctor, specialized in Internal Medicine, Neurology and Neurophysiology. My name is Norma E Agosto Maury, from Puerto Rico. I belong to the American Medical Association and I am Board Certified by the American Board of Electroencephalography and Neurophysiology as well as member of the American Neurological Association, and I am Catholic.

On February 13, 1994, I was in Montaña Santa, San Lorenzo, Puerto Rico, at the Conference of Rev Father O'Carroll, Mrs Vassula Rydén and Agustin Acosta. Where with Dra Dalmau, Dra Colon and some nurses we were taking care of the medical emergencies which may arise from the great multitude; in fact there were many emergencies that day.

I was there to serve the Church, because Bishop Hernandez was to celebrate mass and Dra Merced, Dra Colon, Dra Dalmau had asked me to go. However, relative to Mrs Rydén I had my intellectual reserve, despite my cousin, Dra Dalmau, had lent me Vassula's books and videos, for the same reason I found no time to review them.

As a Neurologist and Neurophysiologist, as well as in my training that included more than three years in Psychiatry, I had read many cases of Freudian's hysterical reactions, automatic writings and so forth. Later I learned, in the hardest way that she is none of them. By that time I told myself: "let's work" and forget about this matter. Then I heard inside of me: "let's pray." Between patients in the emergency room and while listening to the conferences I knelt and prayed.

After the conferences we went to Holy Mass and Communion, there I prayed for God to enlighten me. Then I was invited to have supper with Rev Bishop Hernandez, and Vassula was at his right and Rev Father O'Carroll in front of her. By the time I was introduced to her, her face faded out and turned to look like Jesus face. At that moment I realized I was in front of her but also and as well in front of Him, this was for about thirty seconds. I looked around and again at Vassula's face and still His face was there looking at me with the greatest kindness I have ever seen, and a crown of thorns was on His head. Despite He was smiling to me He was in some sort of deep pain; I wanted to kneel. Then a soft voice coming from Vassula said something to me but I could hardly answer. Again I saw his face. By this time the group noticed something was happening; I was speechless. Now, as Thomas I also repeat "because I have seen, I believe."

I thank Jesus for having answered my questions and as I was eating my meal, I had an emergency call from a nun due to a nearby severe car accident and I had to leave immediately.

I met Vassula for less than fifteen minutes, but was enough to learn that this is God's work, and Jesus is really working in her.

I can say this is the truth, as it happened. I back this up with my good mental health, judgement, my scientific formation and above all God's grace. There is no purpose of personal pride for this privileged moment, neither for Mrs Rydén exaltation but to give testimony of Jesus, the Third person of the Holy Trinity, in this time of Mercy for the whole world.

God Bless you all!

Norma E Agosto Maury, M.D.

Eddy Aguilar Saba
Montaña Sagrada
Puerto Rico

San Juan, February 15, 1994

While I was listening to Vassula, when she was delivering one of most important messages of God, I heard someone whispering "Oh God! Look at the sun." Suddenly, my eyes moved towards the sun and I was just experiencing the most incredible scene I have ever seen. The sun looked so big and so close to me. Somehow it looked transparent, changing colors constantly. It moved up and down very fast. My eyes began to water, my whole body could not move, I knew what I was seeing, but could not say a word. In the meantime, Vassula continued delivering the message of God and the sun was ratifying it. That unexplainable brightness and movement of the sun began disappearing little by little and while this was happening all I could say was "Oh God...Dear God!" I tried to find my friends Carlos and Alice by looking over my shoulders but I could not see them. Vassula was just finishing the message.

Oh God! What a wonderful experience.

Eddy Aguilar Saba

Antonio Pinto
PO Box 364148
San Juan PR 00936-4148

February 14, 1994

To Whom it May Concern

On February 13, I attended a meeting held at the Holy Mountain in San Lorenzo, Puerto Rico. I was assisting as a "Yellow Angel" when, at the precise moment I left the stage, moving towards its front in order to hear the message, I looked up to the sky and saw the sun hiding behind the clouds. These clouds turned into a beautiful golden color, and seeing this, I started taking pictures.

Immediately, the sun came from behind the clouds with unique brilliance. Right then, a veil covered the bright circle and I observed its movements as if it was a clock's pendulum.

The event lasted approximately 3 minutes, and occurred as Vassula was speaking about what Jesus Christ wants from each one of us.

Other people, including my husband Antonio Pinto, witnessed this magnificent experience.

I inform of it so that it be stated, and remain.

Very truly yours,

Cecila Pinto

Alice Quilichini
A #18
Villa Verde, Gudynabo
Puerto Rico 00966

I was all ears, listening to Vassula Rydén present Our Lord's message when a few people behind me started commenting to each other about the sun. My friend Fafico, sitting next to me, wanted to know what was going on. "It's just the miracle of the sun" I said, somewhat despectively. Inside, I felt happy: I'm not the type to be going everywhere looking for signals. I don't need to see. I believe! Besides, I was not sure that this was really happening. People want these types of things to happen and they end up seeing what they want to see. Not becoming elated by the miracle made me feel self-righteous, too, as I remembered a similar incident in Montaña Santa, when Medjugorje visionary Marija indicated that it was more important to pay attention to the heavenly message than to watch these signs.

However... (I guess it was my Guardian Angel) something made me stand up and that's when I saw it:

And for a split-second there I was confused, as I wondered what time it was already, because a huge and beautiful full moon was out. Immediately, I realized this was not the moon. It was the color of the moon and it was round like a full moon, but it was clean and beautiful and holy, like the Holy Host. And then it moved upwards and sideways to the center of the heavenly stage. There, the solar disk became dark as a halo of colors swirled at lightning speed around it.

All this time I just stood there, feeling the greatest joy, thanking Abbá for one more gift of love to His children and also for teaching me a lesson in humility.

Alice Quilichini

Millie Subirá
Centro Paz de Puerto Rico

February 11th, 1994

It was 1.00pm, we got to the restaurant and it was full of people. I felt a little tense because it was very loud and you could hardly talk. We were given a table for six almost immediately. The sitting arrangement came out that I was in front of Vassula and Father O'Carroll in my left. Gogui was beside Vassula. Radamés was in my right corner. Everybody sat down and I looked at Vassula because she was standing in front of her chair. She looked undecided whether to sit or not.

Finally she sat and the menus were brought to us. Father O'Carroll asked
Vassula if she wanted some wine. She said: "no, just water." There was a silence
and I looked at her to try and establish a conversation. When I looked, I saw a
terrible anguish in her languid eyes. It was such a sad sight that I had to lower my
eyes because I was touched by the sadness and grief I saw and felt. I could not bear
it, so I did not dare to look at her.

I said to myself "This is not possible, why can't you look straight at Vassula's
eyes? Why do you feel so moved and uncomfortable, at the same time in front of
her?"   Stubbornly, I tried to establish a normal conversation and I asked her about
Haiti, where they just had a presentation. When she looked at me to answer and she
said "Haiti" in a very distant voice, I saw in her profound eyes such sadness, but at
the same time such a tenderness, that I started to feel I was unworthy of sitting in
front of such a person. Again I could not bear it and touched, I lowered my eyes in
shame.

At this moment, Father O'Carroll answered that everything went very well in
Haiti and that they had a large audience.

There was silence again. For me it was an eternity because of the loud noise
of the people talking around us. I tried to look at Vassula again. At this point she
looks at me to my eyes - but she was not Vassula anymore. Those were not her
eyes, these were the most pure, sad, clear and tender eyes I had ever seen before.
I could say, that the closest to it has been when contemplating Jesus in a beautiful
statue or a painting.

These eyes looked at me directly to my eyes profoundly and smiled to me with
the most beautiful, loving, tender and pure smile I have ever felt. I started to feel
that I was such a sinner and such an unworthy person and still that smile told me that
I was loved and I was called. Then I grieved for all my continued offenses and my
imperfections. Again, I lowered my eyes and tears came into my eyes before this
Powerful Presence I felt there. Now I could not even hear the loud voices anymore.

At that moment, I see that Vassula turns to Gogui to tell her something to her
ear. Gogui answers to Vassula's ear. An my moment was so intense that I thought
that Vassula was asking Gogui to tell me to leave because I was not worthy to be
there in front of her.

Vassula turns to Gogui again and then Gogui tells me that we have to leave.
Now is when I realized, because I have read Vassula's experience when she suffered
Jesus' Passion in Omaha, that she might have started to have the symptoms and that
it was really Jesus who was reflected in her when she looked at me.

Confused, we all stood up. I told the owner of the restaurant that we had to
leave.   Probably they thought that we were not happy with their service or
something. We started down the stairs. Gogui had Vassula on one side. Father
O'Carroll was behind and I was behind Father O'Carroll. Once in the parking, when
I saw her walking in front of me, it was not Vassula's slender body, it was a much
stronger and larger body, tumbling with a very heavy load that could hardly carry
it, she almost fell down.

Once in the automobile she fell. I went to my car because it was behind theirs.

We left to Gogui's house and I was alone in my car and I started to say the rosary and to cry when I realized how unworthy and small I was and how merciful and loving was God with me. I could not forget that look and that smile.

I could only say two decades of the rosary when I got to Gogui's. We started to try to carry her out of the automobile to a room. We were 5 persons and we could not carry her. I carried just one leg, because I could not carry both. They were too heavy.

Finally we got to a room and put her on the bed. There started the real anguish. It was unbearable to see the suffering because we have been so imperfect. She contorted silently and Father O'Carroll tried to soothe her.

Gogui and I fell to our knees, I closed my eyes and we started to say the Sorrowful Mysteries, as it was Friday.

Before that suffering, the only thing I could think of was on how, because of our sins and putrefaction He was suffering like this. He was really alive. We were totally unworthy of His Sacrifice. I grieved for my sins and those of the whole world.

Throughout the Rosary she moaned faintly. At the fifth mystery, the Death of Our Lord Jesus, the moaning stopped and I opened my eyes and she was in the exact position as Jesus on the cross, her feet, her head slightly to one side and her hands and fingers, just like a crucifix.

In a while, we thought it was over because she asked to be seated down in a chair. So we looked for the chair and at that moment I had a phone call so I went out of the room.

When I came back thinking that it was over, I saw Vassula laying on the bed again, suffering and moaning.

Somebody called again, as we were coordinating Vassula's presentation the next day, so I had to leave the room again.

When I came back she was on the floor, in the crucifix position except for one arm that was holding tightly a crucifix toward her heart. This time the whole body was suspended in the air except for her feet and wrists. The grief continued and in a very low voice she said something to Father O'carroll and Gogui asked me to look for paper and pen. So I ran out again and when I got in she was on her knees, still with her crucifix in one hand, but now both arms extended in an upward position. It was at that moment that she started to say His Message crying desperately "I AM losing so many... I Am losing so many of My children..." While saying this she was clinging to Radamés who was standing in front of her, Gogui was holding her in the back, Father O'Carroll was sitting on bed next to her and I was kneeling writing down the message.

It was 3.00pm. She cried out very loud now... Gogui started saying and I repeated: Jesus, help us help you, Jesus help us help you... like a promise.

After this she fell to the floor and soon it was over. We finally had lunch at 5.00pm.

Millie Subirá

Radamés A Arroyo
3166 Manhattan College
Riverdale, N.Y. 10471

February 16, 1994

To: Father Michael O'Carroll and Vassula Rydén

I am Puertorrican, 24 years of age and an engineer student in Manhattan
College at New York City. I came to Puerto Rico just to listen to the messages of
Vassula Rydén.

On Friday, February 11, 1994 I, Radamés Arroyo experienced a new and an
unforgettable event. I will like to give my testimony.

Everything started around 1.00 pm when Vassula said "I do not feel well, let's
go to the house." We stood up from the table and started walking to the car.
Vassula looked so tired that she could hardly walk to the car, so I tried to help her
to get to the car. From the restaurant's table to the car she fell down one time. I
tried to lift her up, with Father O'Carroll's and Gogui's help, and I realized that she
was kind of heavy.

During the ride from the restaurant to the house she was like in ecstasy. She
moved just once or twice making noises like if she was suffering inside her. All the
others in the car: Father O'Carroll, Gogui and myself were praying all the time.

As soon as we got to the house, Father O'Carroll and myself tried to bring her
out of the car. It was almost impossible. She was so heavy that Father O'Carroll
and me could not lift her up, therefore three other people helped us bring her out of
the car and take her to a bedroom.

I remembered that she fell down one more time when we were carrying her
from the car to the bedroom and the only thing that came into my mind was: "God
please help me, I am the only young man here between three women and an elderly
man." At that time I knew that I was not carrying Vassula's body, I felt it was
Jesus' body.

Finally we lay her down in the bed and suddenly she stretched the arms and
crossed her legs as Jesus in the crucifix. After a few minutes she fell down again
to the floor and took the same position as "Crucified Jesus." After some time she
raised her right arm and started blessing everybody in the room. I was the only one
that did not lower my head, so she touched me and did the cross in my face with two
of her fingers. For the second time she turned her face to look for me and tried to
bless me again. I could not get hold of myself, so I kneeled and she blessed me.
I closed my eyes and started to cry and pray. I could not believe in that moment
what I was experiencing.

When I opened my eyes I saw Vassula levitating, holding all her body just with
the tip of her feet and the top of her head. She had both arms stretched. She was

like 4 inches from the floor for about 4 to 5 minutes. She gave a message and it was written.

All the Passion experience took about two hours: from 1.00 pm to 3.00 in the afternoon.

Gregoria Merced
Acropolis QQ-1 APOLO
Guaynabo
Puerto Rico 00969

Given by: Dr Gregoria Merced, Director Centro Paz de Puerto Rico

On Friday, February 11, 1994, after Vassula Rydén and Father O'Carroll had a televised interview on Channel 11, Millie Subira, a member of Centro Paz, a young man named Radames Arroyo and I invited them for lunch at a restaurant. When seated and water served, Vassula told me in my ear: "I do not feel well." I told her "Do you want to leave?" She said "what about your lunch?" I replied "If you do not feel well we will leave." I immediately told Father O'Carroll and the other two that Vassula was not well and that we must leave. When Vassula stood up she told me in my ear "I am feeling the symptoms of the Passion." When I heard that I felt mixed emotions; I shivered and felt joy at the same time because I realized that I could have a living Jesus; sadness because The Passion is painful and fear thinking that Vassula could fall in front of so many people.

We helped her down the stairs, since the restaurant is located on a second floor. When we were half way to the parking lot where the care was parked, she (Vassula), had her <u>first fall</u>. She looked like Jesus carrying the cross, her expression was of pain, her weight was becoming heavier and more difficult to sustain by us. Father O'Carroll, young Radames and I tried to lift her but we could not. We then had to pull her all the way to the car. In the car, we laid her down on the back seat with her head on my lap; her feet were down. On the way home we could see the signs of pain on her face and the stiffness and weight of her body. When we reached my house and parked the car, we tried to pull her out. A fifth person had to help and we could hold her. At that moment she had her <u>second fall</u>. We had to pull her from the open area where the car was parked, to a bedroom in front of the area.

In the bedroom, we had to use all our strength to lay her on the bed. She immediately took the position of the cross, her arms extended; the index and center fingers extended and rigid, the rest of the fingers down. Vassula was cold and tense; her face revealing pain but at the same time peace. There was not sign of despair

in her pain. Her body was in the same position as a crucified: her feet one on top
of the other, her knees and legs were bent, her head was erect and raised in the air,
(not laying on the bed). Her body, with the exception of one of her heels and the
back of her hands, was levitating around six (6) inches from the bed. Father
O'Carroll gave her a drop of water because she felt thirsty. She retained the above
described position for a long time until she tried to stand up. We again pulled with
all our strength and sat her on a chair. It was impossible to keep her seated, so we
laid her on the floor. She again took the position of the cross. She tried again to
stand up and laid her head on my arm, (I was kneeling beside her). Her head was
down and I caressed her face and her hair and told her: "Jesus, I love you." She
opened her eyes, showing a light blue color with a sweet and loving look that I will
never forget (I want to point out that Vassula's eyes are brown). Her weight was so
heavy that I could not hold her and she had the <u>third fall</u>. I was so shaken with
emotion since I felt and truly believe that I had Jesus in my arms. I asked for help
to accommodate her on the floor. She called me with her eyes and I approached her;
she then made the sign of the cross on my forehead with the two fingers that were
maintained erect and were felt as two bars of ice. It was impossible to bend the
fingers.

We placed her on the bed and I felt in my heart that she was going to give a
message. I told Millie Subirá to get pencil and paper but before Millie came back,
Vassula was whispering in my ear the initial part of the message: "THERE IS NO
PEACE IN THE WORLD. PRAY, PRAY." She gave the messages slowly until
completion. Later on we gave her a cup of tea and she started recuperating from
The Passion. She was very weak and had to go to her room and rest. The rest of
the day, including the evening, she was feeling weak.

This has been the most significant experience I have had in my life.

Gregoria Merced

―――――――――――――

February 14, 1994

My dear sister Vassula

In union to Mary and Jesus Christ, I send you peace and my love and do thank
my Eternal One that He has wished that I write to you my experience of February
12, 1994 in your visit to Manati, Puerto Rico. I postrated (sic) myself to the Blessed
Trinity and pray that my testimony be inspired by the Holy Spirit in Truth and Love,
through the maternal and loving intercession of my dear Blessed Mother Mary and
my Guardian Angel, Fabian.

The graces which Jesus bestowed upon me occurred during your prayer of the Rosary. They began during the first mystery, when I started feeling inner currents of electricity over my body. At the end of the mystery, I began to see a constant and pulsing aureole of white light around your head, Vassula. Then, to my amazement and joy, I began to see that your whole face and figure was becoming that of Jesus. At first it was a glimpse that would come and go on two or three occasions, but later it became more constant. These transformations involved me in an ecstatic state, during which I could only pray mentally the Rosary for I was so overcome in a divine presence in my whole being. The light was now of a golden color. The face of Jesus was similar of that one of Jackie Hass's 'Jesus Our Saviour' but also of a slight resemblance to that of Turin. His aspect was one of hardship and seemed to me how He would have looked while He predicated in His journeys in Jerusalem. Then, the light became a greyish blue around your figure with a certain quietness.

Upon the third or fourth mystery, the experience became more powerful, that the vision of my Lord was constant for about a whole mystery. I should mention my friend Priscilla Martinez, who was seated next to me, because we had simultaneous experiences on two occasions. She was moved to kneel; I followed. My tears would flow profusely upon this loving presence for it was so intense and of total transformation.

Vassula, while you spoke and quoted Jesus' exact words, which you read in Spanish, I also experienced more glow around you. These were words full of authority and loving wisdom.

We have been so blessed by Our Lord Jesus and Our Mother Mary with your visit to Puerto Rico. We shall be praying for you and hope that you can come again. Please pray for us, especially for our bishops and the union of our dioceses.

May the love of the Blessed Trinity always keep us.
Your sister in Jesus and Mary

Nydia

Nydia Hernández
Calle "C" No.25
Garcia Rio
Piedras
Puerto Rico 00926

This is the testimony of Fr Francis Frost, a Catholic priest working in the World Council of Churches:

September 12th 1993

On Good Friday 1991, Vassula decided to visit me in the afternoon, because she wanted to see an Orthodox priest in the main building at tea time. She was accompanied by her friend Beatrice, her spiritual director was then James Fannan and an Orthodox woman who did not chose to sit down with the others in my flat, but went straight to the main building.

The four of us, then, sat down to after-lunch tea in my study-bedroom. Vassula sat between James Fannan and myself; Beatrice was in an armchair on the other side of the room. At a point in the conversation, which roamed over a variety of subjects, none of them particularly spiritual or religious, Vassula turned to me to say something. As she did so, her face became as the face of Jesus in His Passion. The look Jesus gave me was at one and the same time full of immense tenderness and yet mingled with reproach: "I have loved you like this, why do you not love me more?" I could not but think of the "Ecce Homo" in chapter 18 of the gospel of St John, having recently noted that, if one examines the whole structure of the chapter, one finds that these words are pivotal in the whole trial scene. Proof was also forthcoming that I was not deluded, because, as Vassula turned back towards Beatrice on the other side of the room, James Fannan, who was looking across Vassula towards me said: "Francis, what have you seen?" He must have noticed that the effect of what I had seen was to make my eyes rigid in their sockets.

I told him briefly what I had seen, while Vassula was occupied in other conversation. He simply said words to the effect of: "That is a grace for you and you must treasure it." This is the first time that I have tried to write the account of what happened. As I write, I realise that it is as clear to me as if it had taken place yesterday.

Fr Francis Frost

I will conclude this chapter with a letter from the Orthodox Archbishop in Jerusalem, David Sahagian:

Armenian Patriarchate
PO Box 14235
Jerusalem
Israel

Dear Ms Rydén

It is an occasion of great pleasure and personal satisfaction for us to recognize in you a new catalyst of spiritual rejuvenation who can talk to our present generation in a most persuasive language, through the books you are publishing.

Your inspired mission of bringing the message of Christ to others is a source of profound joy to the Church. And your indefatigable zeal of drawing strength from and seeking regeneration and reinforcement in your Greek roots, should set an enviable example of dedicated fidelity, to our tortured youth.

In our days, at a time when crass materialism has taken such a deep root in the hearts of men, it is refreshing to know that all is not lost, that there still are among us people like yourself who are in communion with the Creator, and able to transmit to us the benefit of your inspiration.

We take pride in encouraging your ecumenical mission and pray for your success.

We look forward to reading your next book.

Meanwhile, we send you our blessings from the Holy City of God, and ask the Lord to keep you and guard you.

Archbishop David Sahagian
Chancellor & Grand Sacristan

APPENDIX I

BALAMAND DECLARATION

Declaration of the joint International Commission for theological dialogue between the Catholic Church and the Orthodox Church.

Introduction

1. At the request of the Orthodox Church, the normal sequence of theological dialogue with the Catholic Church was interrupted so that the question known as "uniatism" could be immediately approached.
2. As regards the method which has been called "uniatism", it was declared at Freising (June 1990) that "we reject it as a means of seeking unity, because it is opposed to the common tradition of our Churches."
3. In regard to the Eastern Catholic Churches, it is clear that they have, as part of the Catholic Communion, the right to exist and act in response to the spiritual needs of their faithful.
4. The document drawn up at Arricia by the joint coordinating committee (June 1991) and completed at Balamand (June 1993) shows the method we choose in the actual search for full communion, giving also the reasons for excluding "uniatism" as a method.
5. This document comprises two parts: a) Ecclesiological principles, and b) Practical rules.

Ecclesiological Principles

6. The division between the Churches of the East and the West not only has never quenched the desire for the unity willed by Christ, but frequently this situation opposed to the nature of the Church has been for many an opportunity of achieving a more lively consciousness of the need there is to accomplish this unity so as to be faithful to the Lord's commandment.
7. Through the centuries varying attempts have been made to re-establish this unity. They sought to attain this goal by different ways, at times conciliar, in

accord with the political, historic, theological and spiritual situation of each epoch. Unfortunately, none of these efforts succeeded in re-establishing full communion between the Church of the West and the Church of the East, and at times they even hardened the opposing positions.

8. During the last four centuries in different regions of the Orient, initiatives were taken from within certain Churches and under pressure from external elements, to re-establish communion between the Church of the East and the Church of the West. These initiatives led to the union of certain communities with the See of Rome, and entailed, as a consequence, a break in communion with their mother churches of the East. That took place not without the intrusion of extra-ecclesial interests. Thus were born the Catholic Oriental Churches, and thus a situation was created which became a source of conflicts and sufferings, first for the Orthodox, but also for Catholics.

9. Whatever about the intention and the genuineness of the will to be faithful to the commandment of the Lord, 'That they may be one', one must note that the re-establishment of unit between the Church of the East and the Church of the West has not been attained, and that the division persists, envenomened by these initiatives.

10. The situation thus created was in effect to give rise to tensions and oppositions. Progressively, in the decades following these unions, missionary activity put among its priorities, the effort to convert other Christians, individually or in groups, to have them return to one's own Church. To justify this tendency, which was a source of proselytism, the Catholic Church developed the theological outlook by which it set itself forward as the sole depository of salvation. In reaction, the Orthodox Church, in turn, came to adopt the same outlook, according to which, salvation was to be found only with her. To assure the salvation of "separated brethren", it happened that Christians were re-baptised and the demands of the religious freedom of persons and of their act of faith were forgotten, at the time little importance was attached to such things.

11. On the other hand, some civil authorities made attempts to bring back Eastern Catholics to the Church of their forefathers. To this end, when the opportunity was available, they did not hesitate to use objectionable means.

12. Because of the way in which Catholics and Orthodox see themselves anew in their relation to the mystery of the Church, and are again finding themselves as sister Churches, this form of missionary apostolate just described, known as "uniatism" is no longer acceptable neither as a practical method, nor as a model of the unity sought by our Churches.

13. In effect, especially since the Panorthodox conferences and the Second Vatican Council, the rediscovery and the development of the idea of the Church as communion, as much by Orthodox as by Catholics, has radically changed perspectives and attitudes.

On one side and the other it is recognised that what Christ entrusted to his

Church - the profession of apostolic faith, participation in the same Sacraments, especially in the unique priesthood celebrating the unique sacrifice of Christ, the apostolic succession of bishops - cannot be considered the exclusive property of one of our Churches. In this context it is evident that all re-baptism is ruled out.

14. This is the reason why the Catholic Church and the Orthodox Church mutually recognize themselves as sister Churches, together responsible for the maintenance of the Church of God in fidelity to the divine plan, especially in what concerns unity. According to the words of Pope John Paul II, the ecumenical effort of the sister Churches of the East and the West, based on dialogue and prayer seeks perfect, total communion which will be neither absorption nor fusion but encounter in truth and love (cf. *Slavorum Gentes*, I, 27).

15. While respecting the inviolable freedom of persons and the universal obligation to follow the demands of conscience, there is no question in the effort to re-establish unity, of seeking conversion of persons from one Church to another to ensure their salvation. What matters is to realize together the will of Christ for those who are his and the plan of God on his Church through common search between Churches, for complete agreement on the content of the faith and it implications. This effort is pursued in the ongoing theological dialogue. The present document marks a necessary stage in this dialogue.

16. The Catholic eastern Churches who have wished to re-establish full communion with the See of Rome and are thereto faithful, have the rights and obligations which are linked with this communion to which they belong. To rule their attitude towards Orthodox Churches they have the principles set forth by the Second Vatican Council and given effect by the Popes who specified the practical consequences in different documents published since then. These Churches then must be brought into the dialogue of charity, in mutual respect and revived reciprocal confidence, at the local and universal levels, and they must enter theological dialogue with all its practical implications.

17. In this atmosphere, the preceding considerations and the practical rules which follow, to the degree that they are really accepted and faithfully observed, are capable of leading to a just and definitive solution of the difficulties occasioned by these eastern Catholic Churches for the Orthodox Church.

18. In regard to this, Pope Paul VI had stated in his address at the Phanar in July 1967 "that it is on the leaders and hierarchy of the Churches that it devolves to lead the Churches on the way that will bring them to a refound full communion. They must do this while recognising and respecting each other as pastors of the part of Christ's flock entrusted to them, being attentive to the cohesion and growth of the People of God and avoiding everything that could cause a break or confusion in its ranks" (*Tomos Agapis*, n.172). In this spirit Pope John Paul II and Ecumenical Patriarch Dimitrios together made this explicit statement: "We reject every form of proselytism, every attitude which could be or be seen to be a lack of respect..."

Practical Rules

19. Mutual respect between Churches which are in difficult situations will increase notably to the degree that they follow the practical rules hereafter.
20. These rules will not resolve the problems which weigh on us if there is not first on each side a will to pardon, based on the Gospel, and at the heart of the constant effort towards renewal, a desire ceaselessly revived to recover the full communion which existed for more than a millennium between our Churches. It is here that the dialogue of love must enter with an intensity and perseverance ever renewed, for it alone can overcome mutual misunderstanding, and it is the climate necessary for a more profound theological dialogue which will clear the way for full communion.
21. The first step is to end everything which could maintain discord, contempt or hatred between the Churches. The authorities of the Catholic Church will to this end help the eastern Catholic Churches and their communities to prepare full communion between the Catholic and Orthodox Churches. The authorities of the Orthodox Church will act in like manner with their faithful.
    Thus the extremely complex situation which arose in central and eastern Europe, both for Catholics and Orthodox, can be handled in both charity and justice.
22. The pastoral activity of the Catholic Church both Latin and Oriental no longer seeks to have the faithful pass from óne Church to another; that it no longer aims at proselytism among the Orthodox. It aims at meeting the spiritual needs of its own faithful and has no wish to expand at the expense of the Orthodox Church. In these perspectives, in order to avoid distrust and suspicion, it is necessary to have reciprocal information on the different pastoral projects, that thus between the bishops and officials of our Churches co-operation may begin and develop.
23. The history of relations between the Orthodox Church and the eastern Catholic Churches has been marked by persecutions and sufferings. Whatever these sufferings and their causes may have been, they warrant no triumphalism; no one can take the glory in them or use them as an argument to accuse or belittle the other Church. God alone knows his true witness. Whatever the past has been, it must be left to the mercy of God, and all the energies of the Churches must be bent to ensuring that the present and future are more in keeping with the will of Christ for those who belong to him.
24. On one side and the other also bishops and all those in official positions must scrupulously allow for the religious freedom of the faithful. These must be able to express their opinion freely on being consulted or in grouping to this purpose. Religious freedom really demands that, especially in situations of conflict, the faithful be able to set forth their choice and decide without external pressure whether they wish to be in communion with the Orthodox Church or with the Catholic Church. Religious freedom would be violated when, under

the cover of financial aid, an attempt would be made to attract the faithful of the other Church by promising them, for example, education and the material advantages lacking in their own Church.

In this context social help must be organised in agreement, as every philanthropical activity, to avoid the appearance of new suspicions.

25. In other respects the necessary respect for Christian liberty - one of the most precious gifts received in Christ, should not be an occasion for initiating, without previous consultation with the authorities in these Churches, pastoral projects which would also involve the faithful of these Churches. Not only should all pressure, of whatever kind, be excluded, but respect for consciences, coming from a genuine motive of faith, is one of the principles ruling the pastoral care of the authorities in the two Churches and should be the object of their consultation.

26. This is why open dialogue must be sought and undertaken in the first place between those who have responsibility in the Churches on the spot. The leaders of each of the communities involved will set up local commissions with equal representation, or will ensure the efficacy of those in existence, to find solutions for concrete problems and to have these solutions applied in truth and love, in justice and peace.

If agreement cannot be reached at a local level, the question should be referred to the higher authorities working as joint commissions.

27. Distrust would more easily disappear if both sides condemned violence wherever communities practise it against the communities of a sister Church. As His Holiness Pope John Paul II asks, in his letter of 31 May, 1991, all violence and every kind of pressure must be avoided so that freedom of conscience is respected.

It is for the leaders of communities to help their faithful to deepen their loyalty to their own Church and its tradition, and to teach them to avoid not only violence, be it physical, verbal or moral but everything which could lead to contempt for other Christians, to hostile witness, ridiculing the work of salvation which is reconciliation in Christ.

28. Faith in sacramental reality implies that one respects all the liturgical celebrations of other Churches. Use of violence to take over a place of worship contradicts this conviction. This, on the contrary, demands that in certain circumstances one should facilitate the celebration by other Churches, making one's own church available to them, by an agreement allowing alternative celebration at different times in the same building.

More than that, gospel ethics demands that one abstain from declaration or manifestations liable to perpetuate a state of conflict and to harm dialogue. Does St Paul not exhort us to be welcoming to one another, as Christ was for us to the glory of God? (cf. Rom 15:7)

29. Bishops and priests have the duty before God of respecting the authority the Holy Spirit has given to bishops and priests of the other Church, and to that

end, to avoid interfering in the spiritual life of the faithful of this Church. When cooperation becomes necessary for their good, the leaders are required to act in concert, fixing clear bases, known to all, for this mutual aid, acting then frankly and openly, respecting the sacramental discipline of the other Church.

In this context, to avoid all misunderstanding, and to develop trust between the two Churches, it is necessary that Catholic and Orthodox bishops of the same territory, should consult each other before implementation of Catholic pastoral projects, which entail the creation of new structures in regions traditionally dependent on the jurisdiction of the Orthodox Church, this to avoid parallel pastoral activities which would risk becoming quickly competitive and even conflicting.

30. To prepare future relations between the two Churches, going beyond the out of date ecclesiology of return to the Catholic Church bound up with the problem with which this document is dealing, special attention will be given to the preparation of future priests, and of all those in any way involved in apostolic activity exercised where the other Church is traditionally rooted. Their education must be objectively positive in regard to the other Church. All must be instructed in the apostolic succession of the other Church and of the genuineness of its sacramental life.

   In the same way an honest and overall view of history should be given to all, proceeding towards a historiography which is in agreement and even common between the two Churches. This will help to dispel prejudices and will avoid history being used in a polemical manner. This view will give an awareness that the wrongs of the separation were shared, leaving deep wounds on one side and the other.

31. We shall remember the warning of the apostle Paul to the Corinthians (1 Cor 6:1-7) advising Christians to settle their disagreements by means of fraternal dialogue, which would save them from relying on the intervention of civil authorities for the practical solution of the problems which arise between Churches of local communities.

   This bears especially on the possession or restitution of ecclesiastical goods. These must not be founded solely on past situations, or rely entirely on general juridical principles, but must take account of the complexity of present pastoral realities and of local circumstances.

32. In this spirit the re-evangelization of our secularized world can be faced together. An effort will be made to give the mass-media unbiased news, especially to the religious press, to that inexact or tendentious information will be eschewed.

33. It is necessary that the Churches should associate to express gratitude and respect for all those, known and unknown, bishops, priests or faithful, Orthodox, eastern or Latin Catholics, who have suffered, confessed their faith and witnessed to their fidelity to the Church, and, in general, to all Christians

without discrimination who have suffered persecution.

Their sufferings summon us to unity, and to give, in our turn, a common witness to answer the prayer of Christ, "that all may be one, that the world may believe" (Jn 17:21).

34. The Joint International Commission for Theological Dialogue between the Catholic Church and the Orthodox Church, at a plenary meeting in Balamand, strongly recommends that these practical rules be implemented by our Churches, including the Eastern Catholic Churches, called to take part in this dialogue which must be pursued in the serene atmosphere necessary to its progress, towards the re-establishment of full communion.

35. By excluding for the future all proselytism, and every will to increase the number of Catholics at the expense of the Orthodox Church, the Commission hopes that it has eliminated the obstacle which pushed certain autocephalous Churches to suspend their participation in the theological dialogue, and that the Orthodox Church will be able to come back fully to continue the theological work so happily begun.

Balamand, Lebanon, 23 June, 1993

APPENDIX II

CRITICISM

How to deal with criticism of Vassula presents a problem to one seeking to make her well known, to inform people of her mission, to remove obstacles to their faith in her messages. The first reaction is towards direct confrontation. But the danger here is that bitterness is engendered, charity suffers and in such conditions acceptance of a Christian message is difficult. For the moment the best solution appears to be to avoid personal names and reply to points of criticism made. But there are certain preliminaries it will serve to state.

First, Vassula is a member of the Greek Orthodox Church. As has been made clear in the chapter on the Orthodox, they have been overlooked if not neglected in the ecumenical movement; the respect and sensitivity which in the true spirit of Vatican II they can expect have been at times painfully lacking. Some of the criticism made of Vassula shows no restraint or delicacy. In fact there is a harshness, an aggressive manner, patronizing language totally foreign to enlightened, considerate dialogue. The aim is to crush at any cost.

Without entering into polemical matters I register the fact that in the attitude taken towards her I was thrown back to pre-conciliar days when Catholics thought it appropriate to avoid Protestants, would have thought dialogue a compromise if not betrayal and delighted in every wounding blow that disturbed the "enemy", or undermined his thinking. Offensive language was not discouraged. Since I was engaged in dialogue with Protestants twenty years before Vatican II, I speak from personal experience.

One is tempted to ask: did Vatican II take place? Are faithful sons and daughters of the Church bound to follow its directives, especially in this sensitive area? Do you overlook the advice afforded in the Decree on Ecumenism and in the recently revised Ecumenical Directory, as you line up your preferred target? Do you laugh off the tragic verdict of the joint commission of Catholic and Orthodox theologians? Do you reserve all your most hurtful and inconsiderate language for an attack on the one Orthodox writer in over nine hundred years closest to Catholic theology and devotion? Do you dismiss as irrelevant that this is the first Orthodox writer in history to proclaim the universal primacy of the Roman Pontiff?

The iron law of history operates: men are masters of their words and deeds, but not of the consequences of these. They are bound to consider what these consequences <u>may</u> be. Here they need not delay long. Where there is tension between Catholics and Orthodox, as in parts of Russia, news of ill-treatment of an Orthodox Christian at the hands of Catholics, especially Catholic priests, will confirm the worst fears. Certain members of the Greek Orthodox Church who are tempted to dismiss Catholic overtures towards them as window-dressing, will have here evidence of what they may take to be the real Catholic intention. That is to crush the Orthodox. After all here are Catholic priests trying to do just that to Vassula.

I turn now to the evidence which I have of Catholic criticism directed against Vassula. I note first a grave defect in methodology. The critics attacked the texts without addressing the preliminary questions.

The first question is this: How, apart from an overwhelming divine intervention, does one explain this established fact - a lady who was a glittering success in worldly terms, as a painter, a tennis champion, wife of a high ranking official in aid to the Third World, with access to the social round at the highest level, indifferent to religion, non-practising though certainly not hostile, suddenly breaks with this whole pattern, takes on a mentality, a behaviour, life style and activity related to a value system totally different from the life hitherto lived? Instead of living her days on the tennis court she spends them on her knees in communication with the Lord, this exercise taking five, six or seven hours - quite recently nine hours, daily. Is such a total transformation explainable in terms of the human psyche unaided by special supernatural help? Can the critics cite any previous or contemporary examples of such a psychological phenomenon?

The second question which the critic must address, as a prelude to his investigation and evaluation, is this: What is the origin, apart from direct divine communication, of the body of theological and spiritual doctrine contained in the published works of Vassula Rydén? Anyone acquainted with the literature of theology, theoretical or applied, at a professional or popular level, or with spiritual writings, knows that such works are generally the product of much study, of theological or spiritual formation. With such an advantage they may make very little impact. Rarely does one encounter such writings very widely translated. In the course of the present century there certainly are not many literary successes in the domain of spiritual literature. St Thérèse of Lisieux and Dom Columba Marmion undoubtedly. How many others? But in Vassula we are dealing with a writer translated within four years into twenty-two languages, endorsed by theologians of stature, the whole expansion appearing spontaneously, with none of the machinery normally necessary. There has been no literary agent, no request to anyone to undertake translation. It is volunteers who have come forward seeking authorization to translate.

The essential problem remains: Where did Vassula get the contents? She started a complete blank in matters religious. She had no theological instruction, not even elementary catechetical training. Whatever as a child she had heard about these things had vanished through thirty years of religious indifference. At the time of her conversion in November, 1985, she did not even know the difference between a priest and a parson; she had no sort of idea that souls could receive direct messages from God, Our Lady, St Michael or their guardian angel.

The third question preliminary to assessment of the message turns on the spiritual relationship between Vassula and what may be called a world-wide constituency. Why do people mostly not of her own communion, that is not Orthodox, come in so many different countries to hear her? It was the great Newman, the imperial intellect, who expounded so convincingly the essential role of the faithful in matters of doctrine. He went so far as to say that the faithful saved the day in the greatest crisis in the Church's history, fourth century Arianism. *Sensus fidelium* is the word used to designate this stirring of the Spirit within the body of believers. We are witnesses presently to two clear manifestations of this light or force, Medjugorje and Vassula Rydén.

More than any previous Pope, John Paul II teaches repeatedly that the laity enjoy the charisms of the Spirit.

So we have a methodology dictated by three fundamental problems. If the answer to each is that we are in presence of special divine intervention then subsequent study will be respectful and exacting. But first let us not forget the respect for the dignity and rights of the human person. These claims are inscribed in the natural law and they have been emphasized in our time by Popes, notably Pius XII and John XXIII, and by the Second Vatican Council. One such right which most legal systems guarantee is to one's reputation. From some acquaintance with popular writing on alleged visions and private revelations I can say that commentators, and even people in authority, often make little of such a right.

I have some examples of such cavalier conduct in the treatment of Vassula. I have not in over fifty years experience of editors and publishers in many countries encountered anything so nonsensical and shabby as came my way from an American Catholic publication. Three substantial articles were published in criticism of her, and I was given to understand that I would be allowed to reply. I sent an article entitled "Why I support Vassula Rydén", which appears in this appendix. It was not printed and in answer to my query I was told by an editor obviously embarrassed that he had orders that the paper should not "weigh in" on this subject. They had already "weighed in" negatively in three successive issues!

The author of these articles also produced a "first" in my life: he published extracts from a letter I wrote him without the courtesy of seeking my permission. He also misconstrued a remark of mine, unintentionally I hope. As a brother priest I informed him that the Lord had spoken to Vassula about her critics and this would appear, in the normal way, in her published writings. Illogically he characterized this friendly gesture as a "threat". He cannot hope for much mileage there. I've never threatened anyone in the course of a long life. The illogicality is that he should take any notice of what will appear in a series of messages to which he gives no credence. He may suffer from what I call "critics' syndrome." Those who are ruthless in attacking others show amazing tenderness and sensitivity when they are the target, even when a reply based on justice is directed against them.

Another writer in the course of a booklet on apparitions and special graces made the statement which had not been checked with Vassula that she forecast an earthquake in California. She never said any such thing. I pointed this out to the author; my letter was not acknowledged, and I have no evidence that any correction was made.

Worse still was to come from the United States. A weekly Catholic paper published an article on Vassula written in language singularly offensive. One letter of protest from me was published, but in a second I had to reply to a disgraceful allegation that Vassula described her union with Christ in physical terms. In his comment on my letter the editor quoted as proof a passage in which Jesus says to Vassula that his cross will be their "marriage-bed." I then had to inform him that this was the symbolic language of mysticism. He was reading it as would one who took the allegory of the vine as a lesson in botany! I also told him that the very idea, in identical terms, was found in the autobiography of St Margaret Mary Alacoque, a fact unknown to Vassula when she heard these words from Jesus. In this second letter I also pointed out to the editor that Vassula had spoken to Orthodox and Anglican audiences - he had maintained that she, very strangely he thought, spoke only to Catholics.

This important assertion of truth in regard to a person's reputation was not published. Does this paper campaign for justice on behalf of Catholics? Catholics only? Do they publish resounding statements on the "sacred rights of the human person"? Where does the concept of sin arise in behaviour of this kind? Are not calumny and detraction sinful?

The first article in the paper carried an insinuation which one meets from time to time that Vassula profits financially from her mission ("she'll make a lot of bucks"). She does not take a cent from her published writings. She would be perfectly entitled to claim author's royalties; she does not do so. From the sales figures supplied to me by her French publisher, M. F X de Guibert, I have calculated, allowing for a minimum royalty of ten per cent, that on the French edition alone she has now sacrificed half a million French francs! Gifts of money offered to her spontaneously she transfers to charities, preferably to a fund to purchase her books for prisoners. In 1992 she received twenty thousand deutschmarks and gave it immediately to a Childrens' Hospital in Moscow. I am happy to add that her two publishers in the English-speaking world, Pat Callahan of Trinitas (Independence, Missouri) and Mrs Christine Lynch of Belfast, run their publishing on a non-profit basis.

Rejected Letter A:

Why I support Vassula Rydén

Twenty years before Vatican II as a member of the first inter-faith society in Ireland since the Reformation, the Mercier Society, I worked for Christian unity; at the same time as a member of the Pillar of Fire Society I worked for better relations between Catholics and Jews. Neither initiative was, in the closed circuit religious climate of the time, officially welcome. Each was, with the administrative propriety required, terminated. I retained the urge towards Christian unity and as a priest journalist during the Council, supported all that was done for this cause, as I have tried to do since.

I have stated frequently in public and have written that ecumenism launched by the Council and so fully endorsed by the Papacy has shown one mainline defect, inadequate attention to the Orthodox. The preoccupation with Protestants - and I write as one with Protestant relatives and lifelong Protestant friends - has had one disastrous effect on the Catholic body, the assault on Marian theology and devotional practice. To placate certain Protestant bodies this policy was adopted, giving us, in the words of the biblical scholar, Ignace de la Potterie, SJ, at the International Mariological Congress in Huelva last September "a decade without Mary." Hyperbole but a valid point. Attention to the Orthodox would have shown the folly of such an attitude. In that world the wealth of the ages surrounds the Theotokos, and it is not, in the slightest detail, negotiable.

That is an effect of the failure I regret. In substance things were worse. And they remain so. Before anyone decries this harsh judgement let him or her read the report of the joint commission of Orthodox and Catholic theologians issued after the meeting held in the Lebanon in June last.   The division, we read, remains and it is envenomed (*envenimé*) by some of the initiatives taken. So this is our achievement in the twenty-nine years which have elapsed since Vatican II promulgated the Decree on Ecumenism. I am not even dealing with the Russian problem.

In the general area of failure and frustration there has been one sign of hope, Vassula Rydén, who already has a world-wide Catholic constituency, but is Orthodox, increasingly supported by her churches. I am not here entering into polemical matters, I just register the fact generally that in the attitude taken towards her by some of my fellow priests I was thrown back to pre-conciliar days when Catholics thought it appropriate to avoid Protestants, would have thought dialogue a compromise if not betrayal, and delighted in every wounding blow that disturbed the "enemy" or undermined his thinking. Offensive language was not discouraged. I know what I am talking about!

Did Vatican II take place? Are faithful sons and daughters of the Church bound to follow its directives, especially in this sensitive area? Do you overlook the advice afforded in the Decree and in the recently issued Ecumenical Directory, as you line up your preferred target? Do you laugh off the tragic verdict of the joint commission? Do you especially behave thus to the one Orthodox writer in 900 years closest to us? The only Orthodox writer ever to proclaim the universal primacy of the Roman Pontiff?

In studying the work of Vassula I have refused to take this negative approach, intrinsically, as I see it, disobedient and radically cynical. I have no reason to regret my decision. In the book which I have written on her I have shown the quite remarkable content of her writings as judged by two simple criteria: source and degree of harmony with Catholic thinking. Her source was humanly speaking nil. She started to write her books, the series now within four years many times re-edited and translated into nineteen languages with others pending (the translations include Russian, Greek, Arabic, Japanese), *True Life in God*, from a mind utterly blank on theology or spirituality; she did not even have elementary catechetical training and religion had been absent from her life for thirty years.

Vassula writes on the Trinity exactly as St Simeon the New Theologian, whom she had not read before publishing her books. Those who do not accept her own explanation of the source of her knowledge have a problem; where did she get it? Though Orthodox and remaining so, and identifying with her Church, she expounds a spirituality which is entirely acceptable to Catholics. Here I should need space to apply the second criterion, the conformity of Vassula's teaching with that of the Catholic Church. Happily so, for she has helped to revive spiritual insights and ideals which were our glory but were fading, not without some adverse pressure. Central here is the Sacred Heart of Jesus, with which fortunately goes the Immaculate Heart of Mary, and then a vision that is seizing the Catholic world most profoundly, the Alliance of the Two Hearts.

I served on the international symposium sponsored by Filipino leading Catholics and strongly encouraged by John Paul II which pooled elaborate research on this theme, now so vital in Catholic life. What was my astonishment to find it expressed lucidly, forcibly, in the dictated texts of Vassula. Or again, neglect of the Holy Spirit has been an affliction of our Latin Church. Apart from John Paul II there is no more abundant, enlightening, persuasive exponent of the Holy Spirit in the Christian life than Vassula Rydén. Do I have to write of the powerfully personal presentation of God the Father, in terms existential, compelling? Fr Karl Rahner worried up to his death about the Church's failure to make the Trinity totally relevant to everyday life. Here is one, devoid of any formal theological preparation, who makes the Persons each relevant to us and brings all Three to our living acceptance.

Has this mission been fruitful in the Church? I could fill a book with stories of conversion, with reliable records of healing, though Vassula does not claim a healing ministry, with striking instances of people "slain in the Spirit" after personal contact with Vassula. I must mention two aspects of her mission which I omitted from the first edition of my book, but which on advice I have decided to deal with in a new study - they already appear in abbreviated form in the French translation.

Vassula for some time endured the Passion of Christ. I had seen her in this moving experience in Switzerland and in the United States. It had, as a weekly occurrence, ceased some eighteen months ago. It recurred in Omaha on 12 June last, witnessed by five people. Testimonies will appear in due course. A different sign was reported to me by visitors from Dayton, Ohio, for a lecture by Vassula in Notre Dame, South Bend. They saw the "miracle of the sun" over the hall where she was due to speak. I have two written testimonies on the same phenomenon in Kent, England more recently. I have a large file on the change in Vassula's countenance while she speaks - her appearance is that of Christ. This has been witnessed in Switzerland, South Africa, Sweden, Italy, Ireland, Holland, Greece, England, Canada, France, frequently in the Philippines. The most recent witnesses who came to me were detainees in the Muntinlupa prison, Manila, signing statements at once on what they saw during her talk. In Manila also a witness of note was Aurora Aquino, mother of the martyred Benigno, one of the most respected women in the land. Three witnesses were Orthodox, one Anglican.

Why is there so much blatant falsehood printed about Vassula? That she predicted an earthquake in California which did not take place: she never said such a thing. That Jesus told her He wants Christian unity under the World Council of Churches. Never did she say this. That she makes a lot of money. Of the numerous editions and translations she does not take a cent in author's royalties; she would be perfectly entitled to do so; a minimum estimate in France alone is 500,000 francs; she gives away at once, mostly for the benefit of prisoners, gifts she receives. Last year she gave 20,000 Deutschmarks to a Moscow Childrens' Hospital. (Despite repetition, I maintain the text of the letter).

Can people dismiss all this evidence of the divine? Several priests theologically qualified accept it. Others do not - so what? Emile Zola said that if the thousand miracles reported from Lourdes up to his time were authentic he still would not believe.

Rejected Letter B:

Your editorial tail-piece to my letter is the longest of its kind that I have read. I cannot compliment you on its contents, nor on its form. You use the language of invective carelessly, much as your contributor tried his hand at irony. However, my purpose is not to help you to improve your prose style but to remind you of your moral obligation to Vassula Rydén. This you have tried to fudge and dodge.

Briefly:

1. Your original article attributed to her the statement that Jesus wishes to see Christians united under the World Council of Churches. This statement is false and you should withdraw it with an apology if you respect the rights of the human person; these include the right to one's reputation.

    You now shift the criticism, hoping this will pass unnoticed. Jesus wishes to work with the World Council of Churches, a substantially different opinion of course. You try to support it by quoting a passage in which He castigates that body. Some logic! I repeat, that <u>again and again</u>, Vassula records the desire of Jesus that unity must come, will come, under the successor of Peter. Did you know, by the way, that the Holy See is represented at the World Council of Churches? Do you realize the significance of an Orthodox writer's public commitment to the primacy of the Pope?

2. You have really committed an ugly gaffe in your attempt to vindicate the idiotic statement that Jesus called Vassula His bride not only in the mystical but the physical sense. Anyone with knowledge of mystical theology would have saved you from such an error. The statement which you brandish in triumph is in the symbolic idiom of mysticism. As you interpret it you are like a man mistaking the allegory of the vine for a lesson in botany. Read exactly the same idea in St Margaret Mary's Autobiography: "Immediately a large cross was shown me, the extremity of which I could not see, but it was all covered with flowers. Behold the bed of my chaste spouses on which I will make thee taste all the delights of my pure love. Little by little these flowers will drop off, and nothing will remain but the thorns, which are hidden because of thy weakness." You should read the Song of Songs, Sir, and learn that great medieval theologians applied it to Our Lady. Reflect further on these lines from St Margaret Mary: "He deigned to converse with me sometimes as a friend, at other times as a spouse passionately in love." "He gave me further to understand that, after the manner of the most passionate of lovers, He would during that time, allow me to taste all that was sweetest and most delightful in the tokens of love."

3. Why did you not deal with the very serious allegation which you printed that what Vassula writes is blasphemous. I objected to this and still do. I put it to you that it is gravely defamatory and that your tolerance of it is disgraceful. You urge your readers very wisely to frequent the Sacraments. How many of them would dare approach the Sacrament of the Altar if they had unjustly broadcast far and wide a charge of blasphemy against their neighbour? Do not forget, Sir, that it was on a false charge of blasphemy that Our Lord and Saviour, Jesus Christ, was unjustly condemned and put to death.

You ask why does Vassula not speak to Protestant and Orthodox audiences. Elementary research would have informed you that she did just this when she spoke to audiences in the World Council of Churches on 23 January, 1992 - when I also spoke, and on 6 February, 1993, that she has spoken to the Orthodox in Greece and Russia, is invited, and willing to address Protestants in England.

APPENDIX III

A NOTE FROM VASSULA RYDÉN

Followers of the *True Life in God* messages often have questions which they would like answered. The most
frequently received questions are below and I will attempt to answer them as best I can:-

1. Why are some words changed and corrected?
2. What is the explanation for Jesus "broken" nose?
3. Why are passages of text deleted?

WHY SOME INDIVIDUAL WORDS ARE CHANGED

On 5th March 1987, approximately 16 months after I started to receive the messages, God said to me:-

> "SUMMARIZE everything I gave you, <u>correcting them as I will instruct you</u>, completing My Messages. Will you do this for Me Vassula? Vassula, I am sending you someone whom I will enlighten (Fr O'Carroll obviously). When everything is assembled and put in order, I God, will seal it with My Own Hand." [Volume I, *Trinitas*, p.50. Handwritten notebook no.8, p.48-49][1]

With regard to this, one might say, "how is it possible that God can regret certain things He said and even come to alter them?" And yet He can, He can because of the wickedness and spite of man on earth. Have you not read in Scriptures: "Yahweh saw that the wickedness of man was great on the earth, and that the thoughts in his heart fashioned nothing but wickedness all day long. Yahweh REGRETTED having made man on the earth, and his heart grieved. 'I will rid the

---

[1] Volume I, <u>JMJ Publications</u>. March 5, 1987, p.50.

earth's face of man, my own creation,' Yahweh said 'and animals also, reptiles too, and the birds of heaven; for I REGRET HAVING MADE THEM'" (Gn 6:5-7).

In the particular case below the text was open to misinterpretation and therefore for the sake of clarity God gave me a sign to slightly change the wording. [Ref: Volume II, *Trinitas*, again, p.112 and p.113, Handwritten notebook no.23, p.51-52]:-[1]

> "Peter! O Peter recognize the End of Times, how is it that most of you cannot tell the Times? Shadowed by Satan under his wings, Satan has digressed many of you from the Truth! Take My Hand Peter, and I will guide you; hear My cry, assemble your Eastern brothers, call them to meet Me under My roof, assemble your Eastern brothers into My Foundation, call them before Me. How I desire this unity!..."

When Christ dictates to me the messages, only I would know, since I am the receiver, when He talks to all of us, or when He talks to a certain person or if He switches from having talked to one particular person on to another or all of us. The same thing might happen if, eg, the Eternal Father speaks to me, then stops and the Son takes over to tell me something else. But usually in the latter, they introduce themselves in the beginning or the message is so clear that anyone could tell who is who.

Coming back to the above passage that I changed so that I am not misunderstood, this was how it read:

> "Peter! O Peter recognize the End of Times, how is it that most of you cannot tell the Times? Shadowed by Satan under his wings, O come Peter! Take My Hand; Satan has digressed you from the Truth! Take My Hand and I will guide you, hear My cry, assemble your Eastern brothers into My Foundation..." etc...

Here I will note, had I left it as it is when Jesus was speaking to the Pope and when Jesus was speaking to all of us, one might have misinterpreted this passage saying that Jesus is blaming the Pope, but normally no one should have misunderstood it since from the beginning Jesus asks us to honour Peter. Here below I will put in capital letters the parts concerning the Pope. The rest in normal letters will be when Jesus spoke to us. This is the original again:

> "PETER! O PETER RECOGNIZE THE END OF TIMES." (Then Jesus turns to the world and says). "How is it that most of you cannot tell the Times?" (Christ's voice drops here when He says to the world:) "Shadowed by Satan under his wings..." (then there was a pause here before Jesus cried out again).

---

[1]Volume I, JMJ Publications, p.313. April 18, 1988.

"O COME PETER! TAKE MY HAND." (Jesus had paused here again. The semi-colon represents a stop, notice there are no full-stops in the original handwritten version of *True Life in God*, just like in the Old Testament in Hebrew, no stop or capital letters were used, which is rather significant and interesting too since it is the living Word of God and God is the Alpha and the Omega - the Beginning and the End. Then Jesus said to us:) "Satan has digressed you from the Truth! (Again turning to Peter He said) "TAKE MY HAND AND I WILL GUIDE YOU, HEAR MY CRY, ASSEMBLE YOUR EASTERN BROTHERS INTO MY FOUNDATION...etc"

We can always tell when Jesus started to say "Peter? O Peter recognize the End of Times," that He was talking to Peter (the Pope), and it is by what follows that is very important because we can see that Christ was turning to speak to us too, since He said: "How is it that MOST OF YOU cannot tell the Times?"

Many of the passages are to be taken metaphorically, not literally, but God knew that in our weakness and hardness of heart, we were bound to misinterpret His Word and He REGRETTED it. When Jesus said "Destroy this Temple, and I will raise it up again in three days" the Pharisees took him literally which was of course a total misrepresentation. In the same way, when Jesus speaks in metaphors in *True Life in God* one must look for the deeper meaning of the message - this is why I was instructed by God to delete certain passages for He "saw that the wickedness of man was great on the earth, and that the thoughts in his heart fashioned nothing but wickedness all day long."(Gn 6:5)

DELETED PASSAGES OF TEXT

There were a number of reasons for deletion of certain passages:-

a. Some of them were deleted under instruction from God.
b. Most that I had deleted were tasks I had to accomplish.
c. Some of the passages were personal messages for individuals.

Most of the passages I had deleted were things that I had to accomplish and MOST OF THEM NOW HAVE BEEN ACCOMPLISHED. Many of the deleted passages were instructions to go and HAND OVER to the Pope the Messages by my own hand. Some of these passages were regarding Garabandal and the children - these HAVE been accomplished too. One particular passage which was deleted made reference to the Greek Orthodox and Anglicans saying the Stations of the Cross with John Paul II - this has been partly accomplished. Firstly, I will deal with the deleted passages concerning Garabandal.

Garabandal:

Our Blessed Mother was asking me to go to Garabandal and bless the sites where She had appeared and pray over there. This has already been accomplished again in a very simple way. Then Jesus had asked me to meet the children. He had asked me to bless them. I never looked for them or "panicked" not knowing their whereabouts, because God had already taught me how He works. He asks for something quite impossible in anyone's capacity, He expects you to trust Him and lean on Him entirely, then He lays out Himself the way for you to accomplish in peace what He had asked, so long as our spirit is one with His Spirit, every detail He asks is fulfilled. And so I have met Conchita the main seer and talked to the others by phone. Someone had arranged everything for me while I was in the States and Conchita wanted to meet me. This too has been accomplished without me trying. I was invited to go.

Secondly, I will deal with the numerous deleted passages referring to the Pope:-

Pope John Paul II:

The way we were invited to enter the Vatican and meet the Pope on the 6th November 1993, is very important, for it reminded me of the prophecies I deleted in my books. God did not want me to go in a pompous way, with special invitations from high authorities. This is why several times, in the deleted passages He calls me "barefoot messenger," and that I should go to Peter "barefoot," which of course if we know the biblical terms, it means "simple and poor." When God tells me in these deleted passages that I should bend and "wash Peter's feet" which of course is symbolic (although I had not understood what God meant immediately, just like St Francis was asked to rebuild the Church and he took this literally and went and laid brick upon brick reconstructing a church in ruins), I in the beginning had problems to grasp the deeper meanings. I understood later, that since I am an Orthodox, I represent in a way the Orthodoxy. God wanted in this way to tell us, that the Orthodox (our patriarch of Constantinople) ought to give Peter a return gesture of humility, this gesture of washing his feet, a return to what Pope Paul VI did to the Patriarch Athenagoras. Pope Paul VI had bent humbly and kissed Athenagoras' feet. They were two giants of Unity.

When God said, "Hand over My Message to My beloved servant John Paul II" He was referring to the *True Life in God* messages and this I was able to do at that November visit when I personally handed him books in four different languages (three of which were in Polish).

And now here are the passages concerning the Pope that were deleted but have now been fully accomplished:-

1. Volume II, *Trinitas*, p.2. Handwritten notebook no.17, p.4-5:-[1]
   "...You will enter My Domain barefoot, Vassula, now you have given me a vow, every vow is kept. Little one will you do this for Me? From thereon remain barefoot for Me, be My barefoot bearer..."
   Volume II, *Trinitas*, p.3. Handwritten notebook no.17, p.8-12. This message regards the same thing.[2]

2. Volume II, *Trinitas*, p.24. Handwritten notebook no.18, p.33-34[3] AND Volume II, *Trinitas*, p.35. Handwritten notebook no.19, p.10-11:-[4]
   "...Hand over My Message to My beloved servant John Paul II, have My Peace..." Just before that, on page 33 of notebook, I deleted a private message to Beatrice.

3. Volume II, *Trinitas*, p.25. Handwritten notebook no.18, p.37-38:-[5]
   "...and into your House you will receive a barefoot messenger, and the mighty shall wait for you. You will strip them (the freemasons that infiltrated into the Church, enemies of the Pope), from their weapons, disarming them, beseeching you. My Messenger will also speak for you, (the Pope), yours will be the voyage of courage, the great challenge. Vassula, My messenger, you will hand over My Message to My well beloved John Paul, he will recognize you, (he seemed to know about me since others before me had handed in to him my books, and especially when we met later on Cardinal Sodano, because when they introduced me to him he seemed to have already heard of me) when you will enter My House, let us be together entering My House." (And I asked: "Jesus will you arrange it?" And Jesus answered: "I will, Vassula").

4. Volume II, *Trinitas*, p.26. Handwritten notebook no.18, p.40 and p.41:-[6]
   "...You are to be My barefoot messenger, keeping faithfully your vow, remembering My instructions. You are to enter My domain humbly, reminding them that I am a humble God who will bend in front of My servant's feet and wash them. This will be My example, I the Lord will bend. Yes, little one they will have to bend to unite. I will be coming humbly (that means to give His message), barefooted. I am not coming loaded with weapons..." (meaning that the message is not loaded with inflexible statements and arguments and menaces).

---

[1] Volume I, <u>JMJ Publications</u>, p.205.   October 13, 1987.
[2] Volume I, <u>JMJ Publications</u>, p.207.   October 16, 1987.
[3] Volume I, <u>JMJ Publications</u>, p.227.   November 14, 1987.
[4] Volume I, <u>JMJ Publications</u>, p.239.   December 4, 1987.
[5] Volume I, <u>JMJ Publications</u>, p.230.   November 16, 1987.
[6] Volume I, <u>JMJ Publications</u>, p.231.   November 18, 1987.

5. Volume II, *Trinitas*, p.48-49. Handwritten notebook no.19, p.63-64:-[1]
"...You are My messenger carrying My Word which should be given to My servant John Paul, it is I who showed you how you will appear in My Domain. John Paul will not refuse you..." (the Pope seemed pleased to receive the books with the messages in his hands, and he did not refuse them).

6. Volume II, *Trinitas*, p.51. Handwritten notebook no.20, p.5:-[2]
"...take My Message to My servant John Paul, I will fulfil the prophecies of My servant Johannes, (Pope John XXIII called the Pope of Unity), prophecies which will come to light (about unity). I, the Lord, have foretold this event of My messenger and to whom I have entrusted My Word.
"You will speak from My Mouth and the mighty will fear, (the freemasons and the enemies of the Church), for I will speak of them, disarming them. My messenger will also speak of the tribulations that My Church will undergo. This revelation is My Voice. Recognize the Signs of the Times..."

I will not continue to add everything, since it is repetitive. But I wish to mention just where in the Volume II this message is repeated:

1. Volume II, *Trinitas*, p.56-57. Handwritten notebook no.20, p.27-29.[3]
2. Volume II, *Trinitas*, p.64-65. Handwritten notebook no.20, p.56-58, 61.[4]
3. Volume II, *Trinitas*, p.87. Handwritten notebook no.22, p.12.[5]
4. Volume II, *Trinitas*, p.144. Handwritten notebook no.25, p.48.[6]

Finally, I will deal with the deleted passage that this Easter has been partly accomplished. Jesus was asking the Greek Orthodox and the Anglicans to do the Stations of the Cross with John Paul II. As usual, Jesus was speaking in metaphors and this is why again I was advised by God to delete it because many would have misinterpreted this passage again.

Unity and Stations of the Cross

Repeatedly God tells me that I am the sign of the future unity. By this He means that the unity between the Orthodox and Roman Catholics, will be lived as I live it with them (the Roman Catholics). When He tells me: "Unite them", He does not mean that I will have to run to the Pope and the Patriarch and tell them face to face:

[1] Volume I, JMJ Publications, p.253. December 28, 1987.
[2] Volume I, JMJ Publications, p.254. December 31, 1987.
[3] Volume I, JMJ Publications, p.259. End of January 6, 1988 message.
[4] Volume I, JMJ Publications, p.266. January 18, 1988.
[5] Volume I, JMJ Publications, p.287. March 3, 1988.
[6] Volume I, JMJ Publications, p.340. June 26, 1988.

"Go and unite with your brother!" What He wants from me is to pray, pray, pray for the unity of the Church. All the sacrifices I could offer Him will go in the same balance of unity. All the penance and fasting I will do will go there too. All the sufferings, fatigues etc... will go for the unity too. Until the weight of the "balance" is heavy enough and pleasing to God, accumulated also by other instruments' prayers and sacrifices for unity, only then, will unity come. So here is this passage from Volume II, *Trinitas*, p.37. Handwritten notebook no.19, p.16, dated December 6, 1987:-[1]

> "Write Vassula: I the Lord wish you to honour My Stations of the Cross, introduce the light, (meaning to have candles). Vassula, will you ask My servant John Paul to do My Stations the way I have taught you, remember?" The Patriarch Bartholomew of Constantinople this Easter prepared ALL THE PRAYERS for the Stations of the Cross. "I desire to see you all three there," (meaning the Orthodox, the Anglicans and the Roman Catholics), "with My beloved John Paul, first honouring My Mother, offering Her a candle, then I wish to see your knees bend in all of My Stations, honouring Me by holding at My Stations a Light."
>
> Then I asked: "Lord, 'all three there?', who do you mean Lord?"
>
> "I wish to see My beloved servants there too, James and David."

In this message, it is obvious that Jesus speaks vaguely to the Roman Catholic Church, the Orthodox Church and the Anglican Church of celebrating Easter altogether in the same date. Today I understand this message even more. The Stations of the Cross is really representing Easter. The Lord spoke in metaphors asking me and the other two to be together with the Pope and do the Stations of the Cross, but in reality, Christ was asking the three Churches to be together. This has now been accomplished. This past Easter, (1994), when the Pope went to do the Stations of the Cross in the Coliseum of Rome as every year, he invited the Orthodox Patriarch Bartholomew to be with him. As he could not go himself, he sent a representative from Constantinople, Archbishop Polikarpos. We all saw him as he was right behind the Pope. The prayers of the Patriarch Bartholomew were read out by Pope John Paul II. Present also was an Anglican Bishop, thus the 3 Churches were there as Jesus desired.

John Paul II then spoke a lot about unity and mentioning several times the Patriarch of Constantinople. John Paul II during Lent was speaking many times of UNIFYING THE DATES OF EASTER.

---

[1]Volume I, JMJ Publications, p.241. December 6, 1987.

As for the other few messages that are deleted, they were deleted because God instructed me to do so. They are private messages given to individuals that do not concern the readers.

JESUS' "BROKEN" NOSE

We all know that no bone on Jesus was broken according to scriptures. We also all know that most of the nose is not bone but cartilage and cartilage is not a bone. All the experts and best pathologists in this field who studied inch by inch the Holy Shroud, confirm in one voice that the cartilage of the nose was fractured. One can even see it with the naked eye on The Shroud.

Books were written by these experts, and even the famous scientific and documentary video called "The Silent Witness", confirms the words that Jesus gave me. The pathologist in Silent Witness is Dr Robert Bucklin, from Los Angeles, where he says in the film exactly these words: "...separation and possible fracture of the nasal cartilage." Here below are also a few other reports by experts:

In the back cover of the book on the Shroud by Msgr Giulio Ricci, entitled "The Way of the Cross in the light of the Holy Shroud", these words are printed:

"Msgr Giulio Ricci, President of the Roman Center for the Study of the Passion of Christ and the Holy Shroud and of a similar organization in the USA, demonstrates that 'the Man of the Shroud is Jesus.' Basing his research on the sciences, he came to this conclusion after an exhaustive examination of the internal evidence of the Holy Shroud, thus introducing us to a new, realistic vision of the central events of the Christian faith, which find detailed and dramatic confirmation in this precious archaeological document."

On page 25 of his book, there is a picture of the face of Jesus from the Shroud and this is what he writes:

"A second fall can be 'read' on the face of the Shroud in a remarkable swelling of the middle of the forehead and in the fracture of the nasal septum. When the Shroud was brought into contact with the forehead, it did not touch the sides of the forehead; the swelling in the middle came into contact with the material and left its imprint there, while the adjacent areas are shaded. According to the judgement of experts, between the edges of the nasal septum and the beginning of the cartilage, a concave area can be seen, indicative of a fracture caused by some blow."

Another book called "Verdict on the Shroud", written by Kenneth E Stevenson and Gary R Habermas, (I have only the French translation of this book by France-Marie

Watkins), nevertheless in this French copy, picture no.12, after page 152, shows again a portrait of the Head of Jesus on the Shroud. The French words are: "(...) le nez a pu être cassé (...)" in English: "the nose could have been broken."

The last book from which I shall quote from, (there are many more), is French too - called "Le Linceul de Turin", "The Shroud of Turin" by Antoine Legrand, published at Desclée De Brouwer. This is what the author writes on pages 128 and 129: "Ce qui est certain c'est qu'à la base de la joue droite (exactement dans la région zigomatique sur le muscle élévateur naso-labial) il y a une tumefaction résultant d'un coup de bâton qui a également fracturé le cartilage dorsal du nez. Ce coup n'a pu être donné que par une main située à droite et en arrière de la victime qui ne pouvait deviner qui la frappait."

In English the translation is: "What is certain is that at the base of the right cheek (exactly at the zygomatic region on the elevated naso-labial muscle) there is a tumefaction as a result from a strike given by a rod that has also fractured the dorsal cartilage of the nose. This strike could only have been given by a hand situated on the right side and behind the victim who could not guess who was hitting him."

I will conclude this subject by quoting what Scriptures say: "Then they spat in His face and hit Him with their fists; others said as they struck Him, 'Play the prophet, Christ! Who hit You then?'" (Mt 26:67-68). "With a rod they strike on the cheek the judge of Israel" (Mi 4:14).

WHY SOME INDIVIDUAL WORDS ARE CHANGED

I received this message from the Eternal Father given to me in the early times and which will one day go out in print with the very early messages of my angel:

> "Peace be with you. <u>Any word you feel is not right and troubles you, feel free to correct it.</u> I, God, give you the feeling. Vassula, are you happy?" (October 12, 1986).
> "More than happy, overwhelmed." (I cannot describe it when I feel God's Love on me).

I will give a couple of examples of where I changed individual words:

a. If the words "worship" have been changed to "venerate" it is because God permitted me to do so, as you have seen by now from what He had said. (By the way, the word "worship" was used instead of "venerate" in the old times. It does not mean "adore", but it meant to honour. It has been changed for the sake of misjudgement).

b. The word "Hades" has been changed into "purgatory", so that people may understand it better. Again with God's permission. My soul is often exposed in purgatory where with the love I have for God and with my daily prayers for the souls, Jesus brings the souls out of purgatory to Him. This was one of the messages that was deleted in Volume I, *Trinitas*, p.38-39. Handwritten notebook no.8, p.1-2.[1]

I have done what God asked me to do.

Vassula

We recommend as further reading:

1. "When God Gives a Sign" - testimony on Vassula by René Laurentin
2. "Vassula of the Sacred Heart's Passion" by M O'Carroll CSSp

PUBLISHER

---

[1]Volume I, <u>JMJ Publications</u>, p.39. February 18, 1987.

APPENDIX IV

===

LETTER FROM VASSULA TO A FRIEND
IN PUERTO RICO

Vassula has recently released a letter which I consider the perfect Christ-like answer to her critics:

Pully, 17.4.94

Dear Gogui

Let us disarm evil by refusing to answer to Fr ***, or anybody of the kind. Today in Church during the Holy Communion, Jesus said to me: "those who draw the sword will perish by the sword..." "I did not cover my face against insult and spittle."

By replying, you stimulate them to produce new articles. They love it! So let us disarm them and ignore them. In fact if I have anything to tell Fr *** and his kind, I will tell them: "Thank you for augmenting my reward in Heaven. And today with joy I acclaim to our Father in Heaven: Glory be to God! Praised be the Lord! for He has looked upon my wretched soul. How can I merit such gifts, the same gifts His prophets received? And above all His own Son experienced? What have I done to merit the spittle and insult, the persecution and the calumny that His own Son received as well as His prophets? I rejoice and I promise that I will make no resistance to what He is offering me, nor would I turn away from the path He has laid out for me, for I trust in the designs of the Almighty and I will lean on Him entirely."

The more I accept what He is offering me so generously, (the persecutions) the more His Message's fruit will increase, the more altars (souls) He will rebuild, the richer His land will become. I'm indeed happy and rejoicing.

166

May the Peace remain with you all. He has given us His Peace,

All my love in the two Hearts who will soon triumph!

Vassula

(This is what the Lord gave me to read):

Now the days of reckoning have come, the days of reprisals are he
is mad," Israel protests, "this inspired fellow is raving." Ah yes,
your iniquity is so great, your apostasy so grave. Ephraim watc
tent, traps are set for him on all his paths, in the house of his G
him. These men are as steeped in corruption as in the days of Gib
remember their iniquity, he will punish their sins. (Ho 9:7-9)

cc: Fr O'Carroll
     Lynch family
     Pat Callahan

APPENDIX V

BIBLIOGRAPHY

Bibliography of the mystical writings of Vassula Rydén.

<u>List of Published Books</u>:

1. The Vrai Vie en Dieu, O.E.I.L. François de Guibert, Paris, France, 1990-1994, Vol I-IV. Supplement I-V, supplement VI to appear in June 1994.
2. La Vraie Vie en Dieu, Prières de Jésus et Vassula, Paris, France, 1993.
3. True Life in God, Trinitas, Independance MO, USA, 1991, Vol I-VII. Vol VIII to appear May 1994.
4. True Life in God, JMJ Publications, Northern Ireland, 1991, Vol I; 1992 Vol II; 1993 Vol III; Vol IV to appear June 1994.
5. True Life in God, Prayers of Jesus and Vassula, JMJ Publications, N Ireland, 1993
6. Das Wahre Leben in Gott, German, Miriam-Verlag, Jestetten, Germany, 1992-1993, Vol I-IV. Vol V to appear in the course of this year, 1994.
7. La Vera Vita in Dio, Italian, Edizioni Dehoniane, Roma, Italy, 1992-1994, Vol I-VI.
8. Prawdziwe Zycie w Bogu, Polish, Vox Domini, Katowice, Poland, 1993-1994, Vol I-IV. Vol V to appear May 1994, Poland
9. Wasze Modlitwy Moga Zmienic Swiat, Prawdziwe Zcie w Bogu, (Polish prayer book), Vox Domini, Katowice, Poland 1993.
10. A Verdadeira Vida em Deus, Encontros com Jesus, Portuguese, Brasilian, Ediçoes Boa Nova, Requiao, Famalicao, Portugal, 1992-1994, Vol I-V, to appear shortly Vol VI.
11. La Verdadera Vida en Dios, Encuentros con Jésus, Spanish, Mexican, Colombian, Puerto Rican, Ediçoes Bao Nova, Requiao, Famalicao, Portugal, 1993-1994, Vol I-II.
12. Het Ware Leven in God, Dutch, Stichting Getuigenis van Gods Liefde, Eindhoven, Netherlands, 1993-1994, Vol I-II.
13. Mir I Ljubav - Pravi Zivot u Bogu, Croatian, Beograd, Makedonska. 1993-1994, Vol I-III, Vol IV to appear June 1994.

14. Igaz Elet Istenben, Jézus beszélgetései Vassulaval, Hungarian, Marana Tha sorozat 26 Kiado: Az Emmausz Katolikus Karizmatikus Közösség, Budapest, 1993, Vol I, Vol II to appear mid-1994.
15. I Alithini En Théou Zoi, Greek, Politistikos Silogos, Irini Ke Agapi, Athens, 1993, Vol I, Vol II, to appear in May 1994.
16. True Life in God, Russian, Dom Mari, Moscow, and at the Foyer Oriental Chrétien, fr Kozina, Av de la Couronne 206, Brussels, (Prophecies of Russia).
17. Het Ware Leven in God, Flemish, Mevr Lieve Van den Borre, Oostende, 1993-1994, Vol I-XVIII.
18. Sandt Liv i Gud, Danish, Niels Hvidt, Mysundegade 8/V, 1668, Copenhagen-V. 1993-1994, Vol I to appear mid-1994.
19. True Life in God, Korean, Anyang-Shi, Kyeong-gi do, 430-600, R. Spies, Center fr Damien, South Korea. 1993 Vol I, Vol II to appear mid-1994.

List of Books to appear on "True Life in God"

1. Thai: Fr Joseph Likhittham, Thailand
2. Japanese: Ms Sachiko Hitomi, Japan.
3. Arabic: J A Loussi, Bethlehem, Israel
4. Roumanian
5. Norwegian
6. Bangladeshi: Fr James Fannan, Dhaka
7. Ukranian: c/o Fr Cyrill Kozina, Brussells
8. Indonesian

Bibliography of extracts of True Life in God to appear in June 1994, in Northern Ireland

1. Fire of Love, (Teachings on the Holy Spirit), 1994, JMJ Publications, N Ireland.
2. God Comments on His Ten Commandments, 1994, JMJ Publications, N Ireland

Published books about Vassula Rydén:

1. Michael O'Carroll CSSp 'Vassula of the Sacred Heart's Passion', 1993, JMJ Publications, Belfast, N Ireland.
2. Michael O'Carroll CSSp Vassula de la Passion du Sacré-Coeur, 1993, (O.E.I.L.) F X de Guibert, Paris, France.
3. Abbot René Laurentin, 'When God gives a Sign', 1994, Trinitas, Ind, MO, USA.
4. Abbé René Laurentin, Quand Dieu Fait Signe, (Réponse aux objections contre Vassula), 1993, (O.E.I.L.) F X de Guibert, Paris, France

5. Padre René Laurentin, Quando Dio si Manifesta, 1994, Edizioni, Dehoniane, Roma, Italy.
6. Mons Aldo Gregori, Vassula Rydén, Messaggera di Cristo o Profetessa della New Age? 1993, Edizioni Segno, Udine, Italy.
7. Fraternidade Missionaria de Cristo-Jovem, Quem é Vassula? 1993, Ediçoes Boa Nova, Requiao, Famalicao, Portugal.

Books to appear shortly about Vassula Rydén

1. Ovila Melançon SJ, Le Christ appelle sa Messagère: Vassula Rydén, 1994 (O.E.I.L.) F X de Guibert, Paris, France, to appear April 1994.
2. Cyril Auboyeneau, Point de Vue Orthodoxie sur La Vraie Vie en Dieu, 1994 (O.E.I.L.) F X de Guibert, Paris, France, to appear June 1994.
3. Dr Philippe Loron, (neurologue), Analyse Scientifique sur La Vraie Vie en Dieu, 1994, (O.E.I.L.) F X de Guibert, Paris, France, to appear April 1994.
4. Michael O'Carroll CSSp, 'Bearer of the Light - Mediatrix of Divided Christians' 1994, JMJ Publications, Belfast, N Ireland, to appear within one month.

Articles on Vassula that appeared in various publications:

1. Michael O'Carroll CSSp, 'John Paul II, apostle of the Holy Spirit, Dictionary of his Life and Teaching' 1994, article Vassula Rydén; JMJ Publications, Belfast, N. Ireland
2. Michael O'Carroll CSSp, 'Verbum Caro.' A theological Encyclopedia of Jesus the Christ. Liturgical Press, Collegeville, MN 1992, Article Vassula Rydén, p.189f.
3. Howard Q Dee, (Ex-Ambassador of the Vatican), Mankind's Final Destiny, Kyodo Printing Co, 1992, Manila, article Vassula Rydén, p.116.
4. Dr and Mrs Mansour, Our Lady of Soufanieh, Syrian Arab Republic, and Other Phenomena, 101 Foundation, USA, 1991, article Vassula Rydén, p.95-105.
5. Abbé René Laurentin, Comment la Vierge Marie leur a rendu la Liberté (O.E.I.L.) F X de Guibert, Paris, France, 1991, article Vassula Rydén, p.93-97
6. Abbé René Laurentin, 12 Années d'Apparitions (Dans l'horreur de la guerre, l'amour des ennemis), (O.E.I.L.) F X de Guibert, Paris, France, 1993, p.43, 44, 58, 63.
7. Alfons Sarrach, Medjugorjes Botschaft, vom dienenden Gott, 1993, Miriam Verlag, Jestetten, Germany, article Vassula Rydén
8. Jean Mathiot, Icônes surprenantes de al Mère de Dieu, Médiaspaul & Editions Paulines, Paris, France, 1990, article Vassula Rydén, p.71.
9. P Martino M Penasa, Il Libro della Speranza, (Commento al Testo dell'Apocalisse), 1989 Padova, Italy.

10. 101 Foundation, NJ, USA, Messages Pertaining to Russia and the World. 1992, article Vassula Rydén, p.1-3, 5-6, 13, 18, 22, 30.
11. Paul Bouchard, (dir of l'Informateur Catholique, Quebec, Canada), Le Règne de Dieu...au ciel ou sur la terre? 1994, several articles and pages on Vassula Rydén.

Articles in various publications (magazines, newspapers)

French (especially Chrétiens Magazine and Stella Maris), English, Greek, Italian, Portuguese, Brasilian, Dutch, Swedish, Arabic, Canadian (especially L'Informateur Catholique).

APPENDIX VI

Rev. Michael O'Carroll, C.S.Sp. Brief Curriculum Vitae and Outline Bibliography.

C.V.

Education: Blackrock College, Dublin; University College Dublin (B.A. Philosophy; H.Dip. Education) Fribourg University (D.D. Dissertation: Spiritual Direction according to Ven. Francis Libermann, 1939).

Career:

Education:	Professor Blackrock College (Religious Knowledge, History, French Language and Literature);
Journalism:	*Catholic Standard* (14 years sole editorial writer, Features especially on Vatican II in session, book reviews); *The Leader* (10 years identical service); much occasional work elsewhere;
Pastoral Ministry:	*Lay Apostolate*, chaplain to College Scout Troop; Spiritual Director three praesidia Legion of Mary; Adult Education courses in Social Science and Practical Psychology, Dun Laoghaire Technical College; chaplain annually to Irish Handicapped, Banneux Shrine; care of adopted children;
Spiritual Training:	Retreats and lectures; chaplain Blackrock Carmelite Convent;
Ecclesial Collaboration:	Deep cultural and intellectual attachment to the Church in France with diocesan service (Beauvais) annually for twenty years;

Ecumenism: Member of the Mercier Society (1941-1944) for
               dialogue with Protestants, and of the wartime Pillar
               of Fire Society for dialogue with Jews; first chairman
               of Irish branch of the Ecumenical Society of the
               Blessed Virgin May;

Recognition: Elected to General chapters C.S.Sp., 1968 (continued
               to 1969), 1974; Member of the Pontifical Marian
               Academy; *Associé des Bollandistes*; Member of the
               French Society of Marian Studies.

BIBLIOGRAPHY

1. Articles in religious periodicals e.g. The Irish Rosary, Missionary Annals of the
   Holy Ghost Fathers, Blackrock College Annual, *Maria Legionis* (organ of the
   Legion of Mary), Hibernia, Madonna, Knock Shrine Annual;

2. Articles in theological reviews, Clergy Review, Homiletic and Pastoral Review,
   Irish Ecclesiastical Record, Irish Theological Quarterly, The Furrow, Doctrine
   and Life, *Marianum, Ephemerides Mariologicae*; prefaces to a number of books;

3. <u>Contributions</u>: International Mariological Congresses, Rome, Saragossa, Malta,
   Kevalaer, Huelva; dictionaries, *Dictionnaire de Spiritualité* (25 articles);
   Marienlexikon (Regensburg) (24 articles written or requested) Modern Dictionary
   of Theology (1 article) Encyclopedia of Catholic Practice (12 articles);
   commemorative volumes: Dom Columba Marmion, Fr. René Laurentin, Fr.
   G.M. Besutti, O.S.M.; Fr. Theodore Koechler, S.M.; Professor Heinrich Beck
   (Bamberg);

4. Five pamphlets, Ven. Francis Libermann (2), The secret of Knock, African
   Glory (Mgr. Alexander Le Roy), Disciples of St. Thérèse of Lisieux, Lourdes
   Centenary Year.

   Books: twenty on Marian theology, hagiography and the Papacy, among which:
   Joseph, Son of David; *Mediatress of All Graces*; *Medjugorje, Facts, Documents,
   Theology*; *Le Sanctuaire de Knock* (awaiting publication in Paris); *Pius XII,*

Greatness Dishonoured - A documented Study; five theological encyclopedias, *Theotokos* (Our Lady), *Trinitas* (the Holy Trinity), *Corpus Christi* (the Eucharist), *Veni Creator Spiritus* (the Holy Spirit), *Verbum Caro* (Jesus the Christ); *John Paul II, A Dictionary of His Life and Teachings*; *Vassula of the Sacred Heart's Passion*; *Bearer of the Light - Vassula, Mediatrix of Divided Christians*;

THE FOLLOWING ARE THREE PRAYERS JESUS RECOMMENDS US TO PRAY DAILY

NOVENA OF CONFIDENCE TO THE SACRED HEART OF JESUS

O Lord Jesus Christ, To Your Most Sacred Heart I confide this intention... *(Here mention your request)* Only look upon me, Then do what Your Heart inspires... Let Your Sacred Heart decide... I count on it... I trust in it... I throw myself on It's mercy...

Lord Jesus You will not fail me. Sacred Heart of Jesus, I trust in Thee. Sacred Heart of Jesus, I believe in Thy love for me. Sacred Heart of Jesus, Thy Kingdom Come. O Sacred Heart of Jesus, I have asked for many favours, but I earnestly implore this one. Take it, place it in Thy Sacred Heart. When the Eternal Father sees it covered with Thy Precious Blood, He will not refuse it. It will be no longer my prayer but Thine. O Jesus, O Sacred Heart of Jesus I place my trust in Thee. Let me never be confounded. Amen.

PRAYER TO ST. MICHAEL

St. Michael the Archangel, defend us in the day of battle, be our safeguard against the wickedness and snares of the devil. May God rebuke him, we humbly pray, and do thou O Prince of the Heavenly Host, by the Power of God, cast into Hell Satan, and all the other evil spirits, who prowl through the world seeking the ruin of souls. Amen.

MARY, QUEEN OF HOLY ANGELS - PRAY FOR US!

THE MEMORARE OF ST. BERNARD

Remember, O most gracious Virgin Mary never was it known that any one who fled to thy protection, implored thy help or sought thy intercession, was left unaided. Inspired by this confidence, I fly unto thee, O Virgin of Virgins My Mother! To Thee do I come, before Thee I stand sinful and sorrowful. O Mother of the Word Incarnate! despise not my petitions, but in thy mercy, hear and answer me. Amen.

Jesus: May 4, 1988

CONSECRATION TO THE TWO HEARTS

On 21st September 1993, Vassula asked Jesus for a consecration to the Two Most Holy Hearts of Jesus and Mary, he replied with these words "Yes, wholeheartedly, I shall give you one. Write:

Designated in the prophecies of Your
Word O Lord, we know,
we trust and we believe that
the Triumph of Your
Sacred Heart, and the Immaculate
Heart of Mary, is
in the near future;
therefore, we humbly come to
consecrate ourselves, our families,
and our country, to Your Two
Sacred Hearts.

We believe that in consecrating
our country to You, nation will
not lift sword against nation,
and there will be no
more training for war.
We believe that in consecrating our
country to Your Two Loving Hearts,
all human pride and arrogance,
all godlessness and hardening
of the heart
be effaced, and that every evil
will be replaced with love and
good things.
We believe that Your Two Holy Hearts
will not resist our sighs now
and our needs, but in their
Loving Flame will hear us, and
come to us, to heal our deep wounds
and bring us peace.

O Sacred Heart of Jesus, and
Immaculate Heart of Mary,
blow on us a spark from Your
Two Hearts
to flare up our heart.
Make out of our nation the perfect
Dwelling-Place of Your Holiness.
Abide in us and we in You so
that through the Love of
Your Two Hearts, we may find
Peace,
Unity
and Conversion. Amen.

NEW TITLES AVAILABLE

John Paul II - A Dictionary of His Life and Teachings by M O'Carroll CSSp
A quick and fascinating guide to the life and teachings of this outstanding leader of the Church, which will be of great help to Catholics in these confused times. What has he said about the third secret of Fatima? What does the Pope think of Opus Dei? the Orthodox Churches? the Jews? What was his relationship with Monsignor Lefebvre? All these questions have been answered by this comprehensive dictionary, compiled by one of the outstanding theologians of our day, Father Michael O'Carroll CSSp.

Bearer of the Light by M O'Carroll CSSp
This is the second book by Father Michael O'Carroll on Vassula and the messages 'True Life in God.' In this book Vassula's most recent visit to Russia is recorded. Other themes include: pre-history of her conversion; extraordinary signs; the Passion; Chastisement and Purification. The book includes some extraordinary personal testimonies from people all around the world who experienced supernatural events in her presence. A must for any reader of the 'True Life in God' messages.

Volume IV (Notebooks 65-71)
This most recent volume of the messages of 'True Life in God' contains, among other things: prophecies on Russia explained - resurrection of the Church - repairing what was undone - unity by intermarriage. Daniel explained - the Rebel - the "enemy enthroning himself in 'my sanctuary'" - abolition of the Perpetual Sacrifice. Message to Cardinals, bishops and priests (17 March 1993).

Fire of Love
In this book prepared by Vassula Rydén as a gift to her spiritual advisor Michael O'Carroll CSSP, she selects from the complete writings to date of 'True Life in God' what she considers the most important references to the Holy Spirit. This book will be of interest to any reader with devotion to the Holy Spirit.

When God Gives a Sign by René Laurentin
Father Laurentin has long been recognised for his scientific and theological approach to claimed apparitions and his search for the truth. In this book he skillfully and with discernment answers questions arising in relation to Vassula Rydén's charism and the 'True Life in God' messages.
(This book is available in the UK from Sue Ellis, Spring House, Spring Bottom Lane, Bletchingly, Surrey, England Tel: 0883 346365 and in the USA from Trinitas, PO Box 475, Independence, MO, USA 64051)

OTHER TITLES AVAILABLE

Volume I (Notebooks 1-31)

Guardian angel Daniel, prepares Vassula to meet Jesus. Jesus teaches Vassula love of God, the scriptures; describes His passion; His love of 'daughter' Russia and its resurrection; the Great Apostasy. He links Garabandal to Fatima; His desire for unity of the Churches.

Volume II (Notebooks 32-58)

Jesus teaches that God is alive and very near, desiring a return to love, Adoration, sharing His Passion, consoling Him; return of Jesus. He teaches about the state of the Church, His shepherds; the renewal of His vineyards; Devotion to the Two Sacred Hearts of Jesus and Mary; expands on the ten commandments and Beatitudes; Apocalypse 12. The rebellion in the Church and the Great Apostasy; the suffering of His Peter; the minature judgement; unrolling of the 'scrolls.' Many prayers, of consecration, of adoration, of consolation, praise etc... to Father, Son and Holy Spirit.

Volume III (Notebooks 59-64)

Among the contents in this volume: Jesus marks foreheads with the consecration to him, Judgement Day, the time of sorting, the lamb's seal, the three days of darkness, and a strong message when the earth will shake and the sky will vanish.

Prayers of Jesus and Vassula

A beautiful assortment of prayers, some given by Jesus, others by Vassula, inspired by the Holy Spirit. A section on the Devotion to the Two Hearts; Daily Prayers and quotations of Jesus' teaching how to pray.

Vassula of the Sacred Heart's Passion by Michael O'Carroll C.S.Sp.

A 220 page book giving an outline of Vassula's life, her charism and analysis of Jesus' messages in the light of the teaching of the Church. Also a message to cardinals, bishops and priests of 'The Rebel' with a warning not to listen or follow the teaching of anyone except the Holy Father, John Paul II. (17 March 1993)

NATIONAL DISTRIBUTORS (ENGLISH EDITION)

United Kingdom

Chris Lynch
JMJ Publications
PO Box 385
Belfast BT9 6RQ
Northern Ireland
Tel: (232) 381596
Fax: (232) 381596

Australia

Center for Peace
c/o Leon LeGrand
91 Auburn Road
AUBURN Victoria
Australia 3123
Fax: (03) 882-9675
Tel: (03) 882-9822

United States

John Lynch
319 North Virginia Ave
North Massapequa
N.Y.
USA 11758
Fax: (516) 293-9635
Tel: (516) 293-9635

Canada

Caravan Agencies Ltd
6 Dumbarton Blvd
Winnipeg
Manitoba
Canada R3P 2C4
Fax: (204) 895 8878
Tel: (204) 895 7544

South Africa

Winnie Williams
Friends of Medjugorje
PO Box 32817
Braamfontein 2017
Johannesburg
South Africa
Tel: (011) 640-6583
Fax: (011) 339-7185

Republic of Ireland

D.M.Publications
"Maryville"
Loughshinney
Skerries
Co Dublin

Tel: (1) 8491458

Malawi

Rui Francisco
PO Box 124
Lilongwe
Malawi
Africa

Fax: (265) 721504

Denmark: Niels Huidt, Mysundegade 8V, DK 1668, Copenhagen V, Denmark (Fax: 45 331 33115)
Switzerland: Parvis, CH-1648, Hautville, Switzerland (Tel: 41 29 51905)
Holland: Stichting Getuigenis, Jan Van Hooffstraat 8, 5611 ED Eindhoven, Holland (Tel: 040 43 39 89 Fax: 040 44 02 74)

Queries relating to any version, please contact:
'True Life in God', PO Box 902, CH-1800 Vevey, Switzerland

'True Life in God' books are available in the following languages:

Switzerland: True Life in God, PO Box 902, CH-1800 Vevey, Switzerland

Phillipines: Center for Peace Asia, Shaw Blvd Cor. Old, Wackwack Road, Manduluyong Metro, Manila, Philippines. Tel: 795-622. Fax: 922-8358

French: 1. Edition du Parvis, CH-1648 Hauteville, Switzerland
                 2. 'La Vraie vie en Dieu', Editions FX de Guibert (OEIL), 27 Rue de l'Abbé-Grégoire, F-75006 PARIS

German: Das Wahre Lebe in Gott, Mariamverlag, D-7893 Jestetten, Germany

Italian: 'La Vera Vita in Dio', Edizioni Dehoniane, Via Casale San Pio V, 20, 1-00165 ROMA, Italy

Spanish/:   Centro de Difusion 'Grupo Reina', Belisario Dominguez 1302,
Mexican   "Laboratorios Jema", Mazatlan, Sin, Mexico CP 82000 Tel: (91-69) 82-11-59

Portuguese: Ediçoes Boa Nova, 4760 Vila Nova de Famalicao, Famalicao,
and Spanish   Portugal. Tel: 75-165. Fax: 311-594

Polish: Vox Domini, Skr Poczt 72, 43-190 Mikolów, Poland

Greek: Candy Jeannoutsikos, Essex SA, Fokionos 8 Ermou, 10563 Athens, Greece

Russian: Cyril Kozina, Foyer Oriental Chrétien, 206 Ave de la Couronne, B-1050 Bruxelles, Belgium

Korean: Father R Spies, Father Damien Center, PO Box 36, Anyang-Shi, Kyeong-Gi Do 430-600, South Korea

Flemish: Mevr Lieve Van den Berre, Epsomlaan 34, 8400 Oostende, Belguim. Tel: (059) 503-752

Danish: c/o Niels Christian Huidt, Louis Petersenveg, 2960 Rungsted-Kyst, Denmark

Bangladeshi: Father James Fannan, National Major Seminary, Plot 9, Road No.27, Banani, Dhaka 1213, Bangladesh

<u>Indonesian:</u>	Indriati Makki, Jalan Larong no.1a, Kompleks PLN, Kelurahan Duren Tiga, Jakarta 12760, Indonesia
<u>Norwegian:</u>	Ingfrid Lillerud, Lerdalsvn 22, 1263 Oslo, Norway
<u>Ukranian:</u>	Cyril Kozina, Foyer Oriental Chrétien, 206 Ave de la Couronne, B-1050 Bruxelles, Belgium
<u>Dutch:</u>	Stichting Getuigenis van Gods Liefde, PO Box 6290, 5600 HG Eindhoven, Holland
<u>Bulgarian:</u>	Miladora Anastassova, Bd D Grover 20, 1606 Sofia, Bulgaria
<u>Hungarian:</u> <u>Croatian:</u>	c/o Ilma Jordan, Szolyva v 1/b, 1126 Budapest, Hungary Franjo Ereiz, Za Belaka, Za M D Vukić, Palmotićeja 33, 41001 Zagreb PP699, Croatia
<u>Japanese/</u> <u>Chinese:</u>	Serge Bernard Kuhn, Foyer de Charite, Ai to Hakari no Ie, Sendaiji 136, Oaza, 568 Ibaragi-Shi, Osaka-Fu, Japan

<u>Photocopied original handwritter version:</u>

Trinitas, PO Box 475, Independence, MO, USA 64051 Tel: (816) 254-4489

<u>If you have any queries or personal testimonies relating to Vassula and the 'True Life in God' Message contact:</u>

'True Life in God'
PO Box 902
CH-1800 Vevey
Switzerland

<u>OR the author of this book, Father M O'Carroll CSSp at:</u>

Father M O'Carroll CSSp
c/o JMJ Publications
PO Box 385
Belfast BT9 6RQ
Northern Ireland